Bristol City: From Atye(

OTHER DESERT ISLAND HISTORIES OF BRISTOL CITY:

Bristol City: The Early Years 1894-1915   978-1-905328-51-2
Bristol City: From War to War 1915-1946   978-1-905328-43-7
Bristol City: The Post-War Years 1946-67   978-1-905328-93-2
Bristol City: The Modern Era 1967-2007   978-1-905328-27-7

Bristol City

From Atyeo to Dicks
A Personal Memoir

Series Editor: Clive Leatherdale

Edward Giles

DESERT ISLAND BOOKS

First paperback edition published in 2012
First hardback edition published in 2009
by
DESERT ISLAND BOOKS LIMITED
Unit 1, 36 Clifftown Parade, Southend-on-Sea, Essex SS1 1DL
United Kingdom
www.desertislandbooks.com

The right of Edward Giles to be identified as author of this work
has been asserted under The Copyright Designs and Patents Act 1988

British Library Cataloguing-in-Publication Data
A catalogue record for this book is available from the British Library

ISBN 978-1-905328-99-4

Printed in Great Britain
by
4edge Limited, Hockley

The publishers wish to thank The Mike Jay Archive.
Pictures in the central section, pages 91-102, are provided courtesy of Peter Godsiff,
former Sports Editor of the *Bristol Evening Post*, except where stated.
Pictures elsewhere in the book are from the author's own collection

Contents

Dedication

To my daughter-in-law Pippa and son-in-law Tom

Chapter 1

Wedlock's rush job to England regularity

It was a good time to be going West. Sport in general was thriving in and around Bristol. None more so than Association football.

After so many years in the doldrums, both Bristol's top soccer clubs were at last enjoying some playing prosperity as members of the Football League's Second Division. I have dealt elsewhere with the Rovers of that time: the Bert Tann Era of No Buy, No Sell. Here, with some 'poetic licence', straying both before and after in an attempt to put it all into perspective, I am looking back with my personal memoir of Bristol City during the 1950s and 60s – and that largely means the John Atyeo Era.

Peter John Walter Atyeo was born in Wiltshire, at Dilton Marsh, on 7 February 1932. We are told by Wikipedia, the internet's invaluable free encyclopaedia, that he 'was always perceived by fans as being the image of Bristol City at the time, as well as being popular with the ladies with his nearly always slicked hair.' In his fifteen seasons with the club, from the first day of 1951-52 to the last of 1965-66, he shattered their record for both goals and appearances. His 314 League goals (he lost one to another player in a revised reckoning) still have him more than 200 clear of his nearest rival. That was Tom Ritchie, a Scot who was with Sunderland, and on loan to Carlisle, between his two spells at Ashton Gate after Atyeo's retirement. And, with the inclusion of his goals in various cup competitions, big John has an overall total of 350. For appearances, Atyeo leads with 597 in the League and almost 650 in all – more than 60 ahead of the next man on the list, Trevor Tainton, one of the club's numerous Bristol-born players.

Only Everton's Bill ('Dixie') Dean and George Camsell, of Middlesbrough, have exceeded Atyeo's 344 goals in League and FA Cup for one club (there were, of course, no other knock-out competitions when they played, so that is the only real comparison). Camsell did so by just one goal with the addition of his 20 in the Cup; Dean had 28 Cup goals in his overall 377. Atyeo, whose Cup tally was 30, exceeded both for appearances for one club, Camsell reaching 453 (418 League) and Dean 431 (399).

To his City figures, Atyeo added five goals in six appearances for England in full internationals (never on the beaten side) and over a dozen more in his other representative games at youth, Under-23 and 'B' level, and for FA and Football League teams. In common with Geoff Bradford, Bristol's other soccer icon of the time over at Eastville, he would surely have been awarded more caps but for being with a so-called unfashionable club. Both preferred to remain loyal to their roots rather than be lured away to the First Division, not that there was any want of offers. Bradford said that in those days of the maximum wage, he never thought of asking for a transfer, but Atyeo admitted he might have been tempted to move if there had then been increased financial inducements and the chance of playing in major European competitions.

As regards full caps, it also counted against Atyeo that he was a part-timer for most of his career. Walter Winterbottom, England's manager of those years, admitted as much when he conceded that 'it might have been a mistake to have dropped Atyeo at a time when we were badly in need of a prolific scorer, but there was some concern among the selectors over the fact that he was a part-time professional.'

Before Atyeo, of whom more anon, the biggest name in Bristol City history was William John Wedlock, a small and tubby fellow inevitably, but affectionately, known regularly as 'Fatty' and less often as 'the India Rubber Man'. He stood only just over 5ft 4in and weighed no more than 10st 7lb at his peak, yet he was a centre-half whose skill and exceptional heading ability made his short and stocky stature no handicap. Excellent timing enabled him to get the better of taller opponents in the air.

He was beaten by Charles Wreford-Brown to being the first Bristol-born English international (with Old Carthusians against Ireland in 1889), and by Billy Jones to being the first City player to be chosen for England (also against Ireland, in 1901), but he remains the club's most-capped player with 26 call-ups – all but the last one in succession, across seven years and 28 days from 1907 to 1914. That then record sequence began after he had been an efficient late replacement for Newcastle's injured Colin Veitch for the Professionals against the Amateurs. He was summoned to that match in Sheffield at such short notice, in the absence of a previously nominated reserve, that he had to change on the train and only just managed to get to the ground in time. A rush job to England regularity.

Not until his nineteenth international was Wedlock on the losing side. And then it was just the once, against Scotland in Glasgow. England were winners nineteen times, with the six other games drawn, while he was at the heart of their defence, and on ten of those occasions they did not concede a goal. To the travels with England that took him outside the British Isles to Budapest, Vienna and Prague, he added a trip to South Africa, through which the Football Association's touring party went undefeated. But when it came to playing against Wales on his home ground at Ashton Gate he had the misfortune to be ruled out with an ankle injury. England won in his absence – just, by the odd goal of seven – and they were again successful, without having their reguard breached, when Wedlock was recalled for his final cap in Cardiff the following year, just a few months before the outbreak of Great War that is now known as the First World War. Then in his 34th year, even he was surprised to be selected. Considering that he always had great flair in attack as well as defence, it was entirely appropriate that he went out with a goal.

Billy Wedlock was born on 28 October 1881 in the Bedminster area of Bristol, not far from the ground that has been City's permanent home since 1904. He did not play football at his Ashton Gate school, but after leaving there he helped to form a team from boys at his bible class. At 16 he joined Arlington Rovers in the Bristol and District League and with them gained a Gloucestershire Junior Cup winner's medal. That brought him to Bristol City's attention, and he made his debut for them at 18 in a 2-0 defeat of Queen's Park Rangers in a Western League game at their original St John's Lane ground on 18 February 1900. He was given only two more opportunities during that season, however – one in a friendly with Leicester Fosse that City won by an only goal, the other in a 4-0 Southern League defeat at Millwall. After that, he was unexpectedly – and, as it transpired, most unwisely – released, denying him the chance to be in the first team City fielded in the Football League with their election to the Second Division, along with Doncaster Rovers, when New Brighton resigned and Walsall were voted out.

For the next four years Wedlock was a part-time footballer in Wales with Aberdare, whom he twice captained to the Welsh Cup final (though they were beaten in both). By then Bristol City could not fail to have become uncomfortably aware of what they had let slip, though it was mainly due to the persistence of vice-chairman Frank Bacon, who correctly predicted an England future for their prodigal son, that Wedlock returned to the ranks in time for the 1905-06 season. His League debut on the opening day could hardly have been more disheartening – or misleading. City let in five goals away to Manchester United, and three of them were scored by the centre-forward Wedlock was marking. This was Charlie Sagar, who two years before had been an FA Cup winner for the second time in the Bury team that crushed Derby County by the record final score of 6-0.

City were also to be Cup finalists before that decade was out – and again against United. But first the Bristol Babes (as they were known as League newcomers, before the red colour of their shirts made Robins a more natural nickname) won immediate promotion, also in company with the Manchester club, and promptly finished runners-up to Newcastle in the First Division. And Wedlock, rapidly putting his torrid start behind him, was their ever-present inspiration as they recovered from their Manchester mauling to embark upon a sequence of fourteen consecutive wins, from 9 September to 2 December, that equalled the record United had themselves set the previous season (and not matched again for nearly half a century, by Preston North End).

Bristol City's all-conquering run ended in a draw at newly elected Leeds City, against whom Wedlock scored when promotion was ensured in the return at Ashton Gate the following April. City romped away with the title, winning 30 (a club record) of their 38 matches. Six were drawn, and the only other League defeat they suffered after that depressing first day was at home to Leicester Fosse in mid-February. In thus dropping only ten points, they finished four ahead of Manchester United, who also exceeded the highest number in the Second Division achieved by Liverpool's champions with 58 the year before. Under the old system of two points for a win, only Tottenham's 70 in 1919-20 (from 42 matches) exceeded City's 66 in that section (from 38).

The rise to the top sphere of English football was a spectacular start, not only for Wedlock but also for Harry Thickett, the former Sheffield United and England full-back (he won the first of his two caps in Bristol). Thickett was in his first season as City's manager immediately after ending his playing career with the club. Until Easter 1907 there was a real chance of the First Division title being carried off too, but City were then twice beaten at home, either side of a defeat at Newcastle, and wins in each of their remaining four matches, with ten goals against three, could not prise the title from the Tynesiders' grasp. City ended three points behind Newcastle, who had lost to a goal by skipper Wedlock at Ashton Gate on the last Saturday of November.

Two years later Newcastle were champions again, despite conceding nine goals at home to Sunderland in a match refereed by Bristolian A E Farrant. A week afterwards Sunderland were beaten at home by Bristol City, but they had their revenge in the return at Ashton Gate, the week before City met Manchester United in the FA Cup final at Crystal Palace. The semi-final against Derby at Stamford Bridge was the match that Billy Wedlock looked back upon for his happiest and most thrilling soccer memory: 'We were one goal down and time was running out when we were awarded a penalty. Our centre-forward, Wallis Rippon, converted it, and the referee blew for full time. Rippon scored again with a penalty in the replay at Birmingham on the following Wednesday, when we won 2-1.'

Wedlock rated that 1908-09 season his best with City, who were a respectable eighth in the First Division, besides doing so well in the Cup. What was more, it was the season in which Wedlock was joined in the England team by his clubmate and big friend Joe Cottle for a match convincingly won against Ireland in Bradford. Cottle, also born at Bedminster, struck up a fine partnership with Archie Annan at full-back for City, forming a formidable defence with Harry Clay in goal and Wedlock as the pivot during that 'golden age' for the club.

From the delight of their dramatic triumph in the semi-final replay, however, City went to the huge disappointment of defeat in the final. Just one goal gave Manchester United the trophy for the first of what has become many times, scored in the 22nd minute by 'Sandy' Turnbull after a shot from Harold Halse had rebounded off the crossbar. Turnbull, who was persuaded to play by his captain, Charlie Roberts, after being on the verge of dropping out with a knee injury, had been a Cup winner with Manchester City five years before, along with Billy Meredith, the Welsh wing wizard who was also a key figure against Wedlock and his men. Both had joined United after the lifting of suspensions imposed by the FA on themselves and several other Manchester City players over an illegal payments scandal. Turnbull, sadly, did not survive the war. He was killed in action in France in 1917

After that big day at Crystal Palace, Bristol City and Manchester United moved in diametrically opposite directions. The 1910-11 season ended with United League champions for the second time in four years (Meredith and Turnbull were prominent in both), whereas City were relegated with Nottingham Forest – the club they had beaten by four goals, all scored by John Cowell, when threatened with the drop on the last day of the previous season. Past successes under the direction of Harry Thickett counted for nothing when his team pitched up at the bottom of the table in October 1910. Out he went, off to run a pub at Trowbridge, though there was some suggestion that his departure was mainly due to internal strife. Frank Bacon took temporary control until Sam Hollis was reinstated in January for his third spell as the club's manager.

The Nottingham-born Hollis had been the first to hold that post when appointed, from Woolwich Arsenal, at the age of 31 in 1897. That was the year in which City changed their name from Bristol South End, on being made into a limited company, and he was given all of £40 to build a squad capable of competing in the Southern League to which they had just been admitted. Increasing interference from directors led to his resignation within two years, however, and he lost his next job, as secretary-manager of neighbouring Bedminster FC, when that club merged with City in 1900. A year later, by then a publican, he was recalled to lead City into their first Football League season after his successor, Bob Campbell, a Scot who had formerly managed Sunderland, had also fallen out with the board, but he was again dispensed with when three successive finishes as fourth in the Second Division were not good enough to satisfy those impatient directors. Neither could his third coming safeguard the top status won under Thickett, and he left for the last time in April 1913 as City continued to struggle. Even so, his connection with the club was not entirely severed. After a spell as manager of Newport County in Division Two of the Southern League, he became chairman of the Bristol City Shareholders' Association.

Billy Wedlock's stay at Ashton Gate lasted until the end of the 1920-21 season. City finished third, seven points behind the promoted pair, Birmingham and Cardiff City, a year after only narrowly losing to Huddersfield Town in an FA Cup semi-final. Their manager then (and later of Bristol Rovers) was their former trainer Joe Palmer, a disciplinarian who resigned only a few months after Wedlock's exit – yet another to disagree with the directors.

Wedlock, who had missed only 21 of City's 190 matches during their five First Division seasons, was in the team that almost got through to the Cup final again in March 1920, but he played in only the first five of the club's Second Division games in his final season that followed. He made the last of his 362 League appearances (393 in all) at Hull on 11 September 1920. City were beaten that day, but he later helped them to defeat their Rovers rivals in the Gloucestershire Cup final at Ashton Gate, in between captaining them in the benefit match for his colleague Jock Nicholson, a friendly with Cardiff City, and scoring his final goal in victory over an Army side. Wedlock was awarded two benefits – the first against Manchester United at Ashton Gate during the 1910-11 season, which produced receipts of £354; the other against a Scratch XI in 1920-21 that realised £400.

On retiring from playing, Wedlock kept in close touch with City – directly opposite their ground, in fact – in concentrating on running the Star Inn he had taken over during the war. Eventually assisted by his son Denis, he remained there until his death on 25 January 1965, though ill health dogged him in his final years. He suffered from arthritis in both knees, and had difficulty seeing out of one eye. His memory lives on as one of the four men who have had a stand at Ashton Gate named after them. The others? John Atyeo, of course. Des Williams, a former chairman. And Harry Dolman, a farmer's son from Langley Burrell, a village near Chippenham, who was the dominant figure at the club as chairman from 1949 to 1974, and a member of the board for 35 years altogether.

Mr Dolman – as he was always known to the Press in those days when all directors, managers and, yes, referees too, were treated with that respectful mode of address – began his remarkable career in 1921 after serving in the Army and RAF during the war. As a junior draughtsman, he joined the firm of which he became chairman and to which his name was added: Brecknell, Dolman and Rogers. Within six years he was the chief engineer of one section, and he was appointed joint managing director in 1929. The company's products ranged from ticket-issuing machines to egg graders, many of them his own invention. He made millions out of his genius, and poured more than £100,000, a very considerable sum for those days, into Bristol City. There was no bigger soccer influence on that side of the city during the first four decades after the Second World War.

Chapter 2

Cast-off Bourton sends Yo-Yo City to Heaviest Defeat

At the end of their first season after Billy Wedlock's retirement, 1921-22, Bristol City went into further decline, relegated to the new Southern Section of the Third Division. Nottingham Forest, with whom they had descended into the Second Division in 1911, rejoined the elite as champions, whereas City were at the opposite end of the table with nearly two dozen fewer points. Forest had themselves tumbled to that position in the last season before war broke out in 1914, but, as there had then been no lower division of the Football League to accommodate them, they had survived by gaining re-election.

Life for Bristol City between the two world wars was a yo-yo existence. With only the champions promoted from the two sections of Division Three, they went straight back up, six points clear of Plymouth Argyle, hapless runners-up for the second of six successive seasons. But down again City went immediately, once more at the bottom of the heap. Earlier, they had been pushed into last place by their relegation companions from Bradford on goal-average. This time they were four points adrift of Nelson, the Lancashire club whose drop into the Northern Section would soon lead them out of the League altogether.

Three years later, Bristol City were back in Division Two, champions with their record number of goals in a season, 104. Thomas ('Tot') Walsh, fifth to John Atyeo in City's all-time list of League marksmen, scored six of them in one game against Gillingham, still a club record. That was the last in Plymouth's sorry sequence of second places. They finally made it three years later after finishing third and fourth in the meantime, but they were to be back on City's fixture list for only two Second Division seasons. Down the Bristol club went again in 1931-32, ten points worse off then the other relegated side, Barnsley, and with a paltry six wins from their 42 games.

City did put some silverware in their trophy cabinet two seasons later, beating Tranmere Rovers to carry off the Welsh Cup, but there was another big blot on their record on 28 April 1934, when they crashed to their heaviest defeat in conceding nine goals without reply at Coventry. To make matters worse, four of them were scored by a Somerset-born player they had discarded – Clarrie Bourton, who had joined them from Paulton Rovers in 1926 but been given only a few first-team games before leaving for Blackburn (from where he moved to Coventry), along with fellow forward Albert Keating. And that spree was nothing new against his home club. He had included a hat-trick among his five goals in the two matches between the two Cities over Christmas the previous season.

At £750, Bourton, a bustling old-style centre-forward, was one of Coventry's biggest bargains, scorer of 180 goals in 241 League and Cup games in just over six seasons before leaving for Plymouth. Fortunately for Bristol City, they had a second chance to sign him when he failed to settle in Devon, and, again for £750, he was the spearhead of their attack as they went desperately close to promotion in 1938. Millwall pipped them by just one point. Bourton carried on scoring goals until his retirement from playing in 1944, after which he was employed in the pools office at Ashton Gate until shortly before his death in 1981.

As captain, Bourton was also briefly City's first player-manager. That was the outcome of a joint FA and Football League inquiry into payments made to amateur players. City were fined 100 guineas and Bob Hewison, their manager for the past six years, was suspended for the last seven months of the 1938-39 season. Hewison, a bespectacled Geordie who looked more like the manager of a bank than a football team, had become embroiled in another payments scandal when Leeds City, with whom he was a guest during the previous world conflict after being with Newcastle United, had been expelled from the League in 1919. But then he had been an innocent party, asked by the FA inquiry to act as secretary during the winding-up of the Yorkshire club – a job he undertook while recovering from a second broken leg.

After Hewison's reinstatement as Bristol City's manager, he and Bourton were largely responsible for keeping the club going in the 1939-45 war, along with Len ('Lemmo') Southway, then the first-team trainer. When League football was resumed, Hewison again went close to guiding the club back into the Second Division. Southway, who hailed from the Hotwells district of Bristol, had also been a City stalwart during the 1914-18 war, when he and Billy Wedlock had been the club's only two regular players. Southway, also a defender, had remained available because he had been sent to work in the docks instead of into the Forces after losing two fingers in an accident at work in a box factory. Apart from two years away in the 1920s – first with Exeter City, then coaching in Switzerland – he was a familiar figure at Ashton Gate for more than 50 years. He served under five chairmen, nine managers, and was assistant to six trainers either side of being senior trainer himself.

In an interview with Peter Godsiff, who for many years reported on Bristol City for the *Evening Post,* Southway recalled that one Thursday night in 1941 when air raids on Bristol in the Second World War were at their height, he was at Ashton Gate checking on the footballs for Saturday's match when a policeman knocked on the door. 'What are you doing here?' he asked Southway. 'I'm working,' came the terse reply. 'Well, you'd better move smartly,' said the officer. 'One of your stands has just been damaged by a bomb, and there are four more to go off yet.' 'Lemmo' did not need telling twice. The grandstand was totally destroyed that night. Not long afterwards Southway bought a car, a Morris 8. With one stand already wrecked, he reasoned that there would be little chance of another being hit, so he parked his new car beneath it. He had owned it for only three weeks when that stand, and the car, went up in smoke on being hit by incendiary bombs.

Before the war there had also been a fire in one of the stands. Southway and the trainer at the time, Dick Batten, put it out before it could do much damage, but were they thanked? Oh no! Next day, one of the City's directors called Southway to one side and said: 'I've a good mind to give you the sack.' When 'Lemmo' asked him why, he was told: 'Because you put that ******* fire out. We wanted the insurance.' '

Southway, who believed his nickname originated from a drink called 'Lemco' that was widely advertised during the Great War, had high hopes of a Bristol City revival after the Second World War. 'We had a couple of very successful seasons when we almost won promotion. The atmosphere was there after the war. The crowds were big and people were all talking about football. But we lost a valuable player when Roy Bentley left, and to my mind that was a turning point, even though League football had not then resumed. Another slide set in before we got back into the Second Division.'

Roy Thomas Frank Bentley, the Bristol-born son of a rugby player, was one of City's big discoveries of the war years – but only after Bristol Rovers, with whom he was an office boy on leaving Portway School at the age of fourteen, had made the mistake of letting him go, despite his showing great promise in their Western League side. There was not to be a Roy of the Rovers saga. City, alerted to the interest being shown in Bentley by Major Frank Buckley, then manager of Wolves, signed him on professional forms in the late summer of 1941 after he had scored a stack of goals in local football. Service in the Royal Navy restricted his appearances, but City were besieged with offers after his outstanding display in a Cup defeat of Brentford, and in 1946, shortly after his demobilisation, he was snapped up by Newcastle United – without their having seen him play. One of United's directors overheard a remark by the manager of another club to this effect: 'If there is a First Division club looking for an inside-forward their player is Bentley, of Bristol City.' There was just a slight problem about the fee. City wanted £8,500. Newcastle saved themselves the £500 by winning the toss of a coin between the clubs' chairmen.

Bentley failed to fit in on Tyneside, but his career blossomed again with an £11,000 transfer to Chelsea, where he was converted into an unorthodox centre-forward who frequently raided down the flanks. Winner of a dozen England caps, he was the Stamford Bridge club's leading scorer for eight seasons, totalling 149 goals in 366 games, and he captained their first League champions in their Golden Jubilee year of 1955. Another successful change of position, to half-back after moving to Fulham for £8,600, made him a prominent member of a promotion-winning side, and after ending his playing days with Queen's Park Rangers he followed his first stint in management with Reading (a club of which he was later secretary) by guiding Swansea up from the Fourth Division.

'Lemmo' Southway could also have mentioned another Bristolian, Cyril Williams, as a big loss to City as their climb out of the Third Division was delayed until ten years after the Second World War. More so indeed, for Williams did play for the club when the League got back onto a peacetime footing. Having guested for Reading and Tottenham during the war, and made his debut for City when they defeated Bristol Rovers 6-3 at Ashton Gate in a friendly from which the proceeds went to relieve the Bristol rugby club's financial difficulties, Williams scored nearly 30 goals in just over 80 League and Cup appearances in the first two post-war seasons.

The goalkeepers in that friendly between the Bristol clubs, Harold Liley and Joe Nicholls, both stood 6ft 4ins. It was Liley's only appearance in City's first team, although he played for the club in a number of Colts and reserve matches. After his return from National Service in the Army he signed for Rovers because City already had three goalkeepers on their books, but at Eastville he was restricted to being the experienced Jack Weare's deputy before guarding Bath City's goal in more than 200 Southern League matches, 130 of them in succession.

The consistent form shown by Cyril Williams for Bristol City caught the attention of West Bromwich Albion, who in the summer of 1948 agreed an exchange deal involving wing-half Cliff Edwards (later player-manager of Gravesend and Northfleet), plus £500. In his first season at the Hawthorns the crinkly haired Williams, a cultured and constructive inside-forward, was an important member of the team that returned Albion to the First Division. Two years later, after 77 games and 20 goals for the Midlanders, he did what Bentley rejected the chance to do – he rejoined Bristol City.

Bentley became available in 1956, by which time he was into his 30s, because Ted Drake, the former Arsenal and England centre-forward who then managed Chelsea, had decided to switch from his ageing side to his youth scheme. Bristol City put in an offer, along with West Ham and Nottingham Forest, and it was actually accepted. Bentley, however, refused to sign. Not even when City told him they were willing for him to continue living in London and training with Chelsea. Neither could Harry Dolman persuade him with the offer of a job in the capital as a representative of his company. To the accompaniment of 'Keep Bentley' slogans that fans painted on fences around the ground, the affair dragged on for some four months before the reluctant Roy finally threw in his lot with Fulham.

Cyril Williams, on the other hand, jumped at the opportunity to go back to Ashton Gate on the eve of the 1951-52 season, especially as he had no longer been sure of a regular first-team place with Albion after breaking his right leg (in February 1950, on the same day, incidentally, that Billy 'Legs' Linacre, then of Middlesbrough, suffered a similar injury for the third time). Another consideration was that Williams had taken up a clerical post back in Bristol towards the end of his time with West Bromwich. Only a few months before he rejoined City, there had been talk of his going to Queen's Park Rangers in exchange for Don Mills, also an inside-forward, but he had refused the move. Mills, a Yorkshireman who had joined the London club through a tip-off from manager Dave Mangnall's uncle, had gone to Cardiff instead.

Re-signed by his home club for about £5,000, Williams was converted into a first-class wing-half who missed only three matches when he was in another promotion-winning team in 1954-55. He stayed with City for three more seasons, also owning a newsagent's business in Bedminster, and he had some 350 games for the club behind him when he left for the second time to take up a two-year contract as Chippenham Town's player-manager. Afterwards he was manager of Gloucester City. He was only 57 when, early in 1980, he was fatally injured in Somerset as his car crashed into a tree on the Street to Somerton road.

In his first stint with Bristol City, Cyril Williams forged a fine and fruitful understanding with Don Clark, a free scorer and fellow Bristolian who also came to the fore with the club during the 1939-45 War. Clark, who was on the books for 21 years – latterly as assistant secretary, before resigning to join a Bristol firm as their warehouse manager – first attracted City while playing for the North Bristol Central Old Boys junior side. Bob Hewison, impressed by his readiness to shoot, converted him from wing-half to centre-forward and correctly predicted that the goals would flow. Dashing Don had the high ratio of 77 from 128 League games, and set a club record for one season with the 36 (41 in all) that boosted the strong challenge made for promotion from the Third Division South in 1946-47.

Clark scored five more goals in the FA Cup during that campaign – four of them in a 9-3 demolition of Hayes Athletic in the first round, the other, again at home, from the penalty spot that gave them the lead before Gillingham countered with a couple to knock them out in the second. His appetite whetted by a four-goal broadside in a pre-season friendly at Plymouth, Clark twice more repeated that dose in League games – first, again with the aid of a penalty, in a record 9-0 thrashing of Aldershot on the Saturday after Christmas, the other, also including a spot kick, in a 5-0 defeat of Torquay United at the beginning of March.

Clark was quite a penalty expert. Even Harry Baldwin, the Brighton goalkeeper renowned for saving them, was given no chance when Clark took one against him four minutes from the end of an FA Cup-tie in 1951 when both Bristol clubs reached the last sixteen together for the first time (that was the year in which Rovers made the quarter-finals before losing to Newcastle in a mudbound replay; City went out in the fifth round at Birmingham). Baldwin had kept out seven of the last nine spot kicks awarded against the Sussex club, five of them in succession, but Clark blasted the ball past him for the game's only goal. Of course, in common with all other penalty-takers, Clark was not infallible, but an exceptional effort was generally required to foil him. One of the best of them was pulled off by Ted Ditchburn, the Tottenham and England goalkeeper, who pushed aside a typical blockbuster during a match in which Clark played for the RAF against an FA XI at Arsenal's ground.

In the first post-war season that Clark ended as the Southern Section's leading scorer, City got off to a flying start in a spirited bid for promotion, denied top place only on goal-average for several weeks at one stage, but they were subsequently unable to keep up with the pace set by Cardiff and finished third, fifteen points behind the Welsh club. They at least had the satisfaction of being the top scorers in the division, their total of 94 putting them one ahead of Cardiff. Moreover, they also won their Good Friday home match with the champions and drew the Easter Monday return. There was an all-ticket crowd of 36,000 for the Ashton Gate clash; at Ninian Park the gates were closed a quarter of an hour before the kick-off with thousands locked out and 51,621, a record for a Third Division game, packed inside. The City players travelled to the game with the directors on an excursion train, with four coaches specially reserved, and completed the journey to the ground in taxis.

The previous transitional season had also been notable for City's meeting with Cardiff at Ninian Park – not just because they were successful in that one too (with the aid of another Clark penalty), but more for the goal that Ivor Guy, a strong and consistent full-back, scored with a spectacular free-kick from fifteen yards inside his own half. The ball never touched the ground as it zoomed into the net. It was a sight never to be forgotten, but memories were stirred afresh when Ray Cashley, a City goalkeeper of the 1970s, scored with a freak wind-assisted clearance from fully 98 yards – some reports gave it an extra couple – in a home victory over Hull that took the Bristol club to the top of the Second Division.

Six-footer Guy, another of the locally born players who used to be so prevalent in Bristol City – and Bristol Rovers – teams, remained a one-club man for more than 400 League matches and some 30 FA Cup-ties (over 500 in all, including wartime games and the 1945-46 transitional season) after joining the Robins as an 18-year-old in 1944 from Bristol and Suburban League football with the neighbouring village side of Hambrook. Not that there was any dearth of envious eyes being cast in his direction. Newcastle were particularly keen at one stage – they were reported to have been prepared to offer £10,000 if they had been given any encouragement – and Norwich were among a dozen other clubs that made inquiries about him.

Guy, who was known to have kicked a dead ball more than 90 yards, first turned out for City at centre-half, but it did not take Bob Hewison long to decide that 'this chap's a full-back or nothing'. Guy held the right-back position until the arrival of Joe Baillie from Wolves in 1956, but regained it during the following season before being given a free transfer in recognition of his long service. Baillie, who had played three times for the Scottish League while with Glasgow Celtic, was soon on his way out to Leicester City, then Bradford. While with Wolves, Baillie was fined £100 by the Football League on admitting, the League claimed, to asking for an illegal payment from what was termed 'an interested club'. Stan Cullis, the Wolves manager, said his club was not the one concerned, and Blackburn, with whom Baillie negotiated before going to Molineux (a fee of about £4,000 had been agreed), would make no comment.

Ivor Guy might have joined Yeovil Town as player-manager after ending his thirteen years at Ashton Gate if he had not been required to live in Yeovil. He was a qualified engineer, but it was because of his confectionery business in the Fishponds district of Bristol that he felt unable to move home, so he accepted an offer to play for Bath City instead. Two years later, however, he suffered a tragic loss when his wife Nancy, who was his partner in the business, died after a short illness at the early age of 34. She had leukaemia and had been moved to hospital only a few days earlier.

Guy, who died at 60 in August 1986, was described by John Atyeo, in another interview conducted by Peter Godsiff, as one of the greatest characters he came across in football. He said that he always reminded him of 'the old-time amateur who couldn't care less', adding: 'Money didn't seem to matter very much to him. I've heard Sid Hawkins, City's secretary in those days, call to Ivor and say: "Come in and get your wages. I've got six packets here for you." When the team sheet went up, Ivor would say to me: "Now then Johnny, if you're around about Ashton Gate at two o'clock tomorrow drop in, for we might be busy".'

Atyeo also recalled the time he was learning to play solo at cards on the way to a match at Northampton. 'Someone went misere,' he said, 'and I'd got rid of one suit except the four. I didn't think there was much danger, but I got caught. The others cursed me. Near the end of the game that afternoon we were drawing and Northampton had a free-kick on the edge of our penalty area. I was in the defensive wall between Ernie Peacock and Ivor. It was a crucial moment for us, but Ivor turned to me and said: "Hey Johnny, you should have thrown that bloody four away".'

Bristol City in 1947-48
Back: Bill Thomas, Ivor Guy, Frank Clack, Dennis Roberts (capt), Syd Kearney, Jack Bailey.
Front Idris ('Dai') Hopkins, Len Townsend, Don Clark, Cyril Williams, Osman

'Lemmo' Southway

Chapter 3

The Clark-Townsend Strike Force

Bristol City again possessed the Third Division South's leading scorer in the second post-war season of 1947-48. No, not Don Clark. This time it was Len Townsend, a Londoner Bob Hewison persuaded his directors to sign from Brentford, for £2,500, as a precaution because Clark was then still in the RAF and liable to be posted away from the Bristol area.

As it turned out, Clark played one more League match than Townsend that season, missing just two of the 42. So they frequently formed a most potent twin strike force, Townsend scoring 29 goals and Clark 23, with both adding three in the FA Cup. And thereby hangs a rare tale, for those hat-tricks were registered, along with a third from Cyril Williams, in the 9-2 first-round defeat of Dartford after a scoreless extra-time draw at the Southern League club's ground in which home goalkeeper Frank Coombs gave such a brilliant display that City beat Everton to signing him, despite the replay avalanche. There had previously been only three hat-trick trebles for one team in one match, all in the League, and almost fifteen more years went by before another came along.

The Robins also started that season with a flood of goals – 40 in their first thirteen games, of which they won all but three. Townsend scored four times in a 7-2 win at Reading and Clark emulated him a week later in a 6-0 home victory over Norwich. Six goals were also put past Southend, on the opening day, and Leyton Orient, Townsend and Clark sharing nine of the dozen and Williams claiming the three others. This prosperity put City in the running for promotion until late October, but then they lost momentum. All began to go wrong from the moment they surrendered their unbeaten home record to Watford after leading at half-time with another of Ivor Guy's free-kick bombshells, this one from the more modest 45 yards.

On the following Saturday, 1 November, City failed to score in losing away to Queen's Park Rangers. It was a tense tussle between the division's top two, the London club having retained first place despite City's sequence of six wins mainly because they had played two matches more. One of the two goals to which City could not reply came from the penalty spot. The other was scored by Danny Boxshall, winner of the Military Medal in France during the war, who would be signed by City in time for the following season. Boxshall, who assisted Bournemouth, then Rochdale, after his two years at Ashton Gate, was a Leslie Compton discovery. He and the Arsenal defender were in the British Army of the Rhine side. On Compton's recommendation he was given a game with QPR in November 1945 when the boat due to take him to the Channel Islands for another BAOR match was delayed. His display was so convincing that manager Dave Mangnall signed him on professional forms at once.

QPR clung onto the lead Boxshall helped give them against Bristol City despite losing full-back Reg Dudley, carried off with a broken right leg only a few minutes after breaking his nose. City, too, were handicapped. Dennis Roberts, their influential, long-serving centre-half and captain, missed most of the match with a sprained ankle.

Another defeat, at home to lowly Torquay, was suffered before the Cup dates with Dartford, which raised hopes of the striking spark being rekindled when the replay produced a rout. But those hopes proved misleading. City again misfired when in Cup action for the third successive Saturday (no mid-week replays in those early post-war days). Out they went at home to Crystal Palace, beaten by an only goal in the extra time then applied to original ties. One of Palace's most effective players was Joe Millbank, a big centre-half who, while a private in the Army, had joined Bristol Rovers after hitch-hiking for a trial from his unit in the Midlands. The signing had been completed by none other than Sid Hawkins, then at Eastville before becoming City's secretary. From Rovers, Millbank made his way to Palace via Wolves and Millwall. In 1967, Hawkins resumed a link with Rovers by becoming manager of their supporters' social club.

By January 1948, Bristol City were down to ninth, their lowest position all season, but they improved slightly to finish seventh. They completed a double over their Rovers neighbours with a 5-2 win, in which Clark was a missed penalty away from another four-goal broadside, then avenged themselves against QPR's coming champions with two Townsend goals. Townsend spent only one more season with City, again their top scorer, but with his goals tally down to 14 in the League and two in the Cup. He left as he had arrived – as the result of conditions imposed to which he objected. While with Brentford he had sought to secure his post-football future for his wife and daughter by becoming a sales representative for a glue firm, so he had refused their demand that he should make soccer his full-time occupation. He broke with City because they introduced a regulation requiring all players to train at Ashton Gate and live locally.

Before that change of policy, the club's most-travelled player, though not for long, was surely Jimmy Mullen, an Irishman from Larne who ran a confectionery business at Barrow-in-Furness and journeyed to matches from that Cumbrian port on the Irish Sea. He began his professional career with Barrow, then members of the Third Division's Northern Section, and also played for Crystal Palace before his short spell with City. Normally a forward, he was also tried at wing-half.

Townsend, who was transferred to Millwall, lived and trained in London during his two seasons with City – as did his wing partner Idris Hopkins, a Welsh international naturally known as Dai, with whom he had been transferred to City from Brentford shortly after goalkeeper Frank Clack made the same move. Another player City signed from Brentford around that time was

Maurice Roberts, a Bristol-born outside-left, but he never appeared in their League side. In his first practice game with City his eyes began to ache and he noticed that the other players looked blurred. On going for a check-up in hospital, he was told his sight was failing, and soon afterwards he went blind. City held a darts match in aid of his benefit fund, and paid his wages through the 1947-48 season. A London eye specialist then tried a series of inoculations that restored sufficient sight in the left eye for Roberts to resume practically a normal life, and he ran a mobile library at Ruislip. In February 1951 he was Bristol City's guest at their fifth-round FA Cup-tie with Birmingham City. Dai Hopkins had helped the Griffin Park club from Third Division to First in the 1930s, then to victory over Portsmouth in a London Cup final at Wembley during the war, and he was a welcome, if not long-term, addition to City's wing strength in the wake of the departure to Reading of Jack Hargreaves.

It was through his RAF service that Hargreaves, a forceful outside-left, landed on City's doorstep. His posting from Yorkshire to the Bristol Aeroplane Company at Filton, where he worked in the experimental section, was originally for only six months, but he stayed there until his demobilisation. As he had been with Leeds United since before the war, his transfer to City was speedily arranged because Bob Hewison was an old friend of Billy Hampson, a fellow former Newcastle player who was then manager at Elland Road.

At Reading, Hargreaves soon became another victim of a demand to live locally. His home was still in Bristol, where he had only recently started work with Harry Dolman's firm, so he threw in his lot with Yeovil Town in time to take part in the Somerset club's famous FA Cup giant-killing run of 1949 that included victories over Bury and Sunderland. Injury kept him out of the 8-0 trouncing by Manchester United that ended it all, but he looked back on those days as the most memorable of his career. As he put it: 'You just can't beat a good Cup run and the glory which surrounds it.'

After three years with Yeovil, Hargreaves went to Stonehouse with Bill Thomas, a Derby-born inside-forward who played regularly for City during the war and kept his place in their Third South side for much of the first two seasons after it. They helped the Gloucestershire club win the Second Division title in the Western League, but Hargreaves was then provoked into a move back to Somerset, with Minehead, because of a threatened wage cut. He stayed there for three more seasons, as player-manager for the last two, before giving up playing in his 40th year. 'I had to go down there about three times a week, and my work was catching up on me. I just had to pack it in.'

In that work with Brecknell, Dolman and Rogers, Hargreaves switched from being a fitter to working in the test shop, where he checked sugar and flour packing machines – prize inventions by Harry Dolman – before they left the factory for many parts of the world. For some years he also kept in touch with football by combining coaching young players with scouting for Bristol City. That did not leave him much spare time, but in the summer he played cricket well into his 40s for the St Mary Redcliffe club and also managed to fit in 'a bit of gardening' as his favourite relaxation.

Frank Clack left Brentford because his first-team chances were limited by the consistency of Ted Crozier, who guarded Scotland's goal during the 1939-45 War, in which Clack guested for Notts County and Mansfield before his RAF posting to Egypt. It had been the same at Clack's first League club, Birmingham, where, apart from a spell injured, Harry Hibbs, one of England's greatest goalkeepers, had kept him in the background. And if he had stayed there he would also have had to contend with Gil Merrick, another goalkeeper who rose to the international level for which Clack himself was at one time tipped.

There was therefore no question that Clack, who had been an inside-forward for his school and junior teams, was 'a good 'un' – as he was described by the Birmingham scout who was sent to watch him in action for Witney Town, a club he helped to win the Oxford League championship. With Bristol City he at last cast aside his deputy tag – if only for the better part of two seasons, during which he was the one who slammed the first-team door shut on any rivals.

Among them was George Marks, a Wiltshire man in possession at Arsenal when war broke out, and in their team more often than any other goalkeeper before the return of peace. Marks stood between the sticks for the Gunners when they defeated Charlton Athletic 7-1 in the South Cup final at Wembley in 1943, and he also played for England in eight consecutive wartime internationals before a head injury suffered against Wales, also at Wembley. He joined Bristol City from Blackburn, who were then managed by Bristol-born Eddie Hapgood, a former Arsenal colleague, but left for Reading after only a few months. There he was again badly injured, in a plaster cast from head to toe, so he completed his time at the Berkshire club with two years as trainer-coach. A proposed playing comeback at Lincoln was aborted when that club's manager, Bill Anderson, decided to seek a younger player instead.

Clack and Jack Bailey, Ivor Guy's first regular full-back partner, were the players Bristol City most often called upon in the second post-war season, 1947-48. A year later Clack went into the Southern League with Guildford City, then into the Kent League with Dover, but Bailey, a Bristolian recruited in 1944, did not leave until the summer of 1958, when he went to Trowbridge Town. He departed as the only player to have appeared in City's first team in each of the thirteen post-war seasons up to that time. He fell out of favour in 1949-50 when Ken Mitchelson arrived from Charlton, but returned to miss just thirteen of City's 184 League games in the next four seasons. Towards the end of his long service he was called upon less frequently after dropping out with a broken arm, but he enjoyed one last, if brief, lease of League life in which he served up some of the best form and took his total of League and Cup games beyond 400. With the addition of Gloucestershire Cup finals,

Football Combination matches and friendlies, this fast-tackling defender was not far off 500.

For the most memorable of all those encounters, Bailey looked back to 14 April 1945 – to the second leg of a wartime cup-tie with Cardiff City at Ninian Park that lasted 202 minutes. It was the date of his senior debut, called in at short notice from his work at the BAC to deputise for the injured Jack Preece. Bristol City had lost the first leg by the odd goal of three, but Jack Hargreaves wiped out that deficit and Bill Thomas forced extra-time by bringing the aggregate scores level at 3-3 after Cardiff had equalised on the day. The game had to be decided there and then because of the ban on midweek replays to avoid absenteeism in the factories. So, after the normal additional period had expired with the teams still deadlocked, the referee ordered the players to continue until another goal was scored. Cardiff's Billy Rees was the man to get the 'golden' decider, after 112 extra minutes. That put the Welsh club through against Wolves and, although they were again successful in the second leg, it was not sufficient to overcome the earlier margin of defeat at Molineux. Wolves, who had themselves been enmeshed in a marathon (of 153 minutes against Birmingham), then lost their semi-final against Bolton Wanderers, who defeated Manchester United over two legs in the final.

Another of the players on City's books at the time of their Ninian Park endurance test was a forward named Collins – christened Ronald, but always known as Sammy. He was one City mistakenly let go after little more than a dozen League games – to Torquay United, whose scoring records he smashed with 40 goals in the 1955-56 season and a total of 204 in 358 League games. A natural taker of penalty kicks, he scored from the spot in ten seconds against Walsall in 1956.

On 1 May 1953, at the end of the season in which Collins first exceeded Jimmy Trotter's Torquay best of 26 goals in 1930-31, Bristol City were the fitting visitors for Sammy's benefit match, an occasion also marked by the special presentation of a tankard. Collins, who hailed from the Ashton Gate area, gave up playing in March 1959 to concentrate on the newsagent's that he had bought in the Clifton district of Bristol shortly after leaving Torquay the previous summer. His last games were with Gloucester City, whom he captained, before asking to be released from his contract when he found his shop taking up too much of his time.

Bristol City could have done with some of Collins's goals as they slipped on the slide that led to the sacking of Bob Hewison in March 1949, less than three months after his contract had been renewed. Hewison had only recently celebrated his 40th year in football, and was the holder of a Football League long-service medal for his time in management.

The abrupt turnaround in City's attitude towards Hewison resulted from the intervening appointment of four new directors. His departure caused quite a sensation. George Jenkins, the club's chairman for 26 years, also left, after a stormy annual meeting. For several years the directors had been divided, some having never forgiven Jenkins and Hewison for selling Roy Bentley, and a new majority had forced the enlargement of the board after four of Jenkins's supporters had died during the past two seasons. Shareholders also asked why Cyril Williams had been allowed to leave. When Jenkins said it had been 'at his own request', one shareholder who claimed to be a friend of Williams denied this and alleged it was because ten shillings a week had been deducted from his wages.

The fact that feelings were still running high about Bentley had been clearly demonstrated the previous January when he had made a triumphant first reappearance at Ashton Gate in a Chelsea team for which he had scored twice with 'picture' headers in an FA Cup victory gained after City had led with a Clark goal until the last eight minutes. Crowds had welcomed Bentley on his arrival by train at Temple Meads, and he had been cheered both onto the field and afterwards as he went to visit his parents. He had even played a game of snooker with one of the directors before the game.

That Cup exit came during a bleak City run of nine League matches without a win, the worst of them a six-goal pasting at home by Norwich a week after Chelsea's visit. There was therefore a touch of irony when the board meeting at which Hewison was first told of the intention to appoint a new manager was held only four days after the club's first victory since before Christmas, at Torquay. Overdue success, however, was only fleeting. Of their remaining thirteen games, City won only two, finishing 16th, with their goals output down to 44 – their lowest since their descent into the Third Division seventeen years before. The last of those sparse victories, gained with two Boxshall goals against Ipswich, was their first at home for four months. New manager Bob Wright was not there to see it, scouting for talent at one of that afternoon's Combination Cup semi-finals. He returned empty-handed.

Robert Cooper Allen Wright, a Glaswegian defender, had been the first Scot signed by Jimmy Seed. The former England forward, then managing Charlton Athletic, went back to his happy North-East hunting ground to pay Horden Colliery Welfare £100 for Wright in May 1937. After the war, during which he was a captain in the Royal Armoured Brigade, but guested for Middlesbrough when unavailable to the London club, Wright became assistant to Seed at the Valley, and it was from there that he was brought in by Bristol City to succeed Hewison.

Wright's appointment at the age of 34 put him in the novel situation of being junior to one of the players he inherited – Cliff Morgan, a product of Bristol Boys' Brigade football who was then in the last of his eighteen seasons with City. Morgan was rewarded, like Billy Wedlock, for his loyalty and consistency with two benefits – the first jointly with full-back Cyril Bridge when Torquay were the visitors in 1938, the other at a home match with Bournemouth in 1946, when he put City on the path to victory with a second-minute goal from a free kick on his 438th first-team appearance. The first of his League games was played at Tottenham in 1932 when City were narrowly beaten after left-winger Charlie Sargeant had given them a half-time lead but then missed a penalty. Although mainly a wing-half, Morgan also played at the centre of both defence and attack, and in both inside-forward positions. After ending his playing career (which included turning out for Bristol Rovers as a wartime guest), he prolonged his service to City as a scout.

Bob Wright's stay at Ashton Gate lasted just fourteen months. City were sixteenth in the table when he arrived, and only one place better off when he went. He resigned in the 1950 close season, complaining of not being given a free hand, then spent a year over at Eastville as assistant to manager Bert Tann while also running the White Hart public house in Bristol's Lower Maudlin Street.

For Bob Hewison, who had been Northampton Town's player-manager and manager of QPR before taking up the Bristol post, the road out of Ashton Gate led back North – but not for long. Within two months of losing his distinction of being the most durable of the current Southern Section managers (his City reign had dated back to March 1932), he reluctantly signed a three-year contract as manager of Gateshead, the former South Shields club then members of the Third Division North. Reluctantly because, although he originally came from that part of the country, he was so unwilling to give up his home in Bristol that he refused to find a new one in the North-East when asked to do so and resigned that autumn.

After managing Guildford City and scouting for Bristol Rovers, Hewison was appointed team manager of Bath City in May 1957. Three seasons later he piloted the Somerset club to the Southern League title, thirteen points ahead of the runners-up. He put in one more season before retiring in 1961, a couple of months beyond his 72nd birthday. He died, still in his adopted city of Bristol, in the spring of 1964.

Harry Dolman, who saw a lifetime's ambition fulfilled
when City returned to the First Division

Chapter 4

Start of the Pat Beasley era

The manager who Bristol City took on, also at first as a player, to succeed Bob Wright in July 1950 would lead them back to the Second Division five years later.

Pat Beasley, as he was always known, although his real name was Albert, was preceded from Fulham by Sid Thomas, a 5ft 6in Welsh international winger with size 4½ boots. Thomas had polished his game while playing against barefoot natives on the Gold Coast during the war, when he was an RAF driver with an airfield construction company.

Beasley began his own playing career also as a winger of slight build. In his first match for Amblecote School near his Stourbridge birthplace, his team scored 26 goals without response from Kinver School, and young Beasley gobbled up half of them, exploiting his penchant for cutting inside to devastating effect. After leaving school, he joined Cookley, a Kidderminster League side, then, in 1931, turned professional with Stourbridge.

His appearances in that club's Birmingham League side had still to reach double figures when he was sought by both Aston Villa and Arsenal, then the country's top two clubs. He plumped for the Gunners, champions of the Football League for the first time, with Villa as runners-up. It was a difficult decision, for there was formidable competition to be faced with both clubs. Jack Mandley and Eric Houghton were firmly established on the wings for Villa, Joe Hulme and Cliff Bastin for Arsenal.

Consequently, Beasley's fortunes in his five years at Highbury were mixed. With Bastin having spells at inside-forward and Hulme's appearances gradually dwindling, he was chosen enough times to qualify for two League championship medals as Arsenal rounded off their title hat-trick from 1933 to 1935. But when it came to the Cup, Beasley was out of luck, twice denied selection for a final.

In 1932, shortly after his £550 transfer to Highbury, he was overlooked for the final at Wembley in which Arsenal controversially lost to Newcastle, from a cross delivered as the ball ran out of play over the by-line. When the Scottish wizard Alex James failed a fitness test, and Bastin was switched to inside-left, Beasley had every reason to expect that he would be brought in on the wing – he had recently played his first League games in similar circumstances. Instead, manager Herbert Chapman surprisingly moved Welsh international Bob John from left-half (where George Male made his Cup debut) to fill the vacancy at outside-left.

In 1936 Beasley was even more unfortunate. A forward-line reshuffle when centre-forward Ted Drake had to have a cartilage operation enabled Beasley to play from the fifth round through to the semi-final against Grimsby, but out he went for the final in which Sheffield United were narrowly beaten. Drake was deemed fit, just about, to return; Ray Bowden, who had been deputising for him, moved back to inside-right, from where Bastin reverted to the left wing to Beasley's exclusion. Drake did what John had done before – score Arsenal's only goal – but this time it was a winner.

And, after all, there was a happy ending for Beasley as well. Alex James generously offered him his medal. In his book *Football Ambassador,* Eddie Hapgood, Arsenal's captain, recalled: 'Pat refused it at first, saying he would wait until the decision of the FA was made known, following Arsenal's application to have another specially struck for Beasley. The application was refused, so Alex handed his medal over.' James was thus left with the just the one he had gained as a scorer when Arsenal had won their first major trophy by beating Huddersfield Town in the 1930 final.

Beasley eventually graced Wembley after being transferred to Huddersfield, his value raised to £750. In 1938 – in a team for which Joe Hulme bowed out with his record-equalling fifth final appearance, not long after also joining those Yorkshire Terriers from Arsenal – Beasley had to be content with a loser's medal as George Mutch's off-the-bar penalty for Preston in the last minute of extra-time reversed the result of the 1922 final. There again, photographic evidence indicated an injustice. Henry Rose, the *Daily Express* football correspondent, observed that: 'in the split second Mutch was fouled he was just outside the line of the penalty area,' adding that referee Jewell was guilty of 'an honest mistake'.

Beasley would almost certainly not have got that far in the game but for the perspicacity of Tom Whittaker, the trainer who later became Arsenal's manager. Whittaker realised that blood poisoning had set in when he went to the Beasley's home around midnight after Mrs Beasley had 'phoned him to say that her husband had become feverish and run a high temperature since having two stitches inserted in a cut suffered during a game at Highbury that afternoon. Beasley was rushed to hospital, where he spent more than two months recovering after an operation that saved his leg – and possibly even his life – in a situation similar to that in which, during the 1950s, Sheffield Wednesday's Derek Dooley was sadly less fortunate. It transpired that Beasley's infection had arisen from a new kind of fertiliser that had been sprayed over Arsenal's pitch.

To the 89 first-team appearances he had made for Arsenal, Beasley added 123 for Huddersfield, scoring nearly 30 goals, and on 15 April 1939 gained his one England cap against Scotland at Hampden Park. England had not won at the Glasgow stadium for twelve years, and that sorry sequence seemed set to be stretched when trailing with only twenty minutes to go. Then Beasley nipped in to equalise, and with time running out Tommy Lawton, the centre-forward then with Everton, dramatically laid the bogy with a header from a centre by Stoke's Stanley Matthews.

Beasley also went on an FA tour of South Africa that year, before war broke out. After helping Huddersfield to win the North-East regional championship in the first wartime season, Beasley guested for Arsenal before, late in 1945, he was signed by Fulham. After being nominated by the FA to coach in Norway the following summer, he made a return to League action with the Cottagers that was hardly encouraging. They let in seven goals on his debut at Bury but, appointed captain and successfully dropping back to left-half, he led them up to the First Division, as champions, for the first time in their history in 1948-49. By the time he accepted the Bristol City job (chosen from some 30 applicants) he had a further 164 League and Cup games on his CV, and there were to be 66 more for the Robins before he concentrated on management.

Fulham had received offers of up to £8,000 for Beasley, but they waived the fee when he moved to Ashton Gate: 'We'll even pay him his £750 benefit out of our own pockets,' said Bill Dodgin, the London club's manager who was later with Bristol Rovers, 'but Bristol City are only too willing to pay it.'

Sid Thomas, an unsuccessful target for Cliff Britton, the Bristol-born manager of Everton, arrived at Ashton Gate the previous month for about £8,000. That was a nice little profit for Fulham, who had snapped him up as a 16-year-old amateur shortly before the war after he had been spotted by their goalkeeper, Bob McCormick. Thomas, then the local baker's boy, was playing for Machynlleth when McCormick happened to be visiting that small market town in Wales because it was his wife's birthplace. Bristol City were also impressed after seeing Thomas in 'Lemmo' Southway's benefit match, so much so that Harry Dolman and another director, George Jones, hurried there by car to sign him after being tipped off that a First Division club had made inquiries.

Thomas, 29 by the time he joined City, captained his school team at 13, and two years later played in an amateur international trial that was watched by Ted Robbins, then the Welsh FA secretary. Robbins tapped him on the shoulder and told him he would play for Wales one day. While with Fulham, Thomas added four international caps to the representative appearances he had made in West Africa and Germany while serving in the RAF during the war.

But Thomas played for City for only just over two months and 13 games before medical advice rang down the curtain on his career.. He had been ill for some months, advised by a specialist to take a complete rest in mid-October. The last of his games, in a home win against Newport, was the one in which Jack Boxley, a Beasley 'find' from their mutual home town of Stourbridge, made his debut in place of Tommy Rudkin, an outside-left from Southampton who had started out with a few First Division games for Arsenal. Rudkin was one of four players City signed in a week. Bert Hawkins, a centre-forward from Bristol Rovers, and two defenders from Charlton, Ken Mitchelson and Don Freeman, were the others.

The team in which Pat Beasley first played for Bristol City, in a 0-1 defeat at Bournemouth on the opening day of 1950-51, was: Morgan (S); Guy, Bailey;

Peacock, Roberts, Beasley; Thomas, Eisentrager, Rodgers, Lowrie, Rudkin. Four members of that side had been with City since the resumption of League football in 1946 – the Guy-Bailey full-back partnership, and half-backs Ernie 'Ginger' Peacock and Dennis Roberts, who had both previously been with Notts County. Peacock, born in Bristol, went on trial to Meadow Lane with Vic Lambden, a centre-forward who was turned down but made good with Bristol Rovers, and Bobby Allen, a full-back from Shepton Mallet who, like Peacock, arrived at Ashton Gate after playing for Notts during the war.

Allen took part in only one Football League game for both County and City, but Peacock, having rejected Notts' invitation to re-sign at the end of the 1945-46 season, was was a real bargain for his home club at £1,000. He helped City out of the Third Division in exceeding 350 appearances before joining Weymouth as player-coach in 1959. After that he was player-manager of Taunton Town. John Atyeo once described him as a Jekyll and Hyde character – 'when he pulled on a football shirt he would tear your heart out, but off the field he was one of the nicest fellows you could wish to meet; he was always full of life and lived every minute of the game.'

Roberts, a tall and well-built stopper centre-half who in 1949 became the first City player to receive the then maximum benefit sum of £750, appeared in about as many games for the club as Peacock. These included a sequence of 117, of which he was unaware until a newspaper report on the day of that tough match with promotion-bound QPR to which reference has already been made. Fate then took a hand, for play had been in progress only five minutes when Roberts was carried off for attention to the damaged ankle that interrupted his run of appearances.

Born near Huddersfield, Roberts started out as an amateur with the Terriers at 16. He had two seasons before being signed by Notts County, who soon afterwards unwisely gave him a free transfer – a decision they were given reason to regret a decade or so after his move to Ashton Gate in the 1938-39 season. He had been recommended by Joe Riley, a centre-forward who had joined City from their Rovers neighbours in the 1930s and scored all five of their goals in beating Brighton at Ashton Gate. In three Third South meetings Roberts subdued the much-vaunted Tommy Lawton, whose descent into that lowly sphere from First Division Chelsea (replaced by Roy Bentley) was a sensation. On one of those barren occasions for Lawton, Notts turned up at Ashton Gate fresh from scoring seven goals (two for Tommy) against Newport County.

Syd Morgan, the other member of Bristol City's defence when Pat Beasley made his debut, was a Bristolian goalkeeper who had his best run of just over two dozen games in the side in 1950-51. He had keen rivalry for a first-team place during his ten years with the club, and his appearances were still short of three figures by the time he moved to Millwall in 1958. One game, away to Brighton, was notable for its two goals – one for being extraordinary, the other because it needed a delayed second opinion. From a Morgan goal-kick the ball flew off the head of centre-forward Cyril Thompson straight back into an empty net. City's equaliser came from a retaken free-kick. The ball was scrambled away after Peacock's shot struck the underside of the crossbar, and not until the referee noticed the waving flag of a linesman was a goal awarded – and then only after a consultation. It ended a City run of five away defeats.

Of City's attack when Beasley arrived, Alous (Alec) Eisentrager was a stocky 5ft 2in ball player who on the first day of the previous season, in a home victory over Northampton, had become the first German to play in the Football League since Max Seeburg (Tottenham, Burnley and Grimsby, among other clubs, before the First World War.) Eisentrager began playing in Hamburg at the age of eight, and four years later joined Hamburger Sport-Verein, the oldest and best club in that city, playing for their youth team and once for the reserves. With the outbreak of a second world war, he was called up into the Luftwaffe when still only sixteen, and within three months was captured at Breda, in Holland.

On being brought to England in February 1945, he was in prisoner-of-war camps at Herne Bay, Ashford, Chippenham and Yatton. While at Herne Bay he played for a local team, and after being moved to Yatton, near Chippenham, where he was put to agricultural work, he joined Trowbridge Town. There he came to the notice of a Bristol City director, who ensured that his club signed him on amateur forms during the 1949 close season.

Eisentrager, who spoke excellent English, was still an amateur when he became the first German to score four goals in a Football League match, in a 6-0 defeat of Newport on 3 September 1949, after City had gone three games without scoring. Still classified as an alien, he had to continue his work on the land as a condition of his stay in England, but after early-morning starts he was able to train with his team-mates two mornings a week, and then returned to the farm. Not until he had completed his residential qualification as an alien was he able to turn professional – which he did in January 1950, by then aged 22, around the time his elder brother Hans, an amateur half-back, had a trial with City during a two-month holiday in England.

The decision to join the paid ranks denied Alec Eisentrager the chance to represent Somerset in a Southern Counties Amateur Championship match against Devon. By the time he left City for Merthyr Tydfil in 1958, he had scored nearly 50 goals in some 250 appearances. He had been transfer-listed at £3,000 on asking for a move, because he was desirous of a change, but a fee was subsequently quashed when he appealed to the Football League in the hope of making a comeback with another of its clubs. There were no Football League takers for a player in his 30s, however, and after leaving Merthyr he remained in the Southern League with Chelmsford.

It was during Bob Wright's short stewardship at Ashton Gate that Eisentrager joined City. Around the same time Arnold Rodgers and George

Lowrie were also signed as replacements for Don Clark and Len Townsend. The temperamental Lowrie came with the greater reputation, a seasoned Welsh international who had been a prolific scorer as Clarrie Bourton's successor at Coventry, but he was soon to turn 30. Rodgers, in his mid-20s, proved to be the better investment.

Lowrie, who stood more than 6ft and, with his slicked jet-black hair, bore a strong resemblance to Tommy Lawton, was with Swansea, as an amateur, before joining Preston on his 17th birthday in 1937 in exchange for Joe Beresford and Leslie Vernon. He was North End's twelfth man for the following year's FA Cup final. At the end of the next season he cost Coventry £1,750, an astute piece of business when he made nine wartime appearances for Wales (there were four full caps to come later). His forceful shooting helped him to a hat-trick against England at Wembley during the war, in which he served in the Army, but it later deprived him of a goal in a home Second Division match with Bury. The ball burst as it bulged the net, yet the referee refused to allow a goal and the game ended without one.

In the first post-war season, Lowrie's five hat-tricks included five goals in the Army's 8-3 defeat of an FA XI at Stoke, but he lost form in the autumn of 1947 and was dropped from the Coventry team. Stung into asking for a transfer, he went to Bristol, his wife's home city, and trained at Rovers' ground for a fortnight before reporting back, regaining his League place and withdrawing his request for a move. Lowrie was not, however, destined to remain at Highfield Road for much longer. Coventry's deteriorating financial situation compelled them to part with their ace marksman in March 1948.

Lowrie went to Newcastle for £18,500, then the third highest British transfer fee, but a knee injury, for which he needed a cartilage operation, kept him out of action for most of the following season. He had played in only a dozen first-team games in eighteen months when he was transferred to Bristol City for £10,000 in September 1949, after Carlisle, then managed by his former Preston clubmate Bill Shankly, had made an unsuccessful bid. Lowrie's exit from the North-East was a dramatic sequel to his ordering-off at Molineux for allegedly striking Sammy Smyth, Wolves' Irish international inside-forward. 'We will not tolerate this sort of behaviour at Newcastle,' said director Stan Seymour, a former winger with the Geordies. 'When a player is sent off he lets down the reputation of the club as well as his own.'

In his first game for City, Lowrie scored the winner at Eastville after Bristol Rovers had pulled back a two-goal deficit. He then had to serve the 28-day suspension imposed for his Wolverhampton indiscretion, and there were to be only a dozen more Bristol City goals for this fiery son of Tonypandy before Harry Storer, having returned to Coventry as manager, took him back to Highfield Road for £6,000 in February 1952 in an attempt to stave off relegation. A fractured ankle had also restricted Lowrie's appearances for Bristol City, keeping him out for nearly a year until his scoring return against Crystal

Palace at Ashton Gate the previous October. Consequently, he had lost much of the blistering pace that had been one of his biggest assets, and he was unable to supply the spark to avert Coventry's descent. Given a free transfer when he fell out with the club soon afterwards, he went into the Southern League as player-manager of Lovells Athletic.

Arnold Rodgers, a former collier from Rotherham, was one of soccer's best-dressed professionals. He proved an exceptional acquisition for City at £5,000 from Huddersfield, where his clubmates had included Peter Doherty, the famous Irishman who was to succeed Beasley as manager at Ashton Gate. There was also a common managerial link to his move. Bob Wright's opposite number at Leeds Road, George Stephenson, had also been assistant manager at Charlton. Rodgers, whose late winner against Manchester City kept the Terriers in the First Division on the last day of 1948-49, was City's top scorer in each of his first four seasons with them. He achieved the high ratio of almost 120 goals in nearly 200 League and Cup matches before leaving for Shrewsbury in the summer of 1956 – not bad for someone told he would never play again after fracturing his skull with a diving header (with which he scored) while with Huddersfield.

Rodgers, noted for his aptitude for winning penalties, netted about a dozen more times for Bristol City in floodlit friendlies. In one of these, against East Fife, he suffered a serious ankle injury at a stage of the 1952-53 season when City were going well for promotion on the back of his 24 goals. He was again troubled by injury when City finally escaped from the Third Division two seasons later, but still managed to muster a goal for every two of his 26 League games. 'The high spot of my career was undoubtedly playing in the City's promotion side,' he said. 'It was a wonderful feeling, and a wonderful season. City were an excellent club, and the players were excellent men as well as footballers. I had a very happy time during my spell there.'

One of Rodgers's City goals was reportedly timed at a record six seconds in a 5-0 home win against Southend on Boxing Day, 1952, but referee Dellow timed it at nine seconds, saying he always kept his watch in his hand for the first minute or so of a match. As recalled later, Rodgers was also a swift scorer when John Atyeo made his City debut. Such feats are often not truly timed and therefore highly disputable. In the case of Rodgers, the ball went to Cyril Williams and winger Duggie Regan, and then back to Rodgers to hit home. Regan, who came from Yeovil, was regarded as one of Exeter's best discoveries since Cliff Bastin, of Arsenal and England fame, after impressing in a Fleet Air Arm side. Regan's first-team outings dwindled in the four seasons he spent at Ashton Gate, before he went into the Southern League with Weymouth.

Another unusual incident while Arnold Rodgers was with Bristol City occurred on the first Saturday of March in 1953, when Bristol University students, taking part in a rag, 'kidnapped' him in a car near his home. They left a message asking Harry Dolman to discuss terms. The City chairman refused to pay the £200 'ransom money' demanded for rag charities, but Rodgers was still released in good time for that afternoon's home match with Walsall. None the worse for his experience, he scored one of the goals in a 6-1 victory that kept City second to their Rovers neighbours in the table. That was the season in which Rovers reached Division Two for the first time; City fell away to fifth, but their time was soon to come.

Rodgers continued to live in Bristol, and to train at City's ground, after his move to Shrewsbury, against whom he had missed two penalties on their first visit to Ashton Gate in 1952. He shot straight at goalkeeper Pat Egglestone both times, but City still comfortably won. Rodgers could have stayed longer with City if they had not disapproved of his decision to try to safeguard his future by buying a florist's shop in Bristol (his wife had been a florist before their marriage). He did not have the capital for his preferred option, an estate agency, in which he had been employed in his younger days at Huddersfield, but he found flowers so profitable that he soon opened up two more shops in the city. Indeed, he was left with so little time for football that his contract with Shrewsbury was cancelled by mutual consent after only six months.

Even so, Rodgers was not out of the game for long, persuaded to sign for Chippenham Town by their chairman – the appropriately named George Flower, who had sought him before his move to Third Division pastures at Gay Meadow. After a season in which he was Chippenham's top scorer as a part-timer in the Western League, Rodgers intended to finish with football completely when Cyril Williams joined the club as player-manager, but it was with Minehead that he finally put his boots away. His first game for them was, again most fittingly, against a team from Bristol City. He later managed the Somerset clubs Welton Rovers and Bath City.

Chapter 5

Rodgers and Rogers

On 18 November 1950, Bristol City for the first time had a Rogers in their team as well as a Rodgers. Jimmy Rogers, a versatile, battling forward who two years earlier had joined Wolves before RAF service led to the Combined Services team and then to Gibraltar, was introduced into City's line-up at Torquay for one of the games in which Sammy Collins enjoyed himself against his old club.

Collins, benefiting from the craft of Hugh Brown, a Scottish international from Partick Thistle who was also making his Football League debut, scored two of Torquay's four goals. City's lone reply came from Rodgers, who had another recent recruit, Jack Boxley, as his left-wing partner. Rogers, brought in because George Lowrie was unfit, had to wait only one more week for the first of almost 100 goals scored in two spells with City. He got off the mark in a 4-0 home Cup win against Gloucester City that was notable for another of Ivor Guy's long-distance spectaculars, this one from 60 yards.

Rogers, who hailed from Pat Beasley's part of the country (he was born at Wednesbury, a fruitful South Staffordshire source of soccer talent), was given his first chance after promotion-bound Nottingham Forest had ended City's sequence of eight home wins. It took Rogers some time to become established, but he made just over 150 more League appearances before reluctantly leaving City for Coventry in company with Boxley, a fellow Staffordshire man, at a joint fee of £6,500 just before Christmas 1956.

Jimmy Regan, a former Rotherham wing-half, had preceded them from Ashton Gate to Coventry earlier that year, but it was not long before he left to go into the Southern League – first with Yeovil Town, then Burton Albion. With Burton at the foot of the table and their players being accused of not working hard enough in training, their chairman Trevor Grantham remarked: 'I wish they were all like Jimmy Regan, who trains regularly and is always fit. It is unfortunate that they are not all Regans.'

Boxley and Rogers were also reunited at Coventry with trainer-coach Wilf Copping, the 'Iron Man' ex-Arsenal and England wing-half who had left that role with City in November. Copping's departure caught Beasley by surprise: 'Wilf's always been as happy as a sandboy here,' he said, 'and we are very sorry to lose him.' But Copping, though just as sorry to leave Bristol, said Coventry's offer was 'too good to refuse'. It came from Harry Warren, who had become their manager that summer, and with whom Copping had been associated for five years at Southend United. Warren had been an admirer of Copping as a trainer ever since, as Southend's manager, he had persuaded him to leave the Beerschot club in Antwerp a year after the war. 'We had never had an argument at Southend,' said Warren, son of a former Derby, Chelsea and England wing-half. 'Wilf left me only because he got a better offer from Bristol. When George Raynor left us at Coventry I had no hesitation about his successor.'

Jimmy Rogers, who had played in one of Blackpool's junior sides before getting onto Wolves' books, continued to live in the Hanham area of Bristol with his wife Doreen and their two children throughout his time with Coventry. He trained at Ashton Gate, joining up with his new team-mates only on match days, but his work outside football as a travelling salesman for a paint brush company eventually proved unsatisfactory for both club and player. His near-30 goals in 80 games included three hat-tricks – all against Aldershot, and one of them a four-goal blast – but he had been with Coventry less than two years when Billy Frith, Warren's successor, decided to part with him after signing George Stewart from Accrington Stanley.

So it was that Rogers, having asked for a transfer, rejoined Bristol City for £3,500 early in December 1958, by which time there was also a new manager, Peter Doherty, at Ashton Gate. 'I was so pleased that City took me back,' said Rogers, unaware that he had at first been offered to Bristol Rovers. Any chance of a deal in that direction, however, was nullified by the Eastville club's No Buy, No Sell policy. Within two years Boxley was back with Rogers from Coventry after almost 100 appearances fo them. Returning on a trial, Boxley had limited scope before leaving for Chippenham Town (and later Welton Rovers), but he stayed long enough to pass 200 games for the Bristol club in all, and to step off the League stage with a half-century of goals. Rogers, who was re-signed as a full-timer but permitted to carry on with his other job, altogether played more than 270 times for Bristol City in League and Cup before his second farewell took him into the Gloucestershire Northern Senior League as player-manager of Cinderford Town – a post he held for four years before resigning in 1966.

In the 1950-51 season, City's Ashton Gate invincibility before the defeat by Forest that precipitated Jimmy Rogers's entry into League football included one of the finest matches against their Rovers rivals. A first-time shot by Lowrie soon after half-time decided it, but City spent the rest of the game fighting off their neighbours' attempts to avert a first defeat.

Rovers, in that season of unprecedented progress to the Cup quarter-finals, were on an unbeaten run of their own when they obtained revenge in the return in late December, stretching it to 18 games with two Lambden goals to Rodgers's one. At Ashton Gate, Syd Morgan, having seen one of his competitors, Frank Coombs, transferred to Southend in the close season, had been City's saviour. At Eastville, the club's goalkeeper was again their star turn, but by then his name was Sullivan – Con Sullivan, a Bristolian who had taken over a few games previously in Morgan's absence with a septic finger. It was really a tale of two goalkeepers, for few in the 30,000 crowd knew that Sullivan's opposite number, Bert Hoyle, was patched up with a wrist cracked during a drawn Christmas Day game with Port Vale. Hoyle, whose career was so soon to be ended by a car crash, had to keep going because his stand-in was also injured. Rovers' only other goalkeeper was an inexperienced amateur.

Sullivan made over 70 first-team appearances in his five years with City, 46 of them as a League ever-present in 1951-52, before his transfer to Arsenal early in 1954. With the Gunners he took his aggregate of senior games beyond the century mark, then in 1959 was given a free transfer because Jim Standen, later a European Cup-Winners' Cup winner with West Ham (and also a cricketer who helped Worcestershire to the County Championship), was preferred as deputy for Welsh international Jack Kelsey. Sullivan's League debut for City was made on an icy December afternoon when Don Clark was briefly recalled from the obscurity of the reserves for the visit of Bournemouth. Clark, replacing Rogers as Lowrie's deputy, increased a lead gained by Rodgers. The visitors were unable to reply, but they offered strong opposition considering that they had not arrived in Bristol until six o'clock in the morning after a wintry overnight train journey that lasted thirteen hours.

There was to be just one more first-team goal for Clark in the 1950-51 season – the late penalty Cup winner against Brighton. He had a joint benefit with 'Ginger' Peacock when City played against an Overseas XI.

After the comfortable win against Gloucester, Beasley and his men reached that fourth-round tie with Brighton through good fortune and efficient football. In the second round at home to Wrexham, it took them 72 minutes to wipe out their opponents's first-half lead, and only four were left when Rogers nicked the winner from close range. In the third round, again at Ashton Gate, City gave an outstanding display, inspired by their player-manager, in springing one of the day's upsets by seeing off Second Division Blackburn with two goals from Rodgers.

Against Brighton, who also had to travel, City were once more in luck when Luton's Henry Pearce, who refereed the previous year's Wembley final, controversially ruled that centre-half McCoy had fouled Rodgers in the penalty area. But in the next round good fortune deserted City – not only in being drawn away for the first time. Beasley's claim that his team had 75 per cent of the play was perhaps an over-statement, but the first of Birmingham's two goals was a scrappy affair described in one report as 'a muffed free kick, a recovery, a goalmouth mix-up, and a sudden shot that went in.'

That was the season in which, taking into account three replays and two postponements, no fewer than fifteen Third Division clubs went into the draw for the fourth round. In the, regrettably, long-defunct *Sporting Chronicle*, Edgar Turner declared that 'the real reason to my mind lies in the tremendous improvement in Third Division football'. He also revealed that 'Bristol City and Southend United have proposed that Third Division clubs do not meet each other in the first round proper,' a suggestion scarcely practical enough to be implemented.

As it happened, City and Southend shortly met twice in the League – and, after the Essex club had emphatically inflicted only City's second defeat in sixteen home games, the return was one of the roughest and toughest seen at Southend for a long time. One player landed a right hook. Another was lectured for his over-robust play. And at least three more were limping by the end. The home side, who had three 'goals' disallowed, fell behind to an allowed effort by Rodgers, but Joe Sibley salvaged a point for the Shrimpers.

City's forward problems were highlighted anew in that hectic confrontation. Roy Bicknell, who had been signed from Charlton as centre-half cover for Dennis Roberts, was the fifth to be selected for the club at centre-forward that season. And in the very next game Jack Boyd, a Massachusetts-born newcomer who had been outside-left for Gloucester in their Cup defeat by City, became the sixth in a 3-3 draw at home to Walsall. Boyd was among the scorers, along with Beasley and Sid Williams, as City rallied after Don Dearson, a Welsh international formerly with Birmingham, volleyed two right-wing centres past Sullivan in as many minutes, but a late penalty ensured a share of the points.

Sid Williams, a wiry and energetic winger who stood only 5ft 4½in, was an Eastville lad, and a keen Rovers supporter, before the war, but he joined City from Eastville United, along with fellow forward Ken Chilcott, because, he said, 'City seemed more interested in young players than the Rovers in those days.' He played as an amateur in the City Colts team, run by George Crandon, that also included Cyril Williams and future Rovers full-back Harry Bamford before enlisting in the Army and earning selection for Northern Command. It was while he was stationed in the Armoured Corps at Catterick that he met his future wife. After the war Darlington (with whom he had been a guest), Brentford, Leeds and Portsmouth were among the clubs keen to sign him – he even had a trial with Bristol Rovers against City – but he chose to return to Ashton Gate because that, as he put it, 'seemed a natural sequel.'

By then, at 27, Williams felt he was too old to make football a full-time career, so he signed part-time forms and, having served an apprenticeship before the war after leaving school, went back to his trade as a painter and decorator. He trained two evenings or mornings a week with City's other part-timers. 'The club seemed to encourage it,' he recalled. 'They didn't have to pay high wages which they couldn't really afford at that time. So, financially, football was no problem to me as I always had my day-time job to fall back on.'

Williams spent two years with Gloucestershire club Stonehouse on leaving City in the summer of 1952, but after that he decided it was time to give up playing. 'The pitches seemed to be getting larger, and the matches lasting longer.' His break from football was almost complete. He wished he were young enough to be starting out all over again, so that he could benefit from the bigger pay packets then available, but he admitted he found being a spectator boring and attended only the occasional game if he thought it might be interesting. 'I can never really get into a game from the terraces. Even some international games on television bore me. You can say I'm one of the missing millions.' At the time he was speaking, in the 1960s, attendances at Football League matches had dropped below 28 million per season from the early post-war peak of more than 41 million in 1948-49. And over the next two decades they slumped to under 16½ million in 1985-86 before, boosted by the introduction of play-offs and then the Premiership, they gradually climbed back to near 30 million.

For Jack Boyd, the experience of playing at centre-forward against Walsall on the first Saturday of February in 1951 was not entirely new to him, even in the short time since he made his debut on the same day as Sullivan the previous December. In January, his switch from the right wing during a match with Millwall paid off as goals from Rudkin and Rodgers had cancelled out a sliced clearance into his own net by Roberts.

There was yet another leader of City's attack that season when Torquay visited Ashton Gate in April. The subject of that experiment was 18-year-old Michael Lyons, later to make most of his League appearances as a full-back with Bournemouth. Lyons showed some neat touches, but his lack of experience was all too obvious. Torquay arrived without an away victory in twenty attempts on their travels. They left 2-0 winners, and the sole comfort for City was that Collins was not a scorer, though that was only because he was omitted from the Torquay team. Both goals came from left-winger Pembury, the second made by the cultured Hugh Brown. At the final whistle Brown told manager Alex Massie, the former Aston Villa and Scotland wing-half, that he thought his left leg was fractured. With his shin swollen to twice its normal size, he was rushed to hospital for an x-ray, but that fortunately showed the injury to be nothing worse than a torn ligament.

Lyons, another youngster off the Bristol-born production belt, was given one more League game before crossing over to Eastville during the 1953 close season in exchange for forwards Len Pickard and Andy Micklewright. Pickard, a former Devon Boys captain and an accomplished sprinter and long jumper, failed to make his mark with either Rovers or City, but after moving from Ashton Gate to Bradford on a free transfer he was top scorer in his first two seasons at Park Avenue. Micklewright, a product of Birmingham and district football, who had declined an invitation to turn professional with West Bromwich Albion, was also unable to find a first-team place with Rovers despite being a frequent scorer for their reserves, but he enjoyed one good season with City, scoring 15 goals in 36 Third Division games in 1953-54, before being sold to Swindon for a small fee. Afterwards he was with Exeter City and Nuneaton Borough.

As at City, Lyons was allowed only a couple of League opportunities at Rovers, but he had topped 100 senior appearances by the time he also joined Swindon on leaving Bournemouth, where another former Bristol City player,

Tony Nelson, was among his clubmates. Nelson, son of Jimmy, the former Newcastle, Cardiff and Scotland full-back, was signed by City from Newport County, with whom he had won a Welsh amateur international cap against his father's home country before turning professional. At Ashton Gate he was primarily a reserve centre-forward, but after moving to Bournemouth in preference to Aldershot (an exchange deal for full-back Stan Jefferson had been suggested) he, like Lyons, found a first-team place more obtainable in defence, at centre-half.

On returning to Rovers following his release by Swindon, Lyons was trainer to their reserve side for fifteen years, then joined Bath City as trainer-coach. Towards the end of the 1960s, he was secretary of Rovers' Former Players Club.

In their next match, after Lyons had led their front line against Torquay, Bristol City again had a new centre-forward. This time it was 'Ginger' Peacock, moved up from right-half at Aldershot. Peacock was an adaptable player, but he, too, was unable to provide the answer in a scoreless draw. Not that he had a decent chance, for he had to express his versatility in a different and defensive direction, at centre-half, when Roberts was carried off with a leg injury shortly before half-time.

For the remaining few matches Beasley reverted to Rodgers, who had spent much of the season at inside-left but was the only one to have really looked the part in the middle. He responded in home victories with two goals against Ipswich and two more against Swindon, whose own, much-envied, centre-forward, Maurice Owen, was blotted out by Peacock. Those goals took Rodgers to twenty for the season in the League, plus three in the Cup, helping City to a final position of tenth – four places and four points behind Rovers. City were to finish lower in the table before the upsurge that swept them to promotion, but when Rodgers and his clubmates reported back from their summer break in 1951 a giant step had already been taken towards increasing the club's scoring power. The player who was to be the most prolific City marksman of them all had arrived.

Chapter 6

Enter John Atyeo

John Atyeo's footballing career could have taken a very different course but for Portsmouth's refusal to relax two of their rules. As an amaetuer on their books, he wanted to be a part-timer, and also to drive a motor car. The Hampshire club, one of the most successful in the First Division, were willing to sign only full-time professionals and, strange reading though it makes these days, all their players were banned from driving.

Atyeo often wondered how things would have turned out if he had been tempted by the offer of professional terms Portsmouth made to him at Easter 1951: 'I would have accepted it without a shadow of a doubt,' he said, 'if they had been agreeable to the conditions my father and I wanted.' He had almost made up his mind to turn professional after Bob Jackson, Pompey's manager, had promised to take him on the club's post-season tour of America if he signed for them. That trip, rewarding the players who had helped to win the League championship two seasons running, was a big temptation for an 18-year-old country lad, but Atyeo's father would have none of it. Quite apart from the fact that he had misgivings about football as a career, he was insistent that his son remained in his apprenticeship as a quantity surveyor.

In any case, it was in cricket that Atyeo senior, who came from near Yeovil, had his main interest. He even said he would sooner see young John play cricket for Somerset than football for England. And so he might have done, for at Trowbridge High School he was as proficient at the summer game as he was at soccer – and rugby and athletics. In his last year he had a batting average of 80 and achieved his first hat-trick as a bowler. On leaving school, he joined the Frome club, for which he played until he took up golf during the 1960s. He scored a couple of centuries and in one match with Westbury-on-Trym took four wickets in four balls. One of his victims was Tony Brown, an all-rounder who went on to captain Gloucestershire.

Atyeo did get to have trials with Somerset and Hampshire, but, as he said, 'I was then so much involved in football that I didn't take up an offer.' Whereas his father developed his natural aptitude for cricket by bowling to him in the orchard at their home, it was his mother who could be described (which he himself did) as his football coach: 'I remember she had an old tin tray that she used to prop up against an apple tree. I'd try to kick the ball at it from various angles and distances. I didn't really get any expert coaching in football. It just came naturally to me, although when I went to Bristol City I received tremendous help from the senior players.'

The first soccer team for which Atyeo played was Dilton Athletic, the club of the Wiltshire village of Dilton Marsh, on the outskirts of Westbury, where he was born on 7 February 1932. He was a regular scorer despite playing in defence as well as attack, and at 16 he was invited to turn out for Westbury United in the Wiltshire League. On some Saturdays he took part in three matches – for his school team in the morning, Westbury in the afternoon, and Dilton in games specially arranged in the evening for his benefit. When he first played for Westbury, against Calne, he scored four goals, but then had to go off suffering from cramp.

In his last year at school, Atyeo played for England Youth and Portsmouth reserves. 'My first break came when I was invited to have a trial for the Wiltshire Youth team. I was picked at centre-half, and scored a couple of goals early on, but to my amazement, and great disappointment, they called me off. For the next trial, though, I was chosen at centre-forward, and I eventually made the county team.' His first appearance was against Dorset at Devizes and he scored three goals in a 7-0 win. In the next match, against Somerset at Bath City's ground shortly before Christmas in 1949, he scored three more in a 6-3 victory.

Among the onlookers at Twerton Park that day was Wyndham ('Windy') Haines, a Frome man also known as 'Farmer Boy' Haines, who had scored nearly 150 goals for Portsmouth during their rise from Third to First Division in the 1920s. Haines, who later ran a public house just outside Frome, asked Atyeo to sign as an amateur for Portsmouth, and that was how he came to be associated with the Fratton Park club before making his name with Bristol City. Atyeo made his debut for Pompey in a reserve match with Southampton, a club for which Haines had also played, but he was unable to play very often at that time. Not only did he still have school commitments, he was also in the Wiltshire side that made progress in the national youth tournament before being knocked out by Essex at Swindon.

Atyeo took another step up the soccer ladder when nominated as a reserve for an England youth trial at White Hart Lane against a young Tottenham team that included Tony Marchi. A future Spurs captain, Marchi had won England honours at schoolboy, youth and 'B' levels, but would never, unlike Atyeo, graduate to a full international cap. It was enough of an adventure for Atyeo to stay in a London hotel for the first time, but the match itself was to be the greater experience. 'At half-time, he recalled, 'the Spurs side were winning 1-0 and the England team looked a bit of a shambles. The team manager came over to the five reserves and asked if anyone could play outside-left. I immediately stuck up my hand. I'd never played there before, but I would even have played in goal if necessary. I decided to play the way I knew best, so I really played as a sort of inside-left cum centre-forward.'

Those tactics paid off. Early in the second half Atyeo sidefooted an equaliser from a right-wing centre. Soon afterwards he took a return pass to smash what proved to be the winning goal. After that he could scarcely be ignored when the England team was selected to meet Scotland at Carlisle a few days later. He was in at inside-left for his first international, and he snapped up the opportunity with two goals in a 7-1 triumph. After further youth caps against Wales and Ireland, he made his first trip abroad the following summer for a youth tournament in Vienna. He again gave a good account of himself, but England were knocked out by Austria, who went on to win the trophy.

All this happened while Atyeo was studying for his school certificate. And soccer did not have sole claim on his sporting activities. Rugby and athletics also featured prominently. The school played soccer only after Christmas, but rugby in the autumn term, and Atyeo became adept at the oval ball game too. 'I was firmly convinced when I went to the grammar school that rugby was not for me,' he said in an interview with George Baker, an old friend and colleague of mine at the *Evening Post*. 'I'd played soccer all my life and was anti-rugby for the first year at that school. But somehow I got interested. My kicking was always exceptionally good and I took the place kicks playing at either stand-off half or full-back. I used to enjoy running with the ball, and I'm certain that was how I developed my body swerve for soccer. I was rather sorry to pack up rugby, for I began to enjoy it.'

From athletics, Atyeo acquired one of his proudest possessions – a silver medal at the All-England schools championships, though he admitted 'it was really won by gamesmanship'. Two assets that served him so well on the football field were his sprinting and jumping. Hurdling was his speciality, and he was fortunate to have as his PE master 'Jock' Burns, a hurdler of international standard. Burns had coached Johnny Adams, who came from the same village as Atyeo and had won the England title at Hull the previous year. Atyeo was county champion in 1950, and although his time was not good enough for him to be considered automatically for the national event, he gained a place in the Wiltshire team when it was decided to send a larger one because Bath was the venue.

Nothing helped his confidence when, on turning up wearing an old cricket sweater and a pair of flannels, he found other competitors in smart track suits with the names of their clubs emblazoned on them. Neither was his form at the start encouraging. He struggled through the first round, but just managed to qualify in second place. In his semi-final, the leader hit a hurdle and fell, enabling Atyeo to finish second again and get into the final. What happened next is best told in Atyeo's own words:

'The final was held a couple of hours later after torrential rain. There were six of us, and Jock Burns said to me: "You'll finish last. You're the worst of the six." And, of course, I was. But then he said: "I've studied the starter very carefully. He allows no gap between the 'set' and the 'off'. So when he says 'set,' you get going." I was off like a hare with a lead of two or three yards. I ran the race of my life. I led until the last hurdle, when I was overtaken, but I finished second, beaten by a yard.' The winner was David Kay, later athletics coach for the West Country.

With so many other interests, Atyeo played only half-a-dozen Football Combination matches for Portsmouth, but they made it possible for him to buy good equipment from the expenses he was paid. There was not much money coming in at home. His father was later a railway inspector in the Westbury area, but at that time just a relief signalman. As Atyeo recalled, it was 'a thrifty household', and when he obtained his school certificate his father told him to forget about football and get a steady job. So instead of following up the application he had made to attend Loughborough Training College (he got as far as receiving the prospectus, but then shelved it for fifteen years), Atyeo began a four-year course with a building firm at Westbury in preparation for taking diploma exams as a quantity surveyor. He reached an understanding with the firm should he become a part-time professional footballer in the meantime.

That eventuality was not far away. He continued his soccer with Westbury United and Wiltshire, but did not play again for Portsmouth until 'Windy' Haines suddenly called at his home one evening to tell him that Pompey were hard hit by injuries and wanted him for their home match with Charlton that Saturday. The taken-aback Atyeo had first thoughts for the Wiltshire side. He was due to play against Hampshire at Devizes that day, and did not want to let them down, yet the chance of First Division football was too good to miss. So he agreed to play, and on 11 November 1950, having been driven to Fratton Park by Haines, he made his big-time debut in this team: Butler; Stephen, Ferrier; Scoular, Thompson, Dickinson; Harris, Reid, P J W Atyeo, Ryder, Froggatt. To the accompaniment of the deafening Pompey Chimes from a 30,000 crowd, Atyeo did not let the team down in a 3-3 draw. He did not score, but helped put new life into the attack and provided the pass from which big Duggie Reid scored Portsmouth's first. Scoular and Dickinson netted the others for the home side; Charlton replied with a hat-trick from John Evans who two years later was transferred, along with full-back Frank Lock, to Liverpool, then managed by the Athletic's former skipper Don Welsh.

Atyeo was asked to play again for Portsmouth in their following game at Sunderland. On that occasion, however, he refused. He had told Westbury he would be available for their Amateur Cup-tie against Bristol St George, and he did not want to go back on his word. Four more months passed before the next call from Portsmouth. Again he was needed, for Arsenal's visit on Easter Monday, 26 March 1951, because of the injury list. And again he went without a goal but made one for somebody else.

This time he took a pass from Scoular to set up former Gosport forward Albert Mundy to open the scoring. Once more, however, Portsmouth had to share the points. One of Arsenal's own youngsters, left-winger Reuben Marden, equalised a quarter of an hour from the end.

Other deputies, compared with the line-up of Atyeo's debut, were Jasper Yeuell at right-back for Jimmy Stephen, who played for Scotland during the war while with Bradford, and the Belgian Marcel Gaillard for Jack Froggatt, an England international at centre-half as well as outside-left, but skipper Reg Flewin was restored to the centre of the defence.

As the game with the Gunners was followed by Portsmouth's offer of the professional terms that Atyeo and his father felt compelled to reject, that was big John's second and final appearance in the First Division. There was no shortage of offers from other clubs. Managers who went to the Atyeo home to try to tempt him included Ted Drake, then with Reading, Louis Page, in charge at Swindon, and Bert Tann of Bristol Rovers. They all spoke to Atyeo. 'Goodness knows how many others got in touch with my father,' he said. 'Some of them actually walked along the railway track, going from signal box to signal box to seek him out for a chat. After a while it came out that they were representing one club or another.'

Then along came the club official who was to get his man – Harry Dolman. The City chairman had seen Atyeo play, and he also visited his house. Not directly, though. As he was fond of recalling, he was about to pull up in his Rolls-Royce when he spotted a car that he knew was Bert Tann's, so he drove on and returned a little later after the Rovers manager had gone. City, in common with all the other clubs, were prepared to let Atyeo do what Portsmouth had refused – remain a part-timer, and to drive a car. After having talks about terms and conditions with Atyeo's father, who was now more amenable to his only son joining a League club if could be satisfied with what was on offer, Dolman went away to draft a letter that listed all the clauses requested. He returned with it a few days afterwards, signed by himself on behalf of the club. That meant the agreement, described by Atyeo as 'probably the best contract ever signed by a footballer in those days', would still be in force if John remained at Ashton Gate longer than the chairman.

The main conditions were: Atyeo should never be transferred to another club without his own consent (his father had a profound dislike of the transfer system); he should be allowed to continue living at Dilton Marsh; and he should always be allowed to remain a part-time player. He did, in fact, become a full-timer from 1958 to 1963, but then reverted to part-time until he left the club in 1966, changing tack in his other occupation by qualifying as schoolteacher. Mathematics and physical education were the subjects he taught, and he became head of maths at a Warminster school.

For a £10 signing-on fee and the payment of a weekly wage of £12, Harry Dolman had struck his biggest footballing bargain. But all was not immediately shipshape and Bristol fashion.

The Football League first wanted to know why Atyeo wished to turn professional with a Third Division club when he was already on the books of a First Division club as an amateur – and, indeed, had played for them at that level, not once but twice. Several weeks went by before they accepted his registration.

Swindon Town were the only other club Atyeo seriously considered joining. They appealed to him because, like City, they were convenient to his home,
but the pendulum swung against them for two reasons. One was that City's
chairman put such a strong case, the other the fact that Atyeo saw a brighter
future at Ashton Gate than at the County Ground. He was right enough there.
After a couple of near misses, he was in a promotion side in his fourth year as
a professional, whereas Swindon struggled throughout that period and had to
seek re-election at the end of City's first season back in the Second Division.
The man Atyeo felt sorriest for was 'Windy' Haines. 'He had done so much
for me during the previous fifteen months. Although he didn't show it, he
must have been bitterly disappointed, but he never ceased to rub it into
Portsmouth how they had missed me.'

A taxi was waiting for Atyeo at Temple Meads when he got off the train
from Westbury for his first morning's training with Bristol City in July 1951.
Before becoming the proud owner of a car, he took the train regularly for his
first two years at the club, completing the journey on a No 9 bus to the ground
after that one-off special treatment. Because of his work as a quantity survey-
or, he travelled to Ashton Gate only on Tuesday and Thursday mornings, sup-
plementing his training by going for a run at home, often accompanied by his
mother on her bicycle.

Over the years Bristol City kept their word in refusing big offers for Atyeo
(more about them in the next chapter), but after ending his fifteen seasons
with the club he admitted that, although 'never one for the bright lights', he
had often weighed up the prospect of living in a big city such as London or
Liverpool. He went further by saying he doubted that he would have stayed at
Ashton Gate if the money that had since poured into the game had been available in his time, or if there had then been the chance of playing in European
competitions with a bigger club – a particular temptation he said he probably
could not have resisted. He might also have thought again about moving if he
had not made the England team so soon after turning professional, though
there is little doubt that he would not have been so summarily discarded by the
national selectors if he had been playing full time in the First Division.

The simple truth, however, was that he did not really want to go elsewhere.
Dilton Marsh had what he termed 'a kind of hold over me'. He lived there all
his life apart from two years in which he took over a grocery and provisions
shop in the neighbouring village of Westbury Leigh. 'Even when I packed up
playing,' he said, 'I decided to stay in Dilton and get a teaching post nearby.'

Chapter 7

A Dramatic Debut and Penalty-Kick Bet

John Atyeo's debut for Bristol City, at home to Newport County on 18 August 1951, could hardly have been more dramatic. In the first minute he nodded down a high centre for Arnold Rodgers to score the fastest goal of the season. Here again, as so often is the case with such swift strikes, there were varying accounts of the exact time, ranging from 22 to 45 seconds.

In a wartime game, Roy Bentley was credited with a Bristol City goal as early as 23 seconds, and in 1987 Glenn Humphries conceded an own-goal in 35 seconds at Rotherham on his debut for the Ashton Gate club after his signing from Doncaster. But there were to be even quicker City goals, both timed at 17 seconds – by Paul Agostino in an FA Cup-tie in 1996, and by Colin Cramb in a Second Division match in 1998.

A few minutes after Rodgers' shock opener, City were two up – and this time Atyeo himself was the scorer. He pushed a pass out to Alec Eisentrager, who raced away down the wing before crossing. Goalkeeper Pope missed the ball and Atyeo had only to let it hit his head to score. And even that was not all. Just before the half-hour City's new centre-forward broke away down the right, fired in a cross shot the hapless Pope could not hold, and Cyril Williams turned the ball into the net to make it 3-0.

That, however, was the extent of City's scoring, Newport netting the only other goal near the interval. Neither would it continue so straightforwardly for the 19-year-old Atyeo. Although he finished that first season as City's second highest scorer with 14 goals, two behind Rodgers, he admitted that 'it was not before time' when he was dropped for two games. He went further: 'I was green, and I knew it. I was being carried for much of the time by the other players. I learned a lot from Cyril Williams, a most accomplished player. I picked up a few goals, but I still had a lot to learn.'

By early September City were down to tenth in the Third South table after twice hitting the frame and frittering away half-a-dozen chances in losing at Port Vale. After his flying start, Atyeo did not score again until their seventh game, won at home to Millwall, but his next goal, against Bristol Rovers four days later, was one that he and his team-mates relished. Many in the Ashton Gate crowd of nearly 30,000 who left early did not even see it. City fell behind when Con Sullivan got his hands to the ball but was unable to keep out Vic Lambden's header from a free-kick. And that was how the score stayed until the last minute, in which Atyeo drew Bert Hoyle out of goal before slipping the ball past him into the far corner of the net. City finished that thriller with only ten fit men, Pat Beasley no longer being able to take throw-ins after injuring a shoulder in a heavy fall against railings alongside the pitch.

Goals remained in short supply for City in Atyeo's first season despite George Lowrie's return after nearly a year's absence through injury, and the £5,000 signing from Southampton of Ernie Jones, a Welsh international winger. Beasley sought to pep things up by temporarily moving himself forward to inside-left, and then by briefly bringing in Graham Masters, a 20-year-old local-born winger who made his debut in a home defeat by Watford, a fortnight after turning professional following his completion of Army service.

Jones, who earlier in the year had broken an ankle in an FA Cup-tie at Northampton, also started out with City on the losing side, forming a capped triangle on the left flank with Beasley and Lowrie at Walsall after shaking off the flu. He had first been an amateur with his home club, Swansea, and he rejoined them following his demobilisation from the RAF after playing for Bolton Wanderers during the war. At Bolton he was known as Alphabet Jones because of the initials, W E A, that always appeared after his surname in the home match programme. He won the last of his four full caps after his £6,500 transfer to Tottenham in 1947, but left for Southampton two years later in the hope that the bracing air would be beneficial for his daughter's chest trouble.

The deal that took Jones to the Hampshire coast involved the exchange to White Hart Lane of Alf Ramsey, the unruffled England full-back who helped Spurs to promotion and the First Division title in successive seasons, and then, in management, guided Ipswich from Third Division to First and England to the World Cup. It also led to Southampton's loss of manager Bill Dodgin to Fulham, because the deal was conducted in his absence. He considered the offer of £6,000 plus Jones too cheap, after his board had rejected his recommendation that Tottenham's earlier £20,000 bid for Ramsey be accepted.

Jones was back with Southampton as youth team coach after totalling 50 League appearances in three seasons with Bristol City. In November 1957 he was in charge of the Saints side that defeated the Ashton Gate youngsters 9-0 in the FA Youth Cup. He also saw his lads to the semi-finals of that competition before they lost on aggregate to Manchester United.

By Christmas 1951, Bristol City were out of the FA Cup, beaten at Colchester despite one of Jones's finest displays, and hovering uncomfortably close to the re-election zone in the Southern Section of the Third Division. They ended the year, at home to Northampton, with their first League win since late October, and promptly gained two more before falling back into another rut that began with a defeat at Eastville. City's inconsistency was underlined when they hit Southend for six at Ashton Gate but only a few weeks later were swamped by five in the return match. Gillingham also went nap against Beasley's men on the last day of that season, the Kent club thus boosting the goal-average that saved them from having to seek re-election.

A final position of fifteenth, and with 58 goals – only half that of runners-up Reading, who finished five points adrift of promoted Plymouth – was a disappointing outcome for City, but brighter times were immediately ahead. In

1952-53, they were fifth, five points behind promoted Rovers. In 1953-54, when Ipswich went up ahead of Brighton, they rose to third. And in 1954-55 they at last returned to the Second Division after an absence of nearly two dozen years.

For John Atyeo, too, the corner was turned. He was again omitted, for about a dozen games, in his second season with the club, but he really blossomed during a short tour of Devon and Cornwall in May 1953. 'We played at Torquay, Newquay and Penzance,' he said in looking back over his career, 'and I rammed in quite a few goals. As the new season opened I felt I had arrived at last. I suddenly found a confidence that had not been there before. I was a fully-fledged player, and no longer felt I was being carried. Pat Beasley's patience for two years was being rewarded.'

In 1953-54 Atyeo was City's leading scorer for the first time with 23 goals in the League and three in the Cup. But with that surge, which was to be so familiar over the next decade, came those inevitable rumours of his possible transfer and the constant denials by Harry Dolman. It all began with a few tentative articles in the newspapers. First in the queue was Don Welsh, the former Charlton captain, then manager of Liverpool, closely followed by Ted Drake who, with Chelsea, renewed the interest he had shown in the amateur Atyeo while manager of Reading. Les McDowall of Manchester City was not far behind. The firmest offers came from Cardiff, who had recently rejoined the First Division after having sunk to the depths of applying for re-election, and Liverpool, the first post-war champions. The Welsh club dangled a £30,000 carrot; the Merseysiders put in a bid of £20,000 plus two players whose value was set at £8,000. But, said City's chairman, 'although we needed the money badly, we honoured our pledge not to part with John without his agreement.'

The only personal contact Atyeo had in that respect was with Roy Bentley, who was visiting home and training at Ashton Gate. 'He made a special point of seeking me out quietly after training and chatting me up,' said Atyeo. 'He told me of the opportunities I could expect, how important it would be to my future if I were in London with a First Division club, and, above all, the prospects at Chelsea.' Those prospects were undoubtedly to be reckoned with, for it was the following season that the Stamford Bridge club were crowned champions for the first time, but the situation never arose where there was any real chance of Atyeo moving. In letters to the local papers supporters pleaded with City not to sell. There was even the threat of a boycott by a group of militant fans. And, as Atyeo put it, 'the whole thing died a natural death' after Harry Dolman had issued his statement emphasising that under no circumstances would any offers be considered.

As vital a City cog as Atyeo became, it was, of course, by no means a one-man band. Although Pat Beasley retired from playing to concentrate on management after 1951-52, and Dennis Roberts neared the end of his long League road, Ivor Guy was absent four fewer times than Atyeo in missing only ten of the club's 138 Third Division games during the three seasons that culminated in promotion. Other influential players during that period included Bailey, Cyril Williams, Peacock, Boxley, Rodgers and Rogers. There were also two important newcomers to the team, Jack White and Tony Cook.

Beasley was on White's trail for eighteen months before eventually securing his transfer from Aldershot in October 1952 – and then only after negotiations had again fallen through. White, a formidable figure then in his mid-20s, was entrusted with the captaincy for the home win over Gillingham, and he held the role for over 200 more games. In March 1958 he followed Cyril Williams, Colin Rees and Syd Morgan out of Ashton Gate in the wake of Peter Doherty's appointment as manager. White was short-listed for the Chippenham post that went to Williams, then was about to sign for Trowbridge Town when Cambridge City came in with the more attractive offer to become player-manager for their first season as a professional club. After leaving there, while living in Kent, he had some sort of a Bristol City connection by working for Harry Dolman's firm on the sales side.

Three of White's brothers were also with League clubs. Len, a Rotherham and Newcastle forward, was the better-known – a Cup winner with the Tynesiders at the end of 1954-55, when Jack led Bristol City to the Third South championship. Albert also played for Aldershot, Freddie for Bradford Park Avenue. They hailed from Skellow, near Doncaster, and Jack preceded his two years at Aldershot as a Doncaster Rovers amateur after developing his football with colliery teams in South Yorkshire. Jack went to the Shots as a centre-forward, but settled at half-back, and it was at centre-half that he made his City debut. He subsequently filled all three positions in the middle line, and was also selected at right-back. A tough and inspiring character, a bit slow, but invariably dependable and adept at the volley. In one match with Reading he played despite a septic toe. Two weeks later he carried on after breaking his nose against Crystal Palace. And in one game against Bristol Rovers he had to go off with a damaged leg muscle but returned to play on both wings before finishing up at centre-forward.

Goalkeeper Tony Cook was a patient newcomer, for he had to wait three years for his League debut after being signed on Boxing Day 1949. After playing for Clifton St Vincent's in the Bristol Downs League on Christmas Eve, he was visited at his home by Cliff Morgan, who by then was scouting for City, and asked if he was available for the reserves' Football Combination game at Southampton. He was, and played after putting his name to amateur forms on that Boxing Day morning. Next day, he kept goal for St Vincent's in the morning, and for City's return match with Southampton's second string in the afternoon. Asked about turning professional, he said not until he had achieved his ambition of gaining selection as an amateur for Gloucestershire, but two days later he changed his mind and rounded off an eventful week by joining the ranks of the paid.

Cook had a reputation as a 'penalty king'. It was when he twice saved from the spot while playing for a Downs League representative side that City first took note of him, and on that first day for City's reserves he kept out another at Southampton. Indeed, he became so consistently adept at that aspect of his game that ten years later Johnny Watkins, a winger who was also taken onto the Ashton Gate playing staff from Clifton St Vincent's, decided to back his own proficiency as a penalty taker by making a bet: 'I'll give you half-a-crown [12½p],' said Watkins, 'if you save three out of the six penalties I take with you in goal.' The result was a clear win for Cook. He stopped four of Watkins' shots – all taken with the mule-like left kick with which a net had been broken in a Good Friday victory over Ipswich Town at Ashton Gate only the week before.

That was in March 1959, and in the following month at Scunthorpe three attempts were needed, through enforced retakes, to beat Cook from the spot in a 3-3 draw that City forced with the aid of a penalty of their own. Jack Brownsword, the home full-back who was usually reliable from the spot, was so dismayed by his two failures that it was left to his team-mate Peter Donnelly to be third-time lucky. Donnelly also converted another spot-kick that day, but when City conceded a penalty on their return to Scunthorpe at the start of the following season trust was renewed in Brownsword. And that time he made no mistake, gaining a lead which Jimmy Rogers wiped out with his first League goal since his return from Coventry.

Of the nine saves Cook made from the thirteen penalties he faced in 1958-59 (including those two retakes at Scunthorpe), the one that gave him the greatest pleasure was at the expense of his manager. Peter Doherty, who favoured deceptive placing of penalty-kicks to a full-blooded blast, did not miss often. The Irishman once estimated that he had taken over 70 in his playing career and, to the best of his knowledge, had failed with only six. But Cook foiled him when he played at Ashton Gate for an All-Star XI of famous former players in one of the floodlit games in vogue before League and Cup matches were allowed under lights.

Tony Cook's first-team career with Bristol City could be said to have been in two parts. It was spread over eleven years and more than 300 games, but there was a gap in the middle when he lost his place through injury. In one season, 1957-58, he was called upon only once. He played an unusually high number of times with the Colts for a goalkeeper of his experience. Bob Anderson, a Geordie six-footer signed from Bristol Rovers during the summer of 1954, was drafted into the City side midway through the following promotion-winning season after Cook had broken an arm in a heavy fall during a home match with Watford. Cook restaked his regular claim after Anderson had himself been injured, so seriously that it ended his career four years later.

City still sent Watford away pointless, despite moving Ivor Guy from full-back to deputise for Cook for the last hour, but it was not until the last seconds that Jack Boxley broke the deadlock with one of his stunning left-foot specials.

For Bob Anderson, League football began as it was to end – in bitter disappointment. The omens for a successful start with Middlesbrough were not good when he joined them after leaving the RAF, only to find that he was one of seven goalkeepers at Ayresome Park. And he had to retrieve the ball from Middlesbrough's net that many times on his First Division debut at Arsenal on Good Friday in 1948. Ironically, it was the Gunners who might have signed him while he was stationed in Glamorgan on National Service. Albert Lindon, the London club's chief scout, arranged an interview for him with George Allison after seeing him in action at Merthyr, but the then Arsenal manager would not offer professional terms until he had been demobilised. When that time came, however, Allison did no more about it, so instead Anderson accepted the invitation from Middlesbrough manager David Jack, a former Arsenal player.

Denied further first-team chances with Boro after that Easter deluge, Anderson returned to the North-Eastern League – first with Blyth Spartans and then Blackhall Colliery Welfare, from where he was brought back into the Football League by Crystal Palace in October 1951. His next move, in March 1953, took him to Bristol Rovers. It was eye-catching because the Eastville club broke with their famous No Buy, No Sell policy by forking out a fee of £2,000. They were forced to do so at a critical stage of their promotion push by the car accident that ended the career of Bert Hoyle, the goalkeeper for whom they had last had to pay (£350), but chairman Hampden Alpass hastened to emphasise that 'the move represents no fundamental changes in the views of the board'. The transfer went without a hitch, for it suited Anderson down to the ground. His wife's parents lived close to the Eastville stadium in Stapleton Road.

'Seven' again featured prominently in the Anderson story as he made that number of appearances in Rovers' run-in to the Third South title of 1952-53. With City he played in half their 46 games (Cook was in the other half) when it was their turn to be champions in 1954-55. Early in 1956, Anderson was considered the most improved player at Ashton Gate after excelling in narrow defeats at Everton, in the Cup, and Sheffield Wednesday, but another, and far more damaging, downturn in fortune lay in wait. In September 1958 he twice in eight days suffered from a prolapsed disc, the injury affecting a nerve and paralysing him for several minutes.

On both occasions he resumed in goal after a short delay, but was afterwards ordered to wear a plaster jacket for a month. After resuming training, he was all set to resume playing when a specialist made a further examination and the jacket had to be replaced. Soon afterwards he was sent home to Co Durham for a break while City's manager, then Peter Doherty, had discussions with the specialist and the club doctor.

After almost three months in and out of plaster jackets, Anderson, who by then was in his mid-30s, underwent a course of special weight lifting exercises arranged by Bill Watson, a physical culture expert, to strengthen his back. He even got as far as a try-out in the Colts' home match with Minehead in January 1959, but there was to be no comeback. He was not retained at the end of the 1960-61 season, and although he was the Supporters' Club's joint promoter and chief agent for a time, he had to give up those jobs, and coaching with a boys' club, when his condition again deteriorated. An operation became necessary for the removal of the disc, with bone grafted from his hip onto his spinal cord. Six of his vertebrae had to be wired up, but he was spared being paralysed for life, thankful not to be confined to a wheelchair. He found employment as an area manager with a dry-cleaning firm in Bristol until 1986, when he suffered a stroke. He died eight years later, five days after his 70th birthday.

Although the way for Tony Cook's re-establishment in City's team was opened up by Anderson's great misfortune, it came at a time when Cook was actually looking to leave. 'I'm really happy at Ashton Gate, even in the reserve team,' he said, 'but I don't feel I can give my best while I'm worried about my wife.' Marion Cook was homesick for her home town of Guildford, where she was then staying, and had not been well since the birth of their son Kenneth Michael just over eighteen months earlier. A specialist had recommended that she should move. Cook, however, was told that the club could not afford to let him go when Anderson dropped out, so he did not press his request for a transfer. Over the next four seasons this inveterate Woodbine smoker was a first choice, ever-present in 1959-60, and absent only once the season after that, in adding nearly 170 appearances to his total. He eventually left, for Worcester City, in September 1963, and after spells with Cinderford and Cheltenham Town he returned to his Downs League roots as a permit player with the Sneyd Park club. He later worked at Bristol's Horfield prison.

Popular though he was, Tony Cook incurred some rare wrath among his clubmates one day on the journey to a match up north. During one of the card schools on the coach, the air became so blue that he opened a window and threw out the whole pack.

And now, in the next chapter, back to Bristol City's promotion season of 1954-55 in which Cook shared the club's goalkeeping position with the luckless Anderson.

FOOTBALL ASSOCIATION INTERNATIONAL
(Intermediate under 23's)

ENGLAND v. FRANCE

ASHTON GATE ★ BRISTOL
Wednesday, October 17th, 1956   K.O. 7.30 p.m.

Official Souvenir Programme   **6d.**

Chapter 8

Burden, Milton – and Promotion Gained

Burden was a misnomer for the player Bristol City introduced into their team for the last three months of the 1954-55 season they ended as champions of the Third Division South.

Tommy Burden was anything but a burden. On the contrary, he arrived from Leeds United that October as a well-respected and competent captain in five of his six years at Elland Road – a role for which he was naturally fitted, and one that he took up with similar efficiency at Ashton Gate after Jack White stepped down. A leader by example, Burden was an obvious choice to skipper the combined Bristol team (six Rovers, five City) against Arsenal at Eastville on Friday evening, 8 May 1959 in aid of the Harry Bamford Fund, after the Rovers full-back's untimely death.

Pat Beasley signed Burden at Glastonbury, where the player had his home. Burden's wife was Somerset-born, and it was because she had wanted to live there, nearer her family after the death of her brother in an RAF flying accident, that he had asked Leeds for a transfer on reporting back in July 1951. That just over three years elapsed before he did change clubs was testimony to how highly Leeds rated him. During that period he was allowed to live in the West Country, and although it was not ideal for a skipper rarely to see his men until just before a match, he responded by making his continued commitment to United unquestioned. Shortly before his move to Bristol City, however, Burden renewed his transfer request after losing the captaincy to Welsh international John Charles – who, ironically, also asked to leave, but had his application thrown out after a board meeting that lasted nearly three hours.

Burden told Leeds that if he were not listed he would seek release from his contract and retire from football. What a bonus it proved for City when his transfer request was granted. Charles, the Gentle Giant, had to wait for his move until May 1957, when he went into Italian soccer with Juventus at a then world record fee of £65,000.

Although born in Andover, Hampshire, on 21 February 1924, Burden looked upon himself a son of Somerset. He played for that county as a schoolboy – so effectively that he was recommended by his headmaster to Wolverhampton Wanderers, then managed by Frank Buckley. The good major was noted for giving youth its fling, and Burden was still only 16 when, along with other aspiring youngsters such as Billy Wright and Jimmy Mullen, he played for Wolves in wartime football. He showed the versatility that was to be his trademark by playing in both inside-forward positions, and then at wing-half, but declined an invitation to stay at Molineux, preferring to return home to Glastonbury. He was employed at nearby Street by Clark's, the firm of boot and shoe manufacturers with which he became a senior executive after finishing with football.

Called-up into the Army at 18, Burden served with the Northumberland Fusiliers. He was so seriously wounded in his right side during the Normandy landings on D-Day that, like Arnold Rodgers, he was told he would never play football again, but he defied the medical men by completing a physical training course at Loughborough College. Back to full fitness, he was posted to Chester and guested for that club before signing in November 1945, his registration with Wolves having lapsed. When the Football League resumed in 1946-47 he was a force in the Chester side that finished third in the Third (North), scoring 28 goals in 42 appearances.

In the next season Chester sagged to third from bottom, but Burden was their leading scorer, with the reduced output of a dozen goals in his 40 games. He moved to Leeds for £4,000 the following summer when Frank Buckley was again the manager who signed him. With Leeds, Burden dropped back from the attack to settle at wing-half, but further demonstrated his adaptability as an emergency centre-forward – his fifth position since joining the club – by scoring twice in as many minutes in a 2-1 home win against Leicester.

By the time of his transfer to Bristol City, 30-year-old Burden had played over 250 League and Cup games for Leeds. The price City paid was £1,500, plus £500 a year for three years. They were fully repaid, with interest. In their colours he turned out nearly 250 times, occupying his sixth position in two seasons when he filled in at full-back. Although, because of his work in the time and motion study office at Street, he trained only in the evenings, he was one of the fittest players on the club's books.

The first of Burden's appearances for City was as a guest in a floodlit match with Rheims a fortnight before his League debut, a defeat at Northampton on a gloomy first Saturday of November 1954. At the time of that friendly with the French club, Leeds had rejected City's original offer, but terms were agreed while United were in Bristol for a Second Division match in which Rovers beat them 5-1, helped by goals from Meyer and Hooper, future Bristol City players. Burden became an Ashton Gate part-timer, to the disappointment of Jack Smith, the Reading manager who had watched him play for Leeds Reserves.

Despite their failure at Northampton, City retained top place in the Third South, though their lead was halved to two points as their closest challengers, Leyton Orient, stormed to a 7-1 win at Exeter. That setback was only City's second of the season in their renewed pursuit of promotion. Their first defeat, 2-3 at Southend in early October, ended the last unbeaten record in the whole League after an opening run of thirteen games. And it was also Southend who inflicted City's first home defeat in the first round of the FA Cup a fortnight after the Northampton reverse. City led at half-time through Rodgers, but Roy Hollis, formerly of Norwich and Tottenham, countered with a couple of goals after the interval.

Coventry City, early pacesetters that season, were dislodged by Beasley's men in mid-September, when Rodgers scored three of four goals in a home victory against Colchester, while Coventry were slipping up at Gillingham. The leadership stayed in Bristol hands until Gillingham became the season's first League winning visitors to Ashton Gate on the last Saturday before Christmas, persistent Orient taking advantage with a 7-2 win at Torquay. As at Exeter, Vic Groves, a former amateur international soon to join Arsenal, did the hat-trick. Top spot was surrendered only on goal-average, however, and City promptly regained it by beating Reading on Christmas Day, when Orient were without a match. Two days later (Boxing Day fell on a Sunday), City pulled three points clear in completing a double at Elm Park, for Orient lost their scoring touch in a 0-0 home draw with Brighton, another of the promotion hopefuls.

For that return at Reading there was another newcomer in the Bristol City line-up – Theodore Michael Thresher, one of five footballing brothers from the Somerset market town of Chard. Mike Thresher, who moved with his family from his Bradninch birthplace in Devon at an early age, was with Ilminster Town (at 15) and Chard Town before joining City after his demobilisation from the RAF in January 1954, not far off his 23rd birthday. Chosen four times by Somerset before his call-up for National Service, he arrived at Ashton Gate as a utility player, capable of occupying any position in the forward line and also with experience at full-back and wing-half. In one match he scored six goals for City reserves, but it was at full-back, fast in recovery and tenacious in the tackle, that he made his mark. John Atyeo, with whom he became a big pal, likened that tackle to 'a ton of bricks'. With Jack Bailey gradually dropping out of the picture after breaking an arm during the defeat at Northampton, Thresher was a fitting final partner for Ivor Guy. Over the next ten years he outlasted several other partners, exceeding 400 appearances, 378 in the League, before following Guy to Bath City in 1965. In all those games he scored just one goal, in his penultimate season.

Thresher's name was as apt as Burden's was not. Almost every weekend, after a match at Ashton Gate he drove down to Chard, where he was part-owner of a 26-acre farm with his brothers. He went into full-time farming when his footballing days were over. One of his brothers, Brian, an inside-forward who was his junior by about three years, was also with City in the late 1950s, signed as an amateur.

After their Christmas 1954 double over Reading, City fell to a heavy defeat by Orient, who extracted 4-1 revenge for their 0-5 beating at Ashton Gate back in August. That sobering failure was not enough to knock City off the top, but the next one was, 0-1 at home to Norwich a week later. Orient were held to a draw at Northampton that afternoon, but the point put them ahead again on goal average with two games in hand.

The weather had a big say the following Saturday, when City and Orient were among the frustrated clubs. Snow covered practically the whole country

and caused the worst peacetime hold-up. Of the 62 games in the English and
Scottish leagues, 41 were postponed and three others had to be abandoned. All
English horseracing was also off, the Wales v England clash in Cardiff was
part of the near-total cancellation of the Rugby Union programme, and just
two Rugby League fixtures were possible. For only the second time (the other
in 1947), there were no football pools.

City could have wished that their match at Southampton the next weekend
had been among two dozen that had to be put off because of thaw and frost.
But the Third South was the only division unaffected, and while Orient were
5-0 home winners against Shrewsbury, City slipped two points adrift, still with
two games more played, in conceding a second-half penalty that enabled the
Saints to close up a point behind in third place.

From that low-point of their season, however, City zoomed to their highest. They were not beaten again, winning fourteen and drawing four of their
remaining matches in carrying off the title, nine points clear of Orient's runners-up, with Southampton two points further back in third place. City broke
one club record with 70 points from their 46 games (though their Second
Division champions of 1905-06 had fulfilled only 38 fixtures for the previous
best of 66), equalled another, from that same season, by gaining 30 victories,
and were only three goals short of a third – the 104 achieved when City had
last risen from the Third South in 1926-27. The six League defeats for
Beasley's men were four more than the number inflicted on those remarkable
promotion winners of Billy Wedlock's time, but one fewer than in both the
club's previous Third South title seasons (the other one in 1922-23).

Eight of City's victories in the 1954-55 run-in came in succession. The second of these earned a 3-2 home revenge over Southend, after being behind at
the interval, that restored City to the leadership they were not to surrender. On
that same late February afternoon, Orient lost the League's last unbeaten
home record, after fourteen wins and two draws, to a lone Norwich goal. But
the Leyton club, now just one point behind, still held those two games in hand,
and they had a third after being without a match when City trounced Millwall,
who arrived in fourth place but with financial worries, by 5-1 in midweek early
in March. That extended City's lead to three points, and it widened to four
when City won at Exeter while Orient could only draw at lowly Swindon, two
days after again being beaten at home, by Newport.

Orient matched another 5-1 City victory, against Northampton, by returning to form with a 5-0 home win over struggling Exeter. So the issue was very
much in the balance as the season entered April, yet that was when Orient's
challenge faded dramatically. Of their final ten games, they won only three,
and one of those came when it was too late, against Walsall, who had to seek
re-election for a then record seventh time. Southampton also faltered in those
closing weeks, picking up just one more point than Orient's eight. These were
the final leading positions:

1954-55		P	W	D	L	F	A	Pts
1	Bristol City	46	30	10	6	101	47	70
2	Leyton Orient	46	26	9	11	89	47	61
3	Southampton	46	24	11	11	75	51	59
4	Gillingham	46	20	15	11	77	66	55

John Atyeo and Jack White were ever-presents. Ivor Guy missed just one match, Ernie Peacock and Jimmy Rogers two, Jack Boxley three, and Cyril Williams seven. Tommy Burden, Arnold Rodgers, Tony Cook, Bob Anderson Jimmy Regan and Mike Thresher all made at least twenty appearances. Jack Bailey would surely at least have been in that group but for his injury. Of the other players, there was one who was never on the losing side in his fourteen games. Pat Beasley declared himself 'very grateful' to Tom Whittaker, Arsenal's manager, for being 'very reasonable' over the transfer of Arthur Milton, a Bristolian one month short of his 27th birthday, for a fee described as 'moderate', on 16 February 1955.

Fair-haired Clement Arthur Milton was the twelfth and last player to represent England at both cricket and soccer. Lucky though he could be considered in collecting his one cap as a footballer – a late replacement for the injured Tom Finney at outside-right against Austria at Wembley in 1951, after only a dozen League games with Arsenal – he was unfortunate to have to wait so long for the first of his six Tests, against New Zealand at Headingley in 1958 after more than 200 Championship games for Gloucestershire. The football match with Austria was drawn, but England won the Test with more than two hours to spare despite a deluge that prevented play on the first two days.

The circumstances of Milton's call-up into the England football team demonstrate how greatly times have changed. He picked up his boots and caught a bus to meet at the hotel. No posh cars for players then. The news that he had been chosen as the famous Preston winger's deputy was conveyed by Jimmy Logie, the diminutive Arsenal inside-forward who happened to be getting his Wembley ticket from Tom Whittaker when the word came through. Whittaker told Logie: 'You've helped the boy along, so I think you should tell him the good news.' Logie found Milton playing head tennis and called out: 'Congratulations.' Milton paused to ask: 'Am I in?' Logie, who also played only once for his country (for Scotland at Hampden in a draw with Northern Ireland in 1953), answered 'Aye,' and then strolled off, leaving Milton to complete his game before reporting for England duty.

Milton saw so little of the ball against Austria, after setting up an early chance for Ivor Broadis, that he was unable to live up to Whittaker's assessment: 'the greatest wing find since Cliff Bastin', the Arsenal and England forward who won every honour available while still a teenager. But at cricket he had the distinction of being the eleventh England player to complete a debut century – and the first from Gloucestershire since W G Grace.

Milton carried his bat for 104 at Leeds by courtesy of his captain, Peter May, his partner in an unbroken stand of 194 that was only 51 runs short of the England third-wicket record. May delayed his declaration until Milton had got to three figures. With Surrey spinners Lock and Laker making short work of the Kiwis, Milton was the first to be on the field for England throughout a Test.

Another hundred, for the Players against the Gentlemen at Lord's – after playing the ball onto his stumps without disturbing the bails early on – clinched Milton's selection for the ensuing tour of Australasia, though he ended the day in hospital with a broken nose after fielding at short square-leg. He was also a casualty in Australia. Barely had he recovered from a cracked finger, suffered while batting in Adelaide, than he broke another finger on the same right hand in the Melbourne match with Victoria. With no hope of being fit until midway through the New Zealand section of the tour, he had to return home early.

Milton was a natural games player with a big-match temperament. At Cotham Grammar School he played rugby before switching to soccer after Christmas, and was rated by his sports master as a coming international three-quarter. It was also said that he could have made his name as a golfer, but he enjoyed most lasting success at cricket. In a county career spanning 1948 to 1974 he exceeded 32,000 runs (putting him fourth for Gloucestershire behind Grace, Hammond and Tom Graveney) and held over 700 catches. He hit 56 centuries, and the 50th for Gloucestershire made him only the fifth player to reach that total in the county's hundred years of cricket. The others were the three just mentioned, plus Alf Dipper, an opening batsman whose stolid style contradicted a surname indicative of a big hitter.

Soccer was a comparatively minor part of Milton's varied sporting life, yet it might not have been even that but for the expert attention he received from one of the spectators after suffering a groin injury in a Bristol Downs League game between Colston Sports and Durdham Down Adult School. Having refused to leave the field for treatment, he was taken ill only a few minutes into the second half and rushed to the Bristol Royal Infirmary. Ted Davis, Arsenal's chief scout, was at the match to watch Milton, and it was he who accompanied him to hospital – then later that night to his home, where he gave Milton's parents some advice on treatment of the injury.

Davis had been greatly impressed by what he had seen of Milton, and that was why young Arthur became an Arsenal player instead of joining one of the Bristol clubs. To begin with, Milton played at inside-left in one of the Gunners' junior teams. George Petherbridge was among his early wing partners while on trial with the North London club before becoming a Bristol Rovers favourite for so many years. Milton was still only 16 when he was converted into a right-winger, and his team-mates then included George Marks, the goalkeeper who also found his way to Ashton Gate.

While with Arsenal, Milton made 84 League and Cup appearances, scoring 21 goals, but he lost his place to Freddie Cox for the 1952 FA Cup final, and he was again out of the first team when persuaded to bolster Bristol City's final push for promotion. He played a valuable part, never on the losing side as City won eleven and drew three of the games in which he played. On his debut three days after signing, City scored more than twice for the first time since beating Aldershot 6-1 in mid-October, winning 3-2 at home to Brighton with the help of an Atyeo penalty. That victory left them just one point behind Orient, who were held to a draw at Crystal Palace. Beating Southend the following Saturday put City back on top to stay.

One of Milton's three goals for City was the winner at Bournemouth in what was to be his last League game. He did not take part in the final match, won 2-1 at Crystal Palace, and also missed the Gloucestershire Cup final at Eastville the following Tuesday, when City lost to Rovers by the same score. Alec Eisentrager was on the right wing in both matches. Job done, Arthur Milton retired from top football to concentrate on his cricket, but he did play once more at Ashton Gate the following year – on a Monday evening in November under the lights in City's game with an International Managers' All-Star XI. He accepted invitations to appear in other matches played by the managers because they were in aid of charity (players' benefit funds).

There was also a City connection with one of Milton's games for Gloucestershire earlier in 1956. Before the start of play at the County Ground in Bristol, Fred Parsons, vice-chairman of the City Supporters' Club, presented him with a barometer in recognition of his contribution to the promotion that put both Bristol clubs in the Second Division for the first time and made Pat Beasley one of the few men to be associated with championship-winning teams at each of the three Football League levels – with Arsenal in the First Division, Fulham in the Second, and now Bristol City in the Third.

Cliff Duffin (left) is welcomed to Ashton Gate by City secretary Sid Hawkins

Chapter 9

Atyeo Reaches his England Pinnacle

Bristol City's 1954-55 promotion season was especially memorable for John Atyeo, not only because he was again the club's top scorer – with 28 goals, followed into double figures by Jimmy Rogers (24), Arnold Rodgers (14) and Jack Boxley (11). He also climbed his personal soccer ladder, several rungs towards his burning ambition to play for England.

His big break in that respect came in October, when he was selected for an FA XI against the RAF at Highbury. Stanley Rous, the FA secretary who later became president of FIFA, looked on as Atyeo scored twice in a 3-1 win, besides hitting a post with what the City starlet himself called a 'screamer'. Atyeo kept his place against the Army at Hillsborough the next month, and, although he did not score in the 1-1 draw (Dennis Viollet, of Manchester United, was the FA's marksman), he created another favourable impression.

At about that time, having qualified for his diploma as a quantity surveyor, Atyeo faced a showdown. His employers wanted him either to give up playing for Bristol City or working for them. He handed in his notice and obtained employment with a builder at Westbury, Syd Bale, who was willing to allow him as much time off as he needed to further his football. And for the next few years there was quite a lot.

The next step up the soccer ladder made Atyeo the first City player to be called up by England since Billy Wedlock won the last of his 26 caps (and scored) in a 2-0 defeat of Wales in Cardiff on 16 March 1914. On the cold afternoon of 19 January 1955, Atyeo was at inside-right in the England Under-23 side that defeated Italy 5-1 on a sunlit but slippery pitch at Stamford Bridge. He scored one of the goals, heading in from a lofted pass by Fulham's Johnny Haynes in the 47th minute, after the visitors had wiped out a 34th-minute lead gained by Bobby Charlton, of Manchester United, with a typically powerful shot from Atyeo's through pass. Atyeo was also involved in the move that produced England's third goal. He slipped the ball out to Harry Hooper, and Frank Blunstone, the Chelsea outside-left, pushed home the resulting centre. In the *Daily Mail*, Roy Peskett reported that 'Atyeo, of the long stride and intelligent positioning, had his best game of the season'.

There were no changes for England's next Under-23 match against Scotland at Shawfield Park, Clyde, on the evening of 8 February – not, that is, until a freak accident put Bobby Ayre, the Charlton centre-forward, out of action before he had even got a kick at the ball. Inside the first 60 seconds he chased full back Parker, of Falkirk, but fell heavily on the greasy surface. Ayre was found to have dislocated his left elbow, but he was discharged from hospital, spending the night at a Glasgow hotel, after having it set. England were allowed a substitute, at the generous suggestion of Jimmy Currie, chairman of the Scottish second-team selectors, and Stan Anderson, a Sunderland wing-half, was sent on wearing a No 6 jersey. He also carried one numbered No 9, which he handed to Duncan Edwards, and the Manchester United power-house moved up from left-half to form a double attacking spearhead with John Atyeo.

Atyeo scored the second of England's six goals just before half-time, running onto one of the pin-point through passes that were Haynes' speciality and hitting home a fierce shot after juggling the ball round Airdrie centre-half Baillie. After the interval it was Edwards who did most of the sharpshooting. Thriving on the service provided by Haynes, the United player showed a maturity beyond his years with an 18-minute hat-trick during which he also struck a post and registered a near-miss. Three years later almost to the day, Edwards was fatally injured in the Munich air crash that also claimed the lives of seven of his clubmates. Haynes rounded off the scoring against the Scots, who could muster no reply, in the closing minutes from a pass by Blunstone, scorer of the first goal from the Fulham maestro's free kick on the half-hour.

John Atyeo's next representative honour was to be chosen for the Third South team that defeated the Third North 2-0 under the Reading lights on 16 March, but he did not play. A more important call came for the same night. With Haynes, ankle injury, and Ayre, not fully fit, dropping out of the Football League line-up against the Scottish League at Hampden, Atyeo and John Evans, of Liverpool, were the replacements. It was to be Atyeo's only appearance at the famous Glasgow stadium, which lacked its usual atmosphere with just a 20,000 crowd. Neither did he get onto the score sheet. The Scots scored two (one a penalty) of the three goals that came late in the first half, after Evans had given the Football League an early lead. Chelsea's Roy Bentley, the only visitor who had previously played at Hampden, headed the other to equalise immediately before the interval, but the second half was only three minutes old when Joe Marston, Preston's Australian international centre-half, hooked the decider into his own net in attempting to clear a hard-hit centre.

Atyeo played in two more representative games that season. In March he was in the England team that drew 1-1 with West Germany in a 'B' international at Hillsborough, and on Cup final eve, 6 May, he was in the 'Young England' side humbled by 'Old England' at Highbury.

Atyeo was not alone in failing to shine in either game. Roy Swinbourne, the Wolves centre-forward, was the only forward to impress against the Germans, heading the goal that earned a first-half lead and unlucky with three other attempts – especially when netting as he collided with the goalkeeper after battling past four defenders, only to see referee Jack Clough award England an indirect free-kick. Another debatable decision led to the equaliser. Trevor Smith, the Birmingham centre-half, forced a corner with what appeared to be a fine sliding tackle, but was adjudged worth punishing with a penalty.

The five-goal lesson given Young England was inspired by Stanley Matthews. Blackpool's Wizard of Dribble, playing his fourth game of the week after a trip that took in Watford, Devon and Wales, warmed up the 38,000 crowd on a chilly night with the goal that started the rout five minutes from half-time. The others flowed from Tommy Lawton (2), Matthews's club-mate Stan Mortensen, and Bobby Langton, the Blackburn winger. And there would have been even more but for the brilliance of the other Matthews, Reg, the Young England's overworked goalkeeper. The teams for that match make interesting reading, representing the pick of the old and new talent of the time:

OLD ENGLAND: Swift (Manchester City); Ramsey (Tottenham), Eckersley (Blackburn); Johnston (Blackpool), Chilton (Grimsby), Dickinson (Portsmouth); Matthews (Blackpool), Mortensen (Blackpool), Lawton (Arsenal), Baily (Tottenham), Langton (Blackburn). Seven minutes after half-time Swift retired with a pulled leg muscle and was replaced by Jack Kelsey, Arsenal's Welsh international.

YOUNG ENGLAND: Matthews (Coventry); Sillett (Chelsea), Shaw (Sheffield United); Clayton (Blackburn), Smith (Birmingham), Flowers (Wolves); Hooper (West Ham), Atyeo (Bristol City), Hines (Leicester), Haynes (Fulham), Blunstone (Chelsea).

In the following October of 1955, Atyeo netted four times for an FA XI in their 9-0 defeat of the RAF at Ashton Gate. It was the only occasion on which he and Geoff Bradford, who scored twice, were on the same side. They were to have been team-mates later against a Brussels team, when his Rovers counterpart could not play because of a leg injury. 'I had an idea,' Bradford recalled some years later, 'that there were thoughts in the England camp that we would have made a good strike force playing together. It would have given us both great pleasure if this had happened, and we often talked about what might have been. Off the field we were very good friends, and we worked together for the spastics charities.'

Bradford scored for England in Denmark before that game against the air-men, but that was to be his only cap. He was led to believe that he would be with Atyeo in the England team that met Yugoslavia in a 'B' international under the Manchester City lights later that October, after they had shared so many goals at the RAF's expense, but Haynes was preferred and Bradford made twelfth man. The City man filled the other inside-forward position.

Atyeo set England on the way to a 5-1 win with volley following a corner kick by Vic Groves, and the big Bristol striker might have had a first-half hat-trick in an impressive display that had him freely tipped for his first full cap against Spain at Wembley on the last day of November. It was therefore no surprise when he was among the sixteen players called up for special training. In practice matches, the England probables drew 2-2 with Wolves at Molineux and then 1-1 with West Bromwich Albion at the Hawthorns.

The players left their headquarters at the Hendon Hall Hotel to attend the show at the London Palladium on the night before the match with Spain. Atyeo, who distributed the two dozen tickets on which he had spent most of his £50 match fee among those who had helped his career, was in the final selection. This was the team in which Atyeo made his full England debut:

Baynham (Luton); Hall (Birmingham), Byrne (Manchester United); Clayton (Blackburn), Wright (Wolves capt), Dickinson (Portsmouth); Finney (Preston), Atyeo (Bristol City), Lofthouse (Bolton), Haynes (Fulham), Perry (Blackpool).

Atyeo got away to a dream start, best recalled in his own words: 'The game was only eleven minutes old when Ron Clayton chipped the ball across from the right-half position. I caught it on my thigh, and as it dropped I hit it on the turn and it flew into the top corner. A minute later I took part in a move with Lofthouse, and Bill Perry, waved on by the referee, beat the offside trap from Nat's pass down the middle to score the second goal. I also linked with Johnny Haynes to put Tom Finney through in only the sixth minute, but he was brought down and the goalkeeper made a wonderful diving save from his penalty kick. Tom, who was the victim of much obstruction, made up for that miss by scoring a magnificent goal early in the second half. Then Perry netted again just after the hour, and we went on to win 4-1.'

Spain's consolation came after soccer history had been made at precisely 3.23pm on the Wednesday afternoon when, at a signal from the French referee, the floodlights had been switched on for the first time in a full international match in Britain.

'It was the captain's job,' said Atyeo, 'to hand round the caps after the game. Some of the experienced players just slung theirs into their bags, but when Billy Wright handed me mine I fondled it carefully and packed it neatly away. It was the pinnacle of everything I had worked for.'

The same England side represented the Football League against the League of Ireland at Goodison the following Wednesday. On the intervening Saturday, Atyeo did the hat-trick for the third time that season in a 5-1 home defeat of Lincoln that increased City's lead in the Second Division to two points. They had wrestled the leadership from Swansea a fortnight earlier with a 3-2 home victory over Sheffield Wednesday, the champions-to-be. Atyeo's previous trebles were in a 3-1 home win over Bury and a 6-4 success at Blackburn, who had scored eight against Bristol Rovers in an 11-goal extravaganza earlier in the year. The burly Tommy Briggs put all but one of those goals into the Eastville club's net; against City he had to be content with a couple.

Shortly after that Blackburn game, early in November, Atyeo was at inside-right in an FA XI against the Army at Newcastle. The crowd was fewer than 6,000 in a stadium that had accommodated 55,000 for a First Division match with Blackpool only a few days before. The atmosphere was therefore quite a contrast to that created by a Wembley gate of 96,000 on Atyeo's full England debut. Perhaps that was why he and his FA team-mates took time to get going at St James's Park. They fell two goals behind in the second half before Atyeo sparked a revival with a side-footed reply, and Albert Quixall, the Wednesday forward who moved to Manchester United after the Munich disaster, equalised with twelve minutes to go.

Atyeo was also among the Football League scorers in their 5-1 defeat of the Irish part-timers at Goodison Park, getting their third goal late in the opening half. The sky went so black, as if in sympathy with the outplayed visitors, after Roger Byrne had rounded things off from the penalty spot, that the referee, Jack Clough again, would have called for lights if there had then been any to switch on. Instead, he introduced a white ball for the last ten minutes. The prevailing instruction to referees for League games was that the same ball had to be used throughout, but that did not apply to inter-league fixtures.

On 29 February 1956 Atyeo scored again in England's 'B' international with Scotland at Dens Park, Dundee, salvaging a 2-2 draw in the last ten minutes from a cross that the opposition claimed had gone out of play. The provider of that centre was Tommy Taylor, the former Barnsley centre-forward who was to be another of the Manchester United victims of Munich. Atyeo also had a part in the move from which Taylor opened the scoring two minutes before half-time.

The second of Atyeo's six full caps was also at Wembley, against Brazil the following May – two months after he had been given a civic reception by Westbury Urban District Council in honour of his achievements, and a week after Bristol City's first season back in the Second Division had petered out from its bright beginning. They finished mid-table, despite Atyeo's best League tally for one campaign of 30 goals, plus another in the Cup. England won again, beating Brazil 4-2, but although Atyeo was involved in two of the goals he failed with a penalty kick that gave him his best scoring chance.

He had some excuse, however, for there was an unusual delay before he could take the kick. Clear as the case was, when a pair of brown arms, not the goalkeeper's, went up to intercept the ball as Haynes hooked it over the crowded goalmouth, towards where the Sheffield United left-winger Colin Grainger was closing in unmarked, the referee (the same Frenchman who had controlled the Spain game) was besieged by protesting Brazilians. Practically all of them, that is, except inside-right Alvaro, who, as one reporter put it, was 'striding purposefully from the field, clutching the ball with an over-my-dead-body air'. Not until a Brazilian official ordered his players to proceed was the ball surrendered to Atyeo, who, no doubt unsettled by these histrionics, shot straight at the goalkeeper. In League games over the past two seasons, he had put away seven penalties competently enough.

Selected for the ensuing summer tour of Sweden, Finland and Germany, Atyeo retained his place in Stockholm, but was dropped after a goalless draw. Although only inches high with two headers, he otherwise made little impression in a disjointed forward line that lacked punch. England, indeed, were lucky to avoid defeat, especially during a first half in which they faced a blind-ing sun and strong wind. Goalkeeper Reg Matthews had to be at his alert best to keep the Swedes at bay, and was thankful not to face a penalty when the Dutch referee missed a glaring handball by Duncan Edwards. Without Atyeo, England went on to defeat Finland in Helsinki and also West Germany, then the World Cup holders, in Berlin.

City's star man stayed out of the England reckoning until he was among the 22-man squad for three World Cup qualifiers at the end of the 1956-57 season – against the Republic of Ireland, at Wembley and in Dublin, and Denmark, in Copenhagen. For all three matches he was restored to the twin attacking spearhead he had formed against Brazil and Sweden with Tommy Taylor. Between them they scored all but one of England's ten goals, begin-ning with three for Taylor and two for Atyeo in the 5-1 defeat of an Irish team that included Dermot Curtis, a forward who had left Shelbourne to become a full-time professional with Bristol City the previous December. It remains the only time the Ashton Gate club have had two players in an international match at Wembley.

Taylor completed his hat-trick five minutes from half-time, shortly after Atyeo had dived to head home when goalkeeper Kelly touched out Finney's acutely-angled shot. At 4-0, the game was then as good as over, and England eased up during the second half in which Curtis headed the 55th-minute reply. Atyeo rounded off the scoring in the last minute after Finney had flicked the ball back from the by-line, but he earned only muted mention in the national press next day. One critic wrote: 'Whether Atyeo is the answer to the inside-right problem is a matter of doubt. He always manages to get among the goals, yet so much of his play is clumsy and not particularly intelligent that there must still be a question mark against his name.' Damning words indeed for one of the most prolific scorers of his era.

Curtis, who had been the leading marksman in the League of Ireland, while also having a job outside soccer as a panel beater at a Dublin garage, went into that match with England fresh from scoring 13 goals in 17 League games (and another in the Cup) for Bristol City after a spell sharpening-up in the reserves. A week earlier he had done the hat-trick in a 3-1 home win against Swansea, and at that stage he looked well worth the £5,500 invested after Pat Beasley had twice travelled to see him in action – first with director George Jones for a match at Dalymount Park in which the Republic beat West Germany 3-0, then with Jones and another director, Bill Garland, for a game between Shelbourne and Sligo. Curtis did not score against the Germans, though his bustling style won a penalty. Against Sligo, he netted one goal and made anoth-er in victory by the same score. That, with Wolves also reported interested, set-tled it. He put his name to the forms in a Dublin hotel.

The promising start Curtis made with Bristol City was not to be sustained, however. Although remaining an Eire choice, he only just managed to get into double figures for League appearances in his only full season at Ashton Gate, 1957-58, scoring three goals. Neither did the experiment of trying him on the right wing in Football Combination games work out, so in August 1958 he was off-loaded to Ipswich. During his five seasons there he had the misfortune to find himself again squeezed out, as goals from the formidable Ray Crawford-Ted Phillips double act swept the Suffolk club into the First Division. When he next moved, to Exeter City, he had added fewer than 50 games and 20 goals to his League and Cup tally.

A week after the Wembley victory against the Republic of Ireland, England also won the third of their four qualifying games for the 1958 World Cup in Sweden, completing an emphatic double over Denmark. They followed their 5-2 defeat of the Danes at Wolverhampton the previous December (Taylor 3, Edwards 2) with a 4-1 triumph in Copenhagen, where Atyeo's header shared the scoring with Taylor (2) and Haynes. Four days later came the return match with the Republic of Ireland, who stood the chance of a play-off against England on neutral ground if they could beat them in Dublin. And that was what seemed likely to be the outcome from the fourth minute, when Alf Ringstead, the Sheffield United winger, gave the home side a shock lead that was held until the game went into injury-time. Then it was that Tom Finney, a late replacement for the injured Stan Matthews, fastened onto a ball kicked hopefully upfield by Jeff Hall, the Birmingham right-back. This was how John Atyeo described what happened next:

'Tom beat Pat Saward, Aston Villa's left-half, on the inside, sent Noel Cantwell, the left-back who then played for West Ham, the wrong way, and beat Saward a second time as he reached the dead-ball line. He crossed the most perfect centre you could wish to see. I was coming in at the inside-left position, and just nodded the ball down into the net. As soon as the kick-off was taken the match came to an end.'

England qualified for the finals, but by the time they came Atyeo was out of the reckoning. Still only in his mid-20s, he had played his last game for his country, and his only subsequent representative honour was gained in a Football Combination side against a Dutch XI in Rotterdam. But he stepped down from the international stage with surely a unique distinction. He had scored a goal with his last touch of the ball while wearing an England shirt.

Pat Beasley clearing up his books
and papers in his office on his
last day at Ashton Gate

Pat Beasley in his playing days

Chapter 10

Downhill after a Bristol double top

The Second Division table after games played on Saturday, 26 November 1955 made historic reading for Bristol. The city's two Football League clubs were together at the top, attaining an unprecedented joint peak. They had led the way before, but that had been in the Third Division South, from 21 February until Easter Monday, 6 April, during the 1952-53 season in which Rovers romped to promotion but City fell away to fifth. These were the leading positions when they reached their combined highest point in the second tier:

1955-56	P	W	D	L	F	A	Pts
1 Bristol City	18	11	3	4	43	28	25
2 Bristol Rovers	18	11	2	5	46	30	24
3 Swansea	19	11	2	6	41	36	24
4 Sheffield Wed	19	7	9	3	41	27	23

This time, however, the Bristol boom lasted for only one week. It was also blemished because on the afternoon when Rovers hoisted themselves into second place with a 7-2 home win against Middlesbrough, City ended an unbeaten run of ten games in losing 2-3 at Peter Doherty's Doncaster, after going into the second half two up. It was the following Saturday that John Atyeo, fresh from his successful England debut against Spain, did the hat-trick in City's 5-1 home win over Lincoln, but Rovers slipped to fourth behind Wednesday and Swansea in themselves being the victims of a hat-trick, by Ron Wylie, at Notts County.

Lincoln's lone goal was put into his own net by Terry Compton, a Bristolian who deputised at centre-half in 'Ginger' Peacock's first absence of the season with an ankle injury. Compton was both competent and consistent, but, with such players as Peacock and Jack White around, his League appearances were restricted to fewer than 50 in the ten years he spent at Ashton Gate before going into the Western League with Salisbury in 1958.

City only clung onto first place by a fraction of goal-average from Swansea, but with a game still in hand, in surrendering two more points on their visit to the Welsh club. With Rovers also beaten that day, at home to mid-table Port Vale, there was much comment on what one critic termed 'the strange behaviour of the two Bristol clubs' in going from boom to near-slump in a few matches. And on Christmas Eve the double decline continued as City lost the lead in also being beaten by Notts County, and Rovers lost at Doncaster.

Sheffield Wednesday, not Swansea, were the club to take advantage of only the second defeat suffered by City in their first dozen home matches (the first at the hands of Leeds early in September). The Owls comfortably accounted for Stoke, while the Swans lost heavily at West Ham. And Wednesday were at the top to stay, making an immediate return to the First Division. The yo-yo team of the time, they were relegated again two years later, but once more went straight back up.

On Boxing Day, Bristol City sagged to their fifth defeat in six games, conceding five goals without reply at Plymouth, but 24 hours later a Rogers hat-trick spurred them to 6-0 revenge at Ashton Gate.

For the visit of Argyle, Pat Beasley sprang a surprise by bringing in Derek Virgin, an amateur from South Petherton in Somerset, on the right wing in place of Alec Eisentrager. Virgin was retained for the next game, lost at Leeds in the absence of Atyeo with a bruised and swollen toe, and he stayed in for the third-round FA Cup-tie at Everton. City were beaten in that one too, despite Atyeo's scoring return, while Bristol Rovers were stealing the headlines by knocking out Manchester United at Eastville. After that, Virgin was not seen in City's first team for more than two years. In 1958, when, at 22, he was nearing the end of his teaching course at St Luke's College in Exeter, he played for the colts on Good Friday, the reserves on Easter Monday, then made his one League appearance of that season in a 5-0 home win against Barnsley.

The player from whom Virgin took over on that occasion was Wally Hinshelwood, a winger signed for 'a substantial fee' from Reading two years before. Hinchelwood had pulled a thigh muscle in scoring the goal that forced a 3-3 draw with Bristol Rovers at Eastville the previous Saturday. Virgin was a schoolmaster (specialising in physical training) at the Ashton Court primary school near Ashton Gate when he was next called up, in October. A month after signing part-time professional forms for City, he again stood in for Hinshelwood, who had tonsilitis, in a home match with lowly Sunderland – and he scored twice in a 4-1 victory.

City's next opponents, at Eastville, were under the cloud tragically cast by the premature death of Harry Bamford, Rovers' long-serving full-back, from injuries in a road accident. Derek Virgin, though not scoring, helped City's unchanged team to a 2-1 win, but Hinshelwood was then fit to return and the schoolmaster footballer, who taught rugby, had few further first-team opportunities before leaving for Bath City during the 1961 close season.

Wally Hinshelwood joined Bristol City because Pat Beasley remembered him from their Fulham days. Beasley was the London club's captain when Hinshelwood became a professional at Craven Cottage a year after being taken onto the ground staff as a 16-year-old amateur from the Athenian League side Sutton United. If Beasley had had his way, Hinshelwood would have arrived at Ashton Gate earlier than he did, for the manager hoped to obtain him as 'an act of grace' when Sid Thomas, whom Hinshelwood had succeeded in the Fulham team, was forced out of the game by illness soon after joining City. Instead, the Battersea-born Hinshelwood went to Chelsea in part exchange for

Jimmy Bowie, an Aberdonian ball-playing inside-forward, but after only fifteen weeks he was back at Fulham. His second departure from Craven Cottage took him to Reading, where he was converted into an inside-forward by manager Jack Smith. In one Third South match with Coventry, Hinshelwood did the hat-trick as a 0-3 deficit was turned into a 4-3 victory.

While on Army National Service, during which he did duty in Hong Kong, Hinshelwood played against the French and Belgian Army and other Services teams, showing form that had the managers of several clubs casting envious eyes in his direction. In March 1954, as a Reading player, he was in an FA XI at Ashton Gate, with John Atyeo as his inside partner, for the Western League's Diamond Jubilee celebration match. Hinshelwood was an emergency replacement for West Ham winger Harry Hooper, himself a late deputy in being elevated to the England 'B' team, scoring the equaliser against Scotland 'B' at Sunderland the same day. Even so, Hinshelwood would not have played if George Petherbridge, of Bristol Rovers, had been fit to take over instead.

From that accidental link-up, Hinshelwood and Atyeo developed an understanding that made Beasley keener to repeat it with Bristol City, before a snowstorm stopped play with the FA team four goals ahead. Atyeo opened the scoring after four minutes and his City clubmate Jack Boxley, who was on the left wing, increased it ten minutes before half-time. The two other goals were both made by Hinshelwood for Fulham's Bedford Jezzard early in the second half. Jack White, the third City player in the side, staggered off from a collision with Ike Clarke, the Yeovil and former West Bromwich and Portsmouth forward. Another City man, Johnny Watkins, was at outside-left for the Western League, who had Fred Stone, ex-City and then of Chippenham Town, at left-back. These were the full line-ups:

WESTERN LEAGUE: Scott (Barnstaple); Targett (Weymouth), Stone (Chippenham); Lovsey (Trowbridge), Bartholomew (Ilfracombe), Carter (Clevedon); Miller (Bideford), Snook (Bath), Wilshire (Bristol Rovers), Clarke (Yeovil), Watkins (Bristol City).

FA XI: Burton (Swindon); Rutter (Cardiff), Fox (Bristol Rovers); White (Bristol City), Wicks (Chelsea), Sampson (Bristol Rovers); Hinshelwood (Reading), Atyeo (Bristol City), Jezzard (Fulham), Uphill (Reading), Boxley (Bristol City).

On his day, Hinshelwood was one of the best right-wingers in the country, but, to quote Atyeo, 'he only turned it on now and again.' Because of that, he was once described as 'the man Ashton Gate loves to hate'. After more than 150 League and Cup appearances on the wing for City, in which he scored just over a dozen goals, he asked for a transfer on losing his place. One reason was that he and his family wanted to return to London, but he gave another by saying: 'I am not grumbling on my own behalf. I have had good days and bad days, and most of the boos I have had have been deserved. But this Ashton Gate crowd do not try to help a team. When a team are struggling and the players are doing their darndest a crowd should try to rally around and cheer them on. But not at Ashton Gate – although it may be only a small section that makes all the noise.'

Hinshelwood got his wish with a transfer to Millwall in the summer of 1960. He was afterwards in Canadian football, then with Newport County before spells at Canterbury City and Deal Town. His sons Martin and Paul also became League footballers, both full-backs with Crystal Palace. Martin was appointed coach to Chelsea's reserves after giving up playing through injury. Paul's match to remember was one of three penalties. He converted both Palace's spot-kicks against Cambridge United, for whom Steve Spriggs scored the other, on the opening day of the 1981-82 season – the first of them after only 55 seconds.

The in-and-out form displayed by Walter Alexander Hinshelwood became typical of Bristol City as the fortunes of an ageing team faded. This had some bearing on John Atyeo's exclusion from international football. As he said, 'My England career coincided with City's two great seasons, but in the following two seasons things started to go downhill at Ashton Gate. That was the time when I should probably have been thinking about moving to a bigger club, but I didn't think too much then about leaving City.'

Despite their faltering form since November 1955, Bristol City still had an outside chance of reaching the First Division until three games from the finish of what was the most intense scramble for promotion in memory. At a very late stage nearly all the clubs in the top half were in the running. On the Saturday after Easter, City were fifth, just three points behind Bristol Rovers, then runners-up, five points adrift of runaway Wednesday. City had come from behind to beat Doncaster at Ashton Gate. Jimmy Rogers scored three of the four second-half goals, Atyeo the other, as the Yorkshire club yielded a lead given them by Bert Tindill, a versatile forward who was to be Peter Doherty's first signing for Bristol City (more about that in its proper turn).

But that victory was the end of City's challenge. Two of those last three games were away, against Lincoln and West Ham, and they lost both without scoring. In between they beat Blackburn, one of their promotion rivals, but by then it was all over – as it almost was on the same April afternoon for Bristol Rovers, who surrendered second place to Leeds on goal-average when losing at Elland Road. On the following Monday, Leeds pulled two points clear of Rovers by winning the game they had in hand, and on the final day, needing only a draw, they made sure of accompanying Wednesday back to the First Division by accounting for relegated Hull. Bristol Rovers dropped to sixth, three points ahead of their 11th-placed neighbours.

It was during that season that City let slip their grasp on a former Kingswood School and Bristol Boys forward who spread more than 400 appearances and nearly 100 goals among his five other League clubs, besides winning a couple of England Under-23 caps. This was David Burnside, who was signed by City as an amateur, but allowed to leave towards the end of 1955 for West Bromwich Albion. He turned out over 100 times for both Albion and Plymouth Argyle, and in between was with Southampton, Crystal Palace and Wolves (whom he helped to promotion). Released by Argyle in December 1971, he returned to Ashton Gate on a two-month trial, but was substituted in the only League game he played for City, lost at home to Burnley. After that, he rejected a player-coach post at Colchester to join Bath City as player-manager. He was then with Walsall as assistant manager before going out of the League with Cadbury Heath (a club near Bristol), Briidgwater Town and Taunton Town. Later, he became an FA coach and was manager of the England youth team.

While with Albion, Burnside displayed the exceptional ball-playing skills for which he was noted during the half-time interval in a friendly with a Soviet team. He put soccer first in refusing a lucrative contract which he was consequently offered to take part in shows around the world, but later entered a contest organised by a national newspaper to find if Britain possessed a footballer capable of breaking the world's heading record held by a young Austrian with a total of 3,025 in succession. Burnside reached 495.

Bristol City began the 1956-57 season with the newly signed Joe Baillie at right-back in place of Ivor Guy, in this team: Cook; Baillie, Thresher; White, Peacock, Williams (C); Hinshelwood, Atyeo, Rogers, Burden, Boxley. But after five goals had been conceded to promotion-bound Nottingham Forest in the opening home game, the wingers were replaced by Alec Eisentrager and David Smith. For Smith, a former Bristol Boys player who had joined City shortly after leaving Alexandra Park School in the Fishponds district of Bristol, it was a League debut delayed by more than three years. He had, however, played against East Fife in a floodlit friendly soon after turning professional at 18 in March 1953. City had hoped to field him in a Third South game at Colchester a month later, but his registration had not been received by the League before the March deadline for unrestricted signings, and a request for special permission to include him had been refused.

As an amateur, David Smith gained county soccer honours in youth and senior teams and played for England in the youth internationals of 1952 53 against Scotland and Wales. As a professional, he made over 30 first-team appearances for Bristol City before teaming up with Syd Morgan at Millwall, then of the Fourth Division, in 1959. Smith had been listed at £1,500 but granted a free transfer on appeal to the League. Cricket, however, was his strongest suit. Smith was an opening seam bowler with Gloucestershire for 15 summers from 1956, and played for England in five Tests – all in the 1961-62 series in India. In his benefit year of 1968 he became the first bowler of his type to take 1,000 wickets for the county.

There was a preponderance of county cricketers in the Bristol City and Rovers teams of those days, when players could still successfully combine soccer and the summer game at that level. Another one was introduced into the City side four months after Smith, Bobby Etheridge making his debut in another 5-1 home win against Lincoln soon after being a £3,500 signing by Pat Beasley from Gloucester City, in face of competition from Cardiff, Reading and Wolves. He took over at inside-left from Baillie, who had been tried there on Guy's recall at full-back. Etheridge, slim and stylish, started that season as a regular in his home club's Southern League line-up, and with one County Championship game with Gloucestershire, in a defeat of Lancashire in Bristol, to his credit as a wicketkeeper-batsman. He ended it as one of the most improved forwards in the Second Division, with the prospect of establishing himself in county cricket, and soon to sign full-time forms for City on ending his National Service in the RAF.

The date of that demobilisation was Saturday, 13 April 1957. Etheridge became a footballing full-timer on the Monday, but within an hour also signed as a professional with Gloucestershire and joined his new cricketing colleagues at practice. With Peter Rochford, then the county's first-choice wicketkeeper, doubtful because of jaundice, Etheridge was on stand-by, and, although not immediately required, he played in a dozen Championship games that year. At the end of the season Rochford was released, but it was not long before Etheridge was in the middle of a conflict of interests that afflicted two other Gloucestershire players, Barrie Meyer, also a wicketkeeper, and batsman Ron Nicholls (both later of Bristol City), who were shown the door by Bristol Rovers because they made cricket their priority.

In 1958, Etheridge was required for City's close-season tour of Bordeaux and Nice, and was therefore unavailable for Gloucestershire's opening game with Oxford University and their first five Championship matches. That gave Meyer the chance to become Rochford's successor, and he literally took it with both hands – for fifteen seasons in all before spending a good number more as a county and Test umpire.

Etheridge was left to pursue the remainder of his Gloucestershire career mainly in the Minor Counties side, for which he scored his maiden century soon after his return from France. In concentrating on his football before also reaching county standard at bowls, he played in over 250 League games for Bristol City, scoring nearly 50 goals, then left in 1966 for Cheltenham Town. He became that club's player-manager, and after giving up that post for business reasons he rejoined Gloucester City as manager during the 1970s.

Another Gloucestershire cricketer, at second-team level, was Etheridge's first wing partner in Bristol City's League side. This was Johnny Watkins, the penalty-taker who lost his bet with Tony Cook. Watkins, who played his club cricket for Stoke Bishop, one of Bristol's leading sides, was newly into his first extended run on the left flank of City's attack, but he had been with the club since signing part-time forms at the age of 18 in June 1951, after trials with Portsmouth and Stockport and a spell as an amateur with Wolves. A former

England schoolboy international, he was one of a dozen Bristol-born players who were on City's books in the 1956-57 season – and several of the others were also from the West Country.

Watkins and Etheridge came together at a time when City were in flux. John Atyeo, no mean cricketer himself, was out with a thigh injury that also caused him to withdraw from an FA team against the Army in Manchester. David Smith was sidelined too, and Jimmy Rogers, having just recovered from tonsilitis, was about to leave for Coventry with Jack Boxley. For the match in which Watkins began his belated hold on a first-team place, lost at home to Stoke in late November, Hinshelwood was the only member of the attack to keep his place as seven changes were made. Skipper Jack White reverted temporarily to the centre-forward position for which Dermot Curtis was signed soon afterwards. George Walker, Hull-born but recruited from Chippenham Town, was one of Atyeo's deputies but was soon replaced by Eisentrager. Walker was given few further first-team outings over the next two years before being transferred to Carlisle at about the same time that Jim Terris, a full-back, also left for the Cumbrian club. When Etheridge opened his goals account in a 3-3 home draw with Port Vale at the end of 1956, only White, Peacock and Hinshelwood were in the positions they had occupied on the opening day. Boxley and Rogers were unable to complete a match with Coventry until the fourth attempt. Play was twice abandoned – first when the floodlights failed, then because of snow – and the weather next caused a Boxing Day postponement before Boxley scored the winner at Southend.

The chopping and changing at Ashton Gate was having an adverse effect on results. Of their last nine matches of 1956, City won only one – and that was the big defeat of Lincoln in which Etheridge made his debut and Atyeo, briefly back, was among the scorers. From that isolated success City went to letting in six goals at Rotherham on the last Saturday before Christmas and five at Swansea on Boxing Day, plunging to fourth from the bottom of the table – the lowest position they were to occupy all season.

Not the best of times, therefore, for Les Bardsley to be easing into the trainer-coach vacancy left by Wilf Copping's move to Coventry. Bardsley, a former Stockport Boys and Cheshire Boys player, had been snapped up as an amateur by Manchester City on leaving school at 14, and had turned professional three years later, just before the outbreak of war after being apprenticed to an engineering firm as a fitter. He joined the Army as a physical training instructor near the end of the war, and while stationed in Northern Ireland guested for Linfield, with whom he won an Irish Gold Cup winner's medal, and Derry City. Both clubs wanted him to stay, but he opted to join Bury and, converted from inside-forward to wing-half, spent just over seven seasons with the Gigg Lane club before his transfer in September 1955 to Barrow, then in the Third North under the management of former Newcastle captain Joe Harvey.

Soon afterwards, Bardsley was appointed player-manager of Mossley in the Cheshire League, but he did not stay long there either. 'There was a committee of fourteen, and only enough cash for three professionals,' he explained. 'It was good experience for me, but then a friend introduced me to Pat Beasley at Ashton Gate and I was originally taken on there as assistant trainer. It was a big decision to go to Bristol, for my wife Leah was expecting our second son at the time.' But, despite the lean spell into which City slipped soon after his arrival, it was a move that worked out well. While with Bury he had taken advantage of an FA offer for professional footballers to take a physiotherapy course, paying £50 (and the FA £300) to study three afternoons a week in Manchester. So he had excellent qualifications, though Pat Beasley undoubtedly felt the loss of Copping, who had been a big influence since succeeding Eddie Nash. As John Atyeo told George Baker: 'Wilf, a rough-and-ready character who expected everyone to give 100 per cent, was good for Pat, who was quiet, unassuming and a bit of a worrier.'

Atyeo also said that 'as long as you were winning Wilf didn't care a damn. You could please yourself what you did. He kept everyone smiling.' On one close-season tour to Germany, the players had to be in their hotel by 11pm, but, to quote Atyeo again, 'we thought that was too early. So Wilf said: "Don't worry. Stay out a bit longer. I'll get Pat drunk." When we rolled in about midnight there was Pat waiting for us in the lobby, fresh as a daisy. Wilf was slouched out in a chair.'

Chapter 11

John Atyeo's Greatest Goal

For Bristol City and their supporters there were two redeeming features of the 1956-57 season, in which the club declined to 13th in the Second Division. One was the 5-3 defeat of Bristol Rovers in front of an Ashton Gate crowd only 19 short of 40,000, the other a run to the fifth round of the FA Cup, in which John Atyeo scored what he rightly regarded as his greatest goal.

Atyeo and Cyril Williams both scored twice, and Hinshelwood once, in that eight-goal thriller, with Dai Ward (2) and Alfie Biggs replying. Rovers were without their captain, Geoff Bradford, whose comeback from his second serious leg injury was interrupted by a thigh problem. He was omitted from the return at Eastville that provided the contrast of a scoreless draw. In its closing stages Ernie Peacock, City's captain, and Rovers' Jackie Pitt were sent off by Norman Taylor, a referee from John Atyeo's neck of the woods, Westbury in Wiltshire. They clashed after Peacock had moved from centre-half to the wing because of injury, and both incurred a seven-day suspension.

The Cup run began at home to Rotherham, a fortnight after City's crushing League defeat at Millmoor. Atyeo scored twice more in a 4-1 revenge win. City wore Rovers' blue and white quarters because both teams needed to change from their usual red. The fourth round brought to Bristol Cheshire League Rhyl whose win at Meadow Lane in the third had cost Second Division Notts County's manager, George Poyser, and trainer, Vic Potts, their jobs.

Bristol City avoided being humiliated by the little Welsh club. Fresh from a 5-1 home win against Sheffield United, in which Atyeo did the hat-trick, they progressed with three more goals, two from their ace marksman. Those successes, and the one against Rotherham, were well-timed financially. Since the beginning of the year the bonus for a win had been increased to £3 from the £2 that had been in force since just after the First World War. A draw earned a rise of 10s (50p) to £1 10s.

The next obstacle in City's Cup path was the formidable visit to First Division Aston Villa, in front of a crowd of 63,099. That was where hopes were dashed of emulating Bristol Rovers' advance to the quarter-finals six years before – but only by the odd goal of three, and City's was the one that John Atyeo looked back on as his best. This was how he remembered it:

'The pitch was a gluepot. We were losing to a goal by Derek Pace, and were not really in the game. Then the ball was driven out from defence, and I latched onto it. I went past Jimmy Dugdale and then Stan Lynn as I advanced down the left hand side of the pitch. I hit the ball with my left foot from about 25 yards. It popped up a fraction as I connected, and was like a golf ball on a tee before it sped like a bullet past goalkeeper Nigel Sims. It was certainly a spectacular goal, but to no avail as Jackie Sewell, then England's costliest footballer, headed the winner.'

Even then, however, City almost forced a replay. In the last few minutes Atyeo sent the ball over from the right, and Ernie Peacock, who had been injured and limped forward into the attack, only just failed to get a foot to it in front of goal. These were the teams for that memorable encounter:

ASTON VILLA: Sims; Lynn, Aldis; Crowther, Dugdale, Saward; Smith, Sewell, Pace, Dixon, McParland.

BRISTOL CITY: Anderson; Bailey, Thresher; White, Peacock, Burden; Hinshelwood, Williams (C), Atyeo, Etheridge, Watkins.

The League match with Notts County rearranged for the following Wednesday evening, 20 February 1957 because of the Villa Cup-tie, was the first to be played completely under floodlights at Ashton Gate. City won 3-0. Wolves had been the visitors for the first floodlit game at the ground, a friendly that attracted 24,000 on Tuesday, 27 January 1953, and Wolves also provided the opposition when new lights were officially switched on in 1965. The original lights were sold to Burton Albion, and the old floodlight pylons given to Wigan Athletic.

Aston Villa went on to win the Cup, beating Burnley and West Bromwich Albion, both after a replay, and then Manchester United, that season's League champions and European Cup semi-finalists, in a final made controversial by the early injury to United's goalkeeper, Ray Wood, in a collision with Peter McParland.

This was the season in which Bristol City unsuccessfully tried to tempt Roy Bentley back to Ashton Gate. Along with WBA, they also made an approach for Albert Broadbent, a former Notts County left-winger unsettled with Sheffield Wednesday, but he eventually accepted Rotherham's terms instead. Those who were signed, besides Etheridge, included Selwyn Watkins, a former Bath City outside-right who was the younger brother of Allan, the Glamorgan and England cricketer, and Andy Oliphant, a utility player from Taunton Town who had started out with East Fife. Neither, however, followed Etheridge as a first-team regular. Oliphant was later player-manager of Bridgwater Town.

Two other newcomers of greater note were Jimmy Seed, who joined City in an advisory capacity before the Cup-tie with Rhyl, and Alan Williams, an ex-Bristol Boys defender, who made his League debut at Blackburn the Saturday before the Villa Cup-tie.

Seed, an England forward and Cup winner while with Tottenham in the 1920s, and twice captain of Wednesday's League champions in successive seasons after inspiring the Sheffield club's escape from relegation at Spurs' expense, was anxious to get back into football again within four months of resigning as Charlton Athletic's manager, but he did not want to take on full responsibility. At 61 he had had more than enough responsibility in almost a quarter of a century at the Valley, the strain having become unbearable after an eight-goal thrashing at Sunderland left Charlton with no points from their first five games of the season. 'I cannot carry on without Sam Bartram,' said Seed when he departed. 'It was a terrible wrench when Sam left last March to manage York. He had been goalkeeper, friend and often inspiration for 22 years. I realise now that his leaving was the first sign of the crack-up that came to its head at Roker Park.'

Seed had no real thought of retiring, however, when, having phoned to ask for an appointment, he went to the Mayfair offices of timber magnate Stanley Glicksten, the Charlton chairman, at 5pm on the Monday after that heavy defeat. 'We talked for an hour,' he said, 'and Mr Stanley then looked at me and said: "Jimmy, you look tired out." I knew then that it was the end. I told him that I was tired of it all, that I wanted to get out of football for good. He agreed, after making very kind provision for my future. You can call those two hours in Mayfair the saddest of my life, but I realise I am getting old. Football is a game for young men, and it should be run by young men. Many new ideas have been introduced and I have tried to keep up with them. I know that in some ways I have failed.' Glicksten also failed – in, as he stated later, trying to talk Seed out of resigning.

Before meeting the chairman, Seed had his usual morning inquest with the players and afterwards admitted with some regret: 'I was very harsh with all of them except John Hewie [the Scottish international full-back who was one of Seed's signings from South Africa]. I hadn't a good word to say to any of them. It would have been different if I had known this would be my last talk to them. I shall never meet them again after what I said this morning.'

Harry Dolman was at pains to make clear that there was no question of Pat Beasley's managerial authority being undermined when he made his offer to Seed over lunch in London the following January. Seed was brought in 'to do a certain amount of scouting and give advice in talks on tactics and team choosing', but events were to decree that this new set-up would last for barely a year. It brought Seed into association with Sid Hawkins, City's secretary, for the third time. They were first together with Clapton Orient when Seed entered management, and Hawkins was the assistant secretary. Then Hawkins occupied that post with Charlton for a time during Seed's reign at the Valley.

Alan Williams was new to the first team in the 1956-57 season, but not new to the club. Signed from school at 15 in 1954, he was groomed through the colts and reserves, and might have made his debut earlier but for cracking an ankle bone in a practice match. When he got his chance it was not in his normal centre-half position but at left-half, and he had to wait until the following season to become settled in the side. He missed few of City's games during his two years in the RAF, stationed at Gloucester, and was unfortunate not to be capped by England at Under-23 level.

After being reserve for the match with Czechoslovakia at Norwich in the autumn of 1958, Williams was selected to replace Birmingham's Trevor Smith, required for an FA Cup replay against Fulham, in the team to meet Scotland at Ibrox the following February, but that game had to be called off because the pitch was, in the words of one official, 'like concrete.' Two players later with Bristol City, Gordon Low, then with Huddersfield, and Johnny Quigley, of Nottingham Forest, were to have been in the Scots' line-up. The icy weather caused such a backlog of fixtures that it was found impossible to arrange a new date, and Williams was back to being a travelling reserve for the next month's Under-23 match with France in Lyons.

By then, Bristol City had had one change of manager, and were only a year away from having another. The portents for the 1957-58 season were ominous from the start, the team plunging to 20th in picking up only one point and scoring only one goal (and that debited to Liverpool's goalkeeper, Tommy Younger) in their first three matches. The year ended with City just two places better off. A hard-earned 3-2 home win against Bristol Rovers was among the rare bright spots, as five goals were conceded at home to Fulham, at Swansea and Derby, and four at Rotherham, Ipswich, Barnsley and Liverpool.

Time ran out for Pat Beasley after a third-round FA Cup-tie with Accrington Stanley, who that season finished runners-up in the last Third Division (North), as the bottom twelve clubs of the North and South sections went into the new Division Four. City came away with a 2-2 draw on 4 January 1958, and at a board meeting on the following Monday it was 'mutually agreed' to terminate the manager's contract. The directors acceded to Beasley's request to stay on for 24 hours, for the Tuesday evening replay, so he bowed out on a winning note with two goals from Atyeo and one from Curtis in a 3-1 victory. He left admitting to being 'sad and upset', adding: 'I have always tried to give everyone a fair deal. I am sorry to be going for another reason. I feel we have some grand youngsters on our books of whom more will be heard.' At least he left with Harry Dolman saying: 'Pat Beasley and I have always got on well together. He is a gentleman.'

The last team Beasley sent out as City manager was: Cook; Bailey, Thresher; Burden, Peacock, White; Hinshelwood, Atyeo, Curtis, Eisentrager, Smith. This showed one change from the side at Accrington, Bailey resuming in place of Ian Rae. A full-back, Rae had made his debut in October as a second-half substitute in a floodlit friendly with French champions Nice, after signing from Falkirk for a down payment of £1,000 and £500 for each subsequent season he spent with City. A research chemist with a BSc degree, Rae was snapped up by Beasley after moving from Scotland to Cheltenham as chemical engineer with the National Coal Board's research establishment, but his training suffered through living and working so far from Ashton Gate, and he rejoined Falkirk when his contract expired at the end of June 1958.

Rae had been regarded as a potential international during his initial seven years with the Scottish club, so his failure to make the grade with City was especially disappointing. It was his bad luck to be thrust into a side struggling in the League after he had impressed in the 4-0 defeat of Nice. He had made under a dozen appearances when he was left out of a 0-0 home draw with Middlesbrough on the last Saturday of 1957, a week before the Cup-tie at Accrington for which he was recalled. He was brought back again four days after being omitted from the replay, Thresher dropping out with a groin injury. City lost that first game under the caretaker management of Jimmy Seed by four goals at Leyton Orient, and, with Thresher fit to return, that was the last time Rae was seen in the Second Division.

Indeed, Rae afterwards played only a couple of times with the reserves, and for his last few months at City he drew his wages without kicking a ball. His return to Falkirk was also ill-fated. As he had another year in his Cheltenham job, he did not wish to fly back to Scotland to play each weekend, so asked Reg Smith, the Falkirk manager, for a short-term transfer to Southern League Gloucester City, then managed by Harry Ferrier, a former full-back who had briefly been one of John Atyeo's team-mates at Portsmouth. Smith's response was unequivocal: 'Either you play for us or you don't play at all.'

There were two other City debutants in the match with Middlesbrough that Rae missed. Liam Munroe, a diminutive inside-forward from the Northern Irish club Ards, replaced Etheridge as partner for Watkins, and Bristol-born Gordon Parr, a former Bristol Boys captain who had been with City for three years since joining from school at 15, took over from Alan Williams at left-half. For both it was but fleeting recognition.

Munroe did not play in City's first team again; Parr was given two more games that season, then returned to the Combination side for five years. Parr completed an apprenticeship as an electrician at Harry Dolman's factory before his two years' service in the RAF, and, as we shall be see, it was not until he gave up that job in July 1963 to turn full-time that he became a familiar figure in the first team.

Pat Beasley negotiated the 23-year-old Munroe's transfer from Ards, who were then managed by George Eastham, a former Bolton and Blackpool forward whose son George followed him as an England international while with Arsenal. Beasley and Jimmy Seed had seen Munroe score in a 6-1 defeat of Crusaders. That goal took Munroe to a dozen for the season, despite having missed a month with influenza. In the previous season he had scored nearly 40. On that form he looked well worth the £2,000 invested in him, but superstitious folk might have seen an omen when he was prevented from making his debut at Liverpool on the Saturday before Christmas because his registration forms were held up in the post's holiday rush.

FA rules stipulated that a player had to be registered 14 days before being eligible, and, as Sid Hawkins, the City secretary, pointed out, the position was further complicated by the fact that, because Munroe was an Irishman, there were two lots of forms to be completed – first for the Irish FA and Irish League, then for the English authorities in London and Preston. At any rate,

Munroe had to while away his time in the reserves, in which he had created a good impression in their two Christmas games, before leaving for Scunthorpe, newly promoted to Division Two, in the 1958 close season. Early the following year he was back in Ireland with Distillery.

It did not take Pat Beasley long to find a new post. On 4 February 1958, a month since leaving Bristol City, he arrived at Birmingham City's ground at 9.30am hoping to be appointed assistant manager. Much to his surprise he began work shortly afterwards as joint manager, given dual authority with Arthur Turner, a former centre-half at the club who had been in complete charge since November 1954. With Walter Adams, the secretary, they formed a committee of management – Turner and Beasley responsible for the players and playing affairs, Adams for the business side, besides collating reports from the scouting staff. Walter Taylor, who had spent more than 35 of his 73 years with Birmingham, had been assistant manager, but was regarded more as filling the chief scout role to which he was now officially assigned. Directors worried about the team's League position (well down the First Division after letting in eight goals at Preston), and particularly about the reserves. They felt that Turner needed a younger man to help him. Beasley was then in his 46th year.

Chairman Harry Morris, a builder, stated: 'The board decided that the playing staff of 35 to 40 was too much for one man to manage. Mr Turner is the senior partner, but any decisions will be made only after discussions between the two men. The team will be chosen by Mr Turner and Mr Beasley with the help, possibly, of other members of the coaching and training staff. I would point out that no board in the country interferes less with the team selection than does Birmingham City's. I must stress that this decision shows no lack of faith in Mr Turner. If it works, and I think it will, it may set a new fashion in football. One of the two managers will travel with the team to away matches. There will be no need for both to go.'

Turner declared himself 'most happy' with the new set-up, hardly surprising considering that he himself had suggested Beasley to the directors after they had consulted him about obtaining some assistance. 'Pat and I have been pals for many years,' he said, 'ever since we played against each other before the war. Having Pat here will give me more scope. I am certain the tie up will work admirably.' But he and the chairman were wrong.

Although relegation was avoided in reasonable comfort, Turner was soon taking a very different view – so much so that the arrangement lasted for only an uneasy seven months. On 5 September 1958, four winless matches into a new season and two days after a six-goal thrashing at home by West Bromwich, Turner resigned and went with his wife on holiday to Blackpool. At least twice before during those seven months he had been persuaded to change his mind about leaving by the chairman. While manager in his own right he had seen Birmingham to the Second Division title and a Cup final at

Wembley; in harness he had come to regret no longer having the sole say, though his differences were not with Beasley but with some members of the board. He did not feel he had their full backing. 'It was a big shock when Arthur told me he was going,' said Beasley. 'Although people outside the club said it wouldn't work, we got on all right. There has been no dissension between us, and we always came to an amicable arrangement regarding the covering of various matches.'

Back from his seaside break, Turner soon found a new post with Headington United, steering them into the Football League as Oxford United in place of the defunct Accrington Stanley, having resisted an offer from Leeds. Later he was chief scout with Rotherham and Sheffield United.

Beasley carried on as Birmingham's acting manager until appointed team manager in January 1959, but he still did not have full command. Chairman Morris gave a clear hint of that in saying: 'Pat does like a great amount of help which he is prepared to take, and which we have always been prepared to give. It has been successful in the past. I don't see why it shouldn't continue to be successful.' Again it was an over-optimistic assessment. Birmingham ended that season in ninth place, but Beasley's position was weakened when his team lost to Fourth Division Watford in the third round of the FA Cup in January 1960 and then went perilously close to going down in the League. That summer, the board adopted a new policy that would have stripped him of much of his remaining power, so he also resigned. 'I just could not stand for it,' he said. 'When things are going well everybody's your friend. When they are not, it's very different.' This time he declared himself 'not really unhappy to be leaving.'

A year later, after moving his home to Farmborough, a village near Radstock, and sharing his time between running a small poultry farm and scouting for Fulham, Beasley offset the disappointment of having been unsuccessfully short-listed for the Bath City managerial vacancy that Arthur Coles filled by becoming the manager of Dover, another Southern League club. When his three-year contract there expired he retired to the Somerset market town of Chard. He died in Taunton Hospital on 27 February 1986, five months from his 74th birthday.

The vacancy that Beasley left at Ashton Gate early in 1958 was filled for only three matches by Jimmy Seed in his caretaker capacity in collaboration with Harry Dolman, Les Bardsley and 'Lemmo' Southway. After the defeat at Leyton which followed the Cup win over Accrington, Seed made sweeping changes for what was to be his other League game in charge, coincidentally at home to his old club Charlton. Out went Cook, Bailey, Rae, Curtis, Eisentrager and David Smith. Anderson returned in goal, and Burden was switched to right-back, with Thresher as his partner, to mark Johnny Summers, who had recently scored five second-half goals in Athletic's recovery from 1-5 down to beat Huddersfield 7-6, despite being reduced to ten men by the loss of centre-half Derek Ufton with a dislocated shoulder. Hinshelwood, at outside-right, and Atyeo, at centre-forward, were joined in City's attack by the recalled Walker, Etheridge and Watkins

Burden's place at right-half, in a middle line completed by Compton (deputy for the injured Peacock) and White, was filled by Terry Emery, who had made his only previous first-team appearance in City's last game of the previous season. Emery, who was in his late teens, had been signed as an amateur after playing in Boys' Brigade football and for St Paul's Athletic in the Bristol Church of England League, and had turned professional at the same time as Gordon Parr. Unlike Parr, however, he was not eventually to become a regular choice. In June 1959, his senior opportunities having only just got into double figures, he moved to Chippenham Town.

Seed's drastic action promised to pay off when Atyeo gave City an interval lead against Charlton, but again both points were surrendered. Summers could not be kept off the scoresheet, and Jack White conceded an own goal for the winner. The following week Seed, though nearly 63, contradicted his professed unwillingness to accept full responsibility once more by successfully seeking the managership of Millwall, though he stayed on to see City through the fourth-round Cup-tie in which they won 2-1 at Notts County. There were only two minutes to go when a back-pass by Ray Chatham, a former Wolves utility player at right-back for Notts, stuck in the mud, enabling Hinshelwood to race in for a snatched winner.

'I got the smell of the job again through being in charge at Bristol,' said Seed. 'It was difficult not to refuse the call.' Indeed not. Micky Purser, a second-hand car dealer from Bermondsey who was Millwall's chairman, left no doubt that Seed was only too eager to get the job. He revealed that 'Jimmy applied for it as soon as we announced it was vacant.' The post appealed to Seed because he was 'a little tired of travelling and living in hotels'. He added: 'It is hard for me to leave Bristol City because everyone has been very kind and friendly. The City board made it clear that I could have stayed on, but I didn't want to break up my London home. New Cross is only fifteen minutes away from there by car – the same distance I travelled every day when I was with Charlton.'

Ron Gray, a former Millwall trainer who had resigned as the club's manager after a run of poor results that included a big Cup defeat by Gillingham, then the Third (South's) bottom club, was retained as Seed's assistant. Millwall, however, were too far gone to avoid being founder members of the Fourth Division, finishing that 1957-58 season next to the foot of the last Third South table, and that only because their goal average was better than Exeter City's. A good start was made to life in the new lowest League sphere, but Millwall again slumped after being knocked out of the Cup by Worcester City, and in July 1959 Seed stepped down to become an advisor to the club in his new role as a director.

Seed's successor in the managerial hot seat was Reg Smith, who had recently resigned at Falkirk following relegation. The appointment was a shock and disappointment for Charlton, who had just announced that Smith was to be their trainer-coach. It also caused Mickey Purser some embarrassment. He had to tell his new manager not to be misled by an article that had appeared under Seed's name in that weekend's match programme. Of Millwall's new former Aston Villa full-back, Seed wrote: 'Dennis Jackson has stepped into the job as skipper in the manner born, and if he turns out to be the man we are looking for, with player-manager as the target, we will indeed by lucky.' The chairman hurriedly emphasised that Millwall had no longer been looking for a player-manager.

Smith, the son of a South African rugby international (their real name was Schmidt), had won two England caps while a left-winger with Millwall in 1938 and played in three wartime internationals. Leaving Seed to deal with public relations, he enjoyed some success with what he called 'Funnel Football. It made Millwall hard to beat, but also hard for them to win, and he was dismissed early in 1961 after another Cup defeat by a non-League club, Bath City. Ron Gray was then reinstated, but nearly two years later yet another shock Cup exit at the hands of a club outside the Football League, Kettering, also resulted in his sacking.

Jimmy Seed, his health failing, stayed on until shortly before his death on 16 July 1966, the day England defeated Mexico at Wembley on their way to winning the World Cup for the first time.

Jimmy Seed

Les Bardsley

City in 1964-65. Back: Tony Ford, Terry Bush, Jack Connor, Alec Briggs, Mike Gibson, Gordon Low. Front: Ray Savino, Brian Clark, John Atyeo, Gerry Sharpe, Roger Peters

Gerry Gow in action

Norman Hunter (centre), skipper Geoff Merrick (left) and manager Alan Dicks blow out the cake's candle on Hunter's 33rd birthday. It is 29 October 1976, the day after his signing for City

Sid Williams, in FA Cup action
against Brighton in January 1951

Kevin Mabbutt controls
the ball on his chest

Don Gillies, scorer of the winning goal, leaving the Elland Road pitch with coach John
Sillett and skipper Geoff Merrick after the defeat of Leeds in an FA Cup replay in 1974

Jantzen Derrick, who made his League debut at 16, prepares to meet a challenge

Toasts to Pat Beasley at a City dinner

Presentation to John Atyeo by Dick Richards, chairman
of the Supporters Club, in recognition of his 350 goals

Bobby Kellard, who lent his creative
skills to Bristol City and to other clubs

David Rodgers, son of Arnold

Norman Hunter beats Bolton's
Neil Whatmore in the tackle

John Atyeo in 1954, with lace-up
ball, floppy collar, elasticated shorts

The Bristol City squad of 1972-73:
Back: Trevor Tainton, Ray Cashley, Len Bond, Keith Fear. Middle: Gerry Sweeney, John Galley, David Bruton, David Rodgers, David Merrington, John Emanuel. Front: Brian Drysdale, Peter Spiring, Gerry Gow, Geoff Merrick, Les Wilson, Danny Bartley, Trevor Jacobs

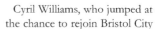

Fred Ford watches Chris
Crowe sign for Bristol City

Cyril Williams, who jumped at
the chance to rejoin Bristol City

The cup that cheers. Manager Dicks drinks
a toast to Gerry Gow (left) and Donnie
Gillies, scorers in the 2-2 draw at Coventry
on the last day of the 1976-77 season

Geoff Merrick evades Liverpool's Phil Neal at Anfield in November 1976

Manager Dicks looks on as Alan Skirton signs
for Bristol City

Len Townsend scored 48 goals in
his two seasons with Bristol City

Peter Cormack at full stretch

Trevor Tainton, second only to
John Atyeo for City appearances

Gary Collier, who started a storm
over the new freedom of contract

Tom Ritchie skips over West
Ham's Frank Lampard (senior)

Ray Cashley leaps to clutch the ball

John Atyeo in action for the England Under-23 team at Stamford Bridge

John Atyeo is tackled from behind in the FA Cup at Villa Park in 1957

Alan Dicks at the microphone

Jack Connor: 'I didn't think I'd last four games,
let alone 400.'

Ray Savino, right-winger in City's promotion team of 1964-65

Brian Drysdale weighs his options

Chris Garland shapes to avoid a tackle

In 'save' hands. Mike Gibson, the goalkeeper Jack Connor rated
'the outstanding City player of my time with the club' (courtesy of the *Bristol Evening Post*)

Paul Cheesley is beaten to the ball by Phil Figgins, the Portsmouth keeper, during the 1-0
win with which City clinched promotion to the First Division in 1976
(courtesy of Mike Jay, and Mark Leesdad & Phil McCheyne Photography of Nailsea)

Chapter 12

Peter Doherty follows Pat Beasley

On 24 January 1958, the evening before Bristol City's Cup-tie at Notts County, Harry Dolman had 'just a chat' with Peter Doherty in Nottingham. 'Nothing has been decided,' the chairman said afterwards. 'There are two or three others in line for the manager's job, and I have still to interview them.' But Doherty, who stayed on to watch the match, was a clear favourite once Tommy Burden had told the chairman that he did not want to be considered. It was believed the post could have been Burden's for the asking. On the Monday after the scrambled Cup win Doherty was duly appointed.

The Irishman was readily available because a week earlier his resignation as manager of Doncaster Rovers had been precipitated by a dispute with a director. Hubert Bates, head of a concrete manufacturing firm, had been accused of criticising some of Doherty's team selections. By the casting vote of Rovers' chairman, 77-year-old Alfred Butler, the nine-strong Doncaster board had demanded that the resignation should come from Bates. When he refused, claiming he had been given no opportunity to defend himself, the matter had been referred to a shareholders' meeting, something it had been hoped to avoid because some of Bates' friends had said they would pool a majority of votes. Consequently, Doherty decided that, 'as the club is greater than either of us,' he would be the one to go.

With him went Geoffrey Dickinson, the Rovers' secretary for seventeen years, and J Paterson Semple, a director who was the club's honorary surgeon. Both said they were resigning 'for the same reasons as Mr Doherty'. Dickinson added: 'It was a matter strictly domestic, and should have remained so.' At the end of that season two other members of the board also stood down – the chairman, disheartened by what he called 'the unhappy spirit in the boardroom,' and Stanley Dixon.

To succeed Doherty, Doncaster tried the joint-management idea Birmingham adopted with Arthur Turner and Pat Beasley. They entrusted the task to chief coach Syd Bycroft and trainer Jack Hodgson, who had helped Rovers out of the Third Division as players. But they were replaced only a few months later by Jack Crayston, the former Arsenal and England wing-half, after being unable to prevent the club returning there.

No finer an inside-forward than Peter Doherty, a tireless, artistic maker and taker of goals who baffled the best with his snake-like body swerve and perceptive footballing brain, has ever come out of Northern Ireland. But for the war of 1939–45 he would surely have been capped more than sixteen times (while with five clubs) in an international career that stretched from February 1935 to November 1950.

As he recalled in his book *Spotlight on Football*, however, there was no indication of the successes to come when he had his first experience of senior Irish football. Spotted playing for Station United, a junior team, he was invited to stand by as a reserve for Coleraine, and had hurriedly to change when word came through that the outside-right had missed his train at Belfast, sixty miles away. Throughout the first half he hardly touched the ball, and during the interval he was completely ignored. He recalled that 'even the boy who brought the lemon slices round gave me a wide berth'. Then came what he never forgot as 'the final humiliation'. The missing winger turned up, and Doherty was told to hand over the jersey to him. Thus did Coleraine lose one of the most gifted footballers of his generation.

Doherty went back to playing for Station United, even when he should have been spending Saturday afternoons working as a conductor on the bus service his uncle operated between Coleraine and Portstewart. As business was usually slack at that time, he left the driver to collect the few fares until he returned, and all went well until a special bus was put on for a golf tournament. On returning, he found the vehicle packed with passengers who did not have a ticket between them, but the ticking-off he got from his relative was not the only reason why he had to find a new job. It was belatedly learned that it was not legal for those below the age of seventeen, as Doherty then was, to be a bus conductor.

Soon afterwards another football door opened for young Peter. Thanks to the recommendation of Billy McSevenny, the owner of a Coleraine sweets shop whose brother Alan was a full-back with Glentoran, he was invited to a trial by the Belfast club. And it turned out so well that on turning seventeen he was signed for all of £2 10s a week. That wage had risen to £3 15s by the time, as proud holder of an Irish Cup winner's medal, he was transferred to Blackpool for £1,500 in November 1933, five months after his 20th birthday. He quickly became one of the Seasiders' most popular players as they strove to regain their newly lost First Division status. He left them in February 1936 only because they urgently needed £10,000 of Manchester City's money (just short of the then record fee) after the death of Sir Lindsay Parkinson, their chairman and main benefactor.

In 1936-37 Doherty was top scorer with 30 goals for the Manchester club's first League champions. The fact that practically the same set of players was relegated a year later, despite again being the First Division's highest scorers (23 more for Doherty), was one of the game's biggest imponderables. Came the war, and after guesting for a variety of other clubs, Doherty struck up his celebrated partnership with Raich Carter at Derby. Doherty had been posted in the RAF to assist the recovery of injured airmen at the medical rehabilitation unit at nearby Loughborough, where Carter was also stationed.

After helping Derby win the Midland Cup, scoring three of his five goals in a 6-0 win within four minutes during the second leg of the final against

Aston Villa, Doherty, like Carter soon afterwards, became one of Derby's own players. That double signing was the key to the club's first winning of the FA Cup in the first post-war final. They were dissimilar in appearance and style, yet on the field they developed an intuitive, often uncanny, understanding. The auburn-haired loose-limbed Doherty, the best seller of a soccer dummy I have ever seen, served up his breathtaking skills with tireless energy, bobbing up in defence as well as attack with bewildering rapidity; whereas the prematurely greying Carter had a stern, even forbidding, manner, making the ball do the work as he schemed ruthlessly, scoring his goals with cold, clinical efficiency.

Although by then well into the veteran stage, Doherty next inspired Huddersfield to cling onto First Division status three times in succession. He then did for Doncaster in 1949-50 what Carter had done for Hull City the year before. He guided them to promotion from the Third Division North in his first season as a player-manager. Doherty's 29 goals, three of them in the Cup, made him top scorer for Doncaster's champions, and he again headed the Rovers' list, with 14, the following season. When he retired from playing at League level in 1953, two years after recovering from breaking a leg, he had totalled 58 goals in his first four years at Belle Vue.

Discounting the two goals he scored in Manchester City's three games of the abandoned 1939-40 League season, that took him to an aggregate 197 in 403 League appearances – and there were 22 more goals for him in the Cup, ten in Derby's Cup-winning run of 1946. Moreover, to that impressive tally could be added his goals in wartime competitions, over 60 for Derby alone over the last two seasons before the game got back to a peacetime footing. At Windsor Park, Belfast, in September 1944, he bagged all four for an Ireland XI against the Combined Services (who, however, responded with eight – four of them by Carter, then still of Sunderland).

For such a popular and respected player, it was incongruous that Peter Doherty should leave three English clubs because of troubles he encountered in the boardroom. He fell out with Manchester City when their directors ordered him to stop guesting for Derby, in the misguided belief that he had deliberately avoided getting away from his duties at Loughborough in time to play for them. His request for a transfer was an inevitable outcome of what he understandably called the 'absurd condition' they finally imposed. Although forbidden from playing for Derby, he was told he could assist Manchester United instead. If he were available to the Old Trafford club, then the same would obviously apply to City.

So he moved to Derby, and he was perfectly happy there until the directors barred him from attempting to safeguard his future by becoming licensee of a hotel not far from the Baseball Ground. They argued that it could adversely affect his football, a view he strenuously refuted. He admitted that his resulting departure was 'a bitter blow', and upset him a good deal. Then, after playing such a prominent part in Huddersfield's three successive narrow escapes from relegation, he flourished at Doncaster until the unpleasantness arising from the Bates affair. In addition to guiding the club out of the Third North, he was helped by the talent spotting of Cliff Duffin, a Yorkshireman who soon rejoined him at Ashton Gate, in turning an overdraft into a comfortable credit balance by offsetting expenditure of £40,000 with income of £100,000 from transfer fees. Duffin, a freelance scout before his ten-year link-up with Doherty at Doncaster, became Jimmy Seed's successor as chief scout with City, then combined that post with the role of assistant manager.

In addition to his success at club level until the later stages of his 8½ years with Doncaster, Peter Doherty prospered as manager of Northern Ireland. He was first appointed to that job in 1951, when Jack Vernon, the West Bromwich centre-half who was then captain of the national side, welcomed him as 'at last a man in charge who knows what he is talking about'. The November before he joined Bristol City, Doherty masterminded Northern Ireland's first away win against England for 30 years, attributing the secret of their success to 'team spirit in a happy family atmosphere'. And in 1958 he was described by Danny Blanchflower, the contemporary captain, as 'the dominating figure in the most successful era in Irish football' after a first qualification for the World Cup finals had brought more glory. In Sweden, Doherty's men, along with Wales, outdid the more fancied England and Scotland by reaching the quarter-finals before both went out, weakened by exhausting group play-offs.

Another achievement by Doherty as a manager worth mentioning resulted from his challenge to any first-class club in the world to play Doncaster under floodlights at Belle Vue. Despite raw and rainy weather on a Tuesday evening in November 1952, there were about 15,000 spectators for the match in which Glasgow Celtic accepted the challenge. And the famous Scottish club were duly beaten.

So, on his hugely impressive past record, Bristol City clearly acquired one of soccer's most accomplished and experienced personalities. Harry Dolman succeeded where he had failed in first seeking Doherty's services at the time of the irrepressible Irishman's move from Huddersfield to Doncaster. Sadly, as will be recalled more fully in its proper turn, the appointment did not work out well, after a start that strongly indicated otherwise, largely due to some ill-fated dabbling in the transfer market. To begin with, Doherty had to face a battle against relegation that was even more desperate than the one he had left at Doncaster. After his last match in charge at Belle Vue, a 0-0 draw at Stoke, they were 17th in the Second Division with 20 points from 27 games. He picked up the reins at Ashton Gate with Bristol City 20th with 19 points from 26, only one point above the bottom pair, Swansea and Lincoln.

By a quirk of the fixture list, it was back to Doncaster that Doherty had what he termed 'an embarrassing journey' for his first match as City's manager. In a farewell letter to the Rovers' players, passed on to them by their captain, Tommy Cavanagh, who was also to follow him to Ashton Gate, he asked them to promise him that they would 'fight with all your might to remain in the Second Division'. And that is precisely what they proceeded to do at his new club's expense. A 1-2 defeat plunged City next to the foot of the table, and the first of Doncaster's goals was scored by the versatile forward who became Doherty's first signing for the Bristol club only two days later. This, at a cost of £6,000, was 29-year-old Bert Tindill, scorer of more than 130 goals in over 400 games for the Yorkshire club. He had rejected a move to Blackburn since asking for a transfer after Doherty's resignation. In staying loyal to the Irishman by following him to Ashton Gate, Tindill missed the chance of playing in the First Division. Blackburn were promoted that season as runners-up to West Ham.

For that first match at the City helm, Doherty reintroduced Jim Terris at right-back, for only his second senior appearance, and switched Tommy Burden back to left-half. This was the team: Anderson; Terris, Thresher; Emery, Williams (A), Burden; Hinshelwood, Walker, Atyeo, Etheridge, Watkins. On the same afternoon, this second team was fielded at home to Swansea reserves: Cook (A); Briggs, Cook (C); McCall, Parr, Morris; Mawditt, Munroe, Curtis, Eisentrager, Smith (D).

Sheffield-born Alec Briggs, signed as a junior, was to be a mainstay of the first team in almost 400 games throughout the 1960s; Charlie Cook, who hailed from Cheltenham, had arrived from Gloucester City, where he had been in the same side as Bobby Etheridge, but he returned there in the 1958 close season after only a couple of League appearances. Of the others not already mentioned, only fair-haired Peter McCall was often seen in the senior side, exceeding 80 games before Oldham paid £1,000 for him in 1962. He had the misfortune to break a leg when he first had a trial with City in 1954, while on holiday from his King's Lynn home, but was signed after a second try-out and spent much of his time in the Colts before being converted into a wing-half. He was later an England international – at bowls. Cliff Morris was born at Weymouth, where his father, Sam, ended his playing career after being a wing-half with Sunderland, and he came to City's notice while playing for Portland United in the Western League. He moved on to Nuneaton in 1960.

Colborne ('Fred') Mawditt, a centre-forward with Bristol Boys, joined City straight from school and was a regular outside-right in the reserves before going to Trowbridge at the time of David Smith's transfer to Millwall. Mawditt had a rare first-team opportunity in the Somerset Professional Cup final replay against Yeovil at the Huish in 1957. City carried off the trophy for the first time without actually winning it. Dermot Curtis opened the scoring against the run of play midway through the first half from a cross by Mawditt, but Matt Gemmell, a former Portsmouth and Swindon forward, equalised before the interval. It was still 1-1 after extra-time, so it was agreed that the managers, Jimmy Baldwin (ex-Leicester) and Pat Beasley, should toss a coin to decide the issue. Beasley called correctly. Unsatisfactory as that outcome was, the game was also remembered for a more undesirable reason. Yeovil finished with only nine men, City with ten. Cyril Williams and 'Micu' Nagy, the home centre-half, were ordered off in the second half, and soon afterwards Yeovil also lost their left-winger, Johnny McKay, who was carried off with a leg injury suffered in a tackle by full-back Charlie Cook. McKay resumed for the last ten minutes, but was again off the field for the whole of extra-time.

There had been no goals for Bert Tindill in Doncaster's 2-2 draw on their visit to Bristol City in September 1957, but he had been the man of the match, with mixed fortunes, in a 3-2 home win against Bristol Rovers a couple of months later. Back after suspension, he scored twice, failed with two penalties, made Doncaster's other goal, hit the crossbar twice and had a header cleared off the goal-line by full-back 'Josser' Watling. At left-half for Doncaster that day was Gordon Hopkinson, who also rejoined Doherty at Ashton Gate. He had written for a trial on being given a free transfer at the end of that season. Hopkinson was first spotted by Cliff Duffin, along with his brother Len, while playing for Beighton Miners' Welfare in the Yorkshire League. Gordon gained a place with City mainly as a right-back, making just over 70 appearances in the first team before leaving for Cheltenham Town in 1961; Len left Doncaster for Lincoln, and was later with Cambridge City.

Tindill was to make an important contribution to City's escape from relegation in 1958, despite the handicap of an injury suffered on his debut in a home defeat by fellow strugglers Rotherham. That was the week in which soccer was stricken by the Manchester United disaster at Munich airport. Tragedy on such a devastating scale put in proper perspective City's loss of two more valuable points through their inability to counter a lone second-half goal from Albert Broadbent, the former Notts and Wednesday winger they had tried to sign before Pat Beasley's departure.

Not until near the end of that season did Tindill reveal the handicap under when he had been playing: 'In my first game for City,' he said, 'I was in a collision and I felt my stomach aching afterwards. After the game the club's doctor decided that I had strained the fibres attached to a muscle in my stomach. I should have stopped playing, as rest is the only certain cure, but as I had only just started my career in Bristol, and the club were in such a precarious position at that time, I resolved to continue playing. For most of the week I was getting extensive massage and heat treatment from trainer Les Bardsley. The only training I was doing was on Friday mornings, to keep my muscles from getting stiff. After each match I went through the whole process again.'

With just a few games to go, Tindill benefited considerably from two injections a specialist in Bristol gave him, and he managed to get through not only the season but also the club's summer trip to France before going back home to Yorkshire for his overdue rest. In those circumstances, it was indeed remarkable that he was so influential in City's Second Division survival, their most effective forward in most of his matches. He was ineligible for the next fixture after the defeat by Rotherham, a home fifth-round FA Cup-tie which City lost 3-4 to Bristol Rovers in front of an all-ticket crowd of almost 40,000, but he clinched crucial points by scoring the only goal against Notts County at Meadow Lane and Ipswich at Ashton Gate. On Good Friday he pinched the winner in Cardiff 45 seconds from time. He also did the hat-trick in a 4-3 win at Fulham, but City had to cling on after being four up at half-time. In just fourteen appearances, Tindill ended as City's joint second-highest scorer behind John Atyeo. He and Johnny Watkins had eight goals apiece; Atyeo netted 23, plus two in the Cup.

City made a rousing rally in that Cup defeat by their neighbours – a match for which they became the first club to have three different managers for three consecutive Cup rounds in one season (Beasley, Seed and Doherty). Etheridge and Burden brought the scores level at 3-3 after Rovers had led 3-1 at half-time with goals from Norman Sykes, Dai Ward and Barrie Meyer to one by Watkins. Time was running out when Geoff Bradford put Rovers into the quarter finals for the second time in their history with a goal City were convinced was offside. Bradford was equally convinced that they were wrong. This was how he recalled it: 'We were under pressure when Dai Ward broke away with me on his right. Mike Thresher was covering me, but as Dai went on he had to leave me and go to Dai. I had kept behind Dai all the time, and the linesman was right with me. Dai slipped the ball to me, and I hit it past Bob Anderson as he came out to meet me. I know I wasn't offside.'

As in 1951, when Bristol Rovers first got through to the last eight and then lost to Newcastle after a replay, the sixth round proved too big an obstacle for City's local rivals. Bradford again scored after the interval, but there was no further reply to the three first-half goals by which Fulham progressed at Craven Cottage. Two of them were netted by Arthur Stevens, who was in the side only because Maurice Cook, a centre-forward for whom Watford had recently been paid £15,000, was, like Tindill, Cup-tied.

Bristol City's repeated victory over Notts County, who had also gone down at Ashton Gate, was only their second away from home that season. The defeat of Ipswich a week later lifted them into 18th place above Doncaster, who came a real cropper at Fulham. Five of the Cottagers' six goals were scored in succession by Jimmy Hill, the PFA chairman. City were without a match the following Saturday because their scheduled opponents, Blackburn Rovers, met Bolton in the Cup semi-final at Maine Road, but Doncaster were unable to take advantage in losing a seven-goal thriller at Swansea. Neither could Doherty's former club exploit City's heavy defeats in their next two matches – in the rearranged game at Blackburn, where Peter Dobing put four of five goals into their net, and at home to Sheffield United, for whom Bill Russell scored three out of four. Doncaster were beaten at home by Derby, and then more heavily (three goals out of five for England winger Bryan Douglas) by Blackburn.

In fact, Doncaster tailed away so badly following Doherty's change of clubs that they won only one of their remaining fourteen fixtures – a sudden five-goal flurry against Notts County for their sole away success of the season on the penultimate Saturday. Meanwhile, City picked themselves up after conceding nine goals in two games by dropping only three points in the next six. They drew 3-3 draw at Eastville with the aid of an own goal by Rovers' centre-half David Pyle, and lost at Lincoln in a match postponed from October because nine Imps had gone down with influenza. Doherty's new men completed a double over Cardiff, and totalled nine goals of their own in consecutive victories at home to Barnsley and at Fulham. That took them well clear of trouble, enabling them to finish eight points ahead of Doncaster, who went down with Notts County.

Swansea edged away from the drop by winning at Ashton Gate on the last day, but the big escape act was pulled off by Lincoln, who surged to safety by winning their last six games, having gone without a victory for four months. These were the final positions at the foot of the table:

1957-58	P	W	D	L	F	A	Pts
16. Derby	42	14	8	20	60	81	36
17 Bristol City	42	13	9	20	63	88	35
18 Rotherham	42	14	5	23	65	101	33
19 Swansea	42	11	9	22	72	99	31
20 Lincoln	42	11	9	22	55	82	31
21 Notts Co	42	12	6	24	44	80	30
22 Doncaster	42	8	11	23	56	88	27

John Atyeo felt that his game was adversely affected towards the end of that season because his father was seriously ill. 'He died on Cup final evening, I had the grocery and provisions business at Westbury Leigh at the time, but out of the blue came an offer that was impossible to refuse. So on the death of my father, my wife Ruth and I moved back to my mother's house at Dilton Marsh.'

During that summer, on 21 May 1958, Peter Doherty played for Bristol City in the last match of their French tour, only a fortnight from his 45th birthday. It was seven months since, as an advocate of floodlit football, he had turned out for one of the matches in which he invariably excelled for the All-Star Managers XI, so he was out of training and had to be persuaded by Harry Dolman to play against an amateur team in the small town of Ruffec in the Bordeaux region. The game was arranged by Stephen Kew, a Bristol solicitor who was in the City party (later the club's chairman), and a friend of the soccer-loving local mayor.

As Doherty always carried his boots with him, he said, after some consideration, that he did not think there was anything in the rules to prevent his playing in a small friendly match, so he was in his old inside-left position in this team: Anderson; Terris, Thresher; McCall, Peacock, Bardsley; Bevan, Etheridge, Tindill, Doherty, Watkins. It was two years since Bardsley had retired from playing. Brian Bevan, who was substituted by Peter Wilshire and then went back on as substitute for Tindill, was a winger who made a couple of League appearances before going to Carlisle on a free transfer in 1960. He was also with Millwall, Salisbury and Weymouth then returned to Bridgwater in Somerset. Wilshire, a Bristol-born centre-forward, was unable to break into City's League side after making just one appearance for Bristol Rovers as the injured Geoff Bradford's stand-in, and, his £1,500 valuation cancelled on appeal, he moved to Bath City on a free transfer. He later did some scouting for Bristol City.

For the record, one other substitute was used by the Ashton Gate club during that match in France – Gordon Parr for McCall. City won 4-3 with goals from Tindill, who did the hat-trick, and Bevan.

A Good Friday invasion of Eastville in 1976,
the year of City's long-awaited return to the First Division

Barrie Meyer, who went from soccer to Test cricket as an umpire, pictured in his Bristol
Rovers days with Howard Radford (left) and Peter Hooper (right). Hooper also joined City

Chapter 13

Storming Start and a new Backroom Set-up

Hopes of a bright new dawn for Bristol City under the management of Peter Doherty were raised beyond all expectations by the goal-packed start the club made to the 1958-59 season. On the opening day Rotherham were beaten 6-1 at Ashton Gate; on the following Wednesday evening Barnsley's Lol Chappell had the demoralising experience of scoring all his side's four goals in a home match, yet finishing on the losing side. Rampant City galloped away with seven, though the outcome was in doubt until as late as the 82nd minute in which Bert Tindill made the score 6-4.

Of those thirteen Bristol broadsides, John Atyeo and Tindill each fired four, Bobby Etheridge and Wally Hinshelwood two, and Johnny Watkins the other. Atyeo did the hat-trick at Oakwell, where eight of the goals came in a hectic second half after City had led 2-1 at the interval, but the man of that match was Tindill, who was at his creative best.

There was a glut of goals generally on the first day, the 174 in the Football League's 46 games showing an increase of 47 on the corresponding Saturday of the previous season. Middlesbrough led the way with a club record nine against Brighton, five of them credited to a brash young man named Brian Clough. Bristol City were one of four teams to score six; three others notched five. Only Darlington's visit to Coventry in Division Four drew a blank.

Of course, such an exceptional scoring rate could not be sustained, not least by Bristol City. In their next match they went down the road to Bramall Lane with an unchanged team (Anderson; Peacock, Thresher; McCall, Alan Williams, Burden; Hinshelwood, Tindill, Atyeo, Etheridge, Watkins) and were beaten 0-4. After that, they were never out of the top six until early December, and, although they were quickly back in that leading group, they faltered in the final weeks to finish tenth – four places behind their Eastville neighbours. City's eighteen defeats, seven of them at home, exceeded their victories by one, and they totalled four more goals, 74, than they conceded.

In the third round of the FA Cup, Peter Doherty was required to take his team back to Doncaster. That was one of five ties that had to be postponed due to snow and frost. It again had to be called off five days later, but when it finally took place City won 2-0 with goals from Watkins and Tindill. In a hard-fought encounter, littered with free-kicks, Doncaster were without their cen-tre-half, Brian Makepeace, because of wrenched stomach muscles for the last 75 minutes.

A crowd of 42,594 saw the visit of First Division Blackpool in the next round – only 741 below the Ashton Gate record set at a fifth-round match in which City held Preston to a scoreless draw in 1935. Again there had to be a replay. Tindill gave City a first-half lead, but Ray Charnley, Blackpool's most prolific scorer after Jimmy Hampson and Stan Mortensen, headed an equaliser from one of Stanley Matthews' corner-kicks.

And again City lost the replay, but by only one goal, scored after the interval by Dave Durie, a part-timer and Methodist Sunday School teacher. And again the opposition were reduced to ten men – but for only the last eight minutes. Roy Gratrix, the centre-half who played more than 400 times for Blackpool, crashed heavily into team-mate Tom Garrett and was carried off on a stretcher to have stitches in a head wound.

Behind the scenes at Ashton Gate, the new regime under Doherty's direction was backed by a set-up that promised a brighter future. Cliff Duffin was working on the reorganisation of the scouting system, and Les Bardsley was given full control of the dressing rooms, training, coaching and fitness schedules. A real coup was pulled off when City signed practically the whole Bristol Boys team that won the English Schools Shield in 1958. That rich array of local talent most notably included its captain, fair-haired Brian Clark, son of Don, and Jantzen Derrick, but more about them later.

Peter Doherty's first attempt to keep a promise to Les Bardsley, appointing a trainer-coach to help him out, failed when Ivor Powell, the former QPR, Aston Villa and Wales wing-half who was then assistant trainer at Leeds, reluctantly declined. The post was soon afterwards filled by Bill Harvey, who combined his coaching commitments with looking after one of the junior sides. 'I thought about it,' said Powell, 'but then decided that, much as I would like to be with Peter, whom I admire very much, I couldn't leave Leeds at that time. I had just bought a house, and my two children were at school.'

Powell had been with Leeds for two seasons since giving up playing through injury, after being player-manager with Port Vale and Bradford City. He declared himself 'not keen' on the vacant manager's job at Elland Road at the time of Doherty's approach, but later returned to that role, first with Carlisle and then Bath City, before leaving the game to become a publican in the Manningham district of Bradford.

Harvey joined City, in preference to an offer from the Middle East, on the recommendation of Bardsley. They had met during a summer training course at Lilleshall, and he moved into the club-owned house at Bedminster formerly occupied by Jack White. The dapper, wise-cracking Harvey had no Football League experience as a player, having made his three first-team appearance for his home club, Grimsby Town during the transitional 1945-46 season, and then been with the Uniteds of Boston, Peterborough (in their Midland League days) and Spalding. But he already held a full FA coaching badge, having worked with young players at Spalding and some junior sides. After leaving his job with a water board in Lincolnshire to go to Ashton Gate at the age of 38, he embarked upon a trainer's course, taking the three stages – preliminary, intermediate and final – in turn at Lilleshall each summer. Anatomy and phys-

iology were among the subjects he studied at home in evenings and at week-
ends. In passing a stiff final exam, he became only the third man in the country to hold both FA coaching and training awards. The others: Harry
Medhurst, former Chelsea goalkeeper, and Jimmy Gallagher of Southampton.

Harvey formed an excellent backroom team at Ashton Gate with Bardsley
and the veteran 'Lemmo' Southway before leaving to manage Luton Town in
succession to Sam Bartram, the former Charlton goalkeeper, during the 1962
close season. He resigned after being unable to save the Hatters from relegation to the Third Division a year later, but soon found another coaching post
at Swindon before resuming those duties back at Ashton Gate in 1965. Again,
in January 1968, he left to be a manager, this time with Grimsby Town, and
again he was unable to avert the drop in his first season. His old club went
down to Division Four by 0.008 of a goal. Forced to sell his best players –
among them Graham Taylor, a future England manager – he once more
resigned, a year and a day since his appointment, as the Mariners slid towards
having to seek re-election. After that he was trainer-coach with Cardiff City,
then coach and physiotherapist with Peterborough United.

Towards the end of 1958, Les Bardsley was offered the job of head trainer by Sheffield Wednesday's manager, Harry Catterick, but he turned it down
even though it meant more money. 'I would have been concentrating entirely
on coaching,' he explained, 'but I like variety, and at Ashton Gate I am spending a lot of time treating injuries, which I like doing.' City players were grateful for his expert attention.

Wednesday were top of the Second Division at the time of that invitation
to Bardsley, heading for a prompt return to the First Division with Fulham.
On consecutive Saturdays in November, Bristol City's hopes of beating one of
them to it, scenting a return to the top flight the club had left in 1911, were
uplifted as they drew with Fulham at Ashton Gate and defeated Wednesday at
Hillsborough. Doherty's men were then third on 22 points from 17 games. A
penalty, converted by Etheridge, was needed to hold Fulham, and a 3-2 victory was snatched at Sheffield with two goals in the last three minutes. Atyeo was
the match-winner – five days after scoring four goals in City's 6-5 defeat of a
Managers' XI for which Jimmy Hagan, the former Sheffield United maestro,
also netted four times (Peter Doherty got the other).

It was during this period that a new instruction forebade captains the right
to appeal to referees or linesmen. City's manager was not slow to voice his dis-
approval. 'How can any referee be right every time in his career when called
upon to make split-second decisions match after match?' he asked. 'I feel the
risk of rough play will now become great because we shall have players smoul-
dering over decisions that grieve them. Tempers will be more easily aroused,
and then it's only a short step to dangerous play.'

Just over a year before, cautions and sendings-off had risen to levels that
had threatened to make League soccer its roughest and toughest on record,

with an alarming number of broken legs and arguments with match officials. However, within weeks of Doherty's comments, the Football Association's official publication, *FA News*, observed that not only captains but also other players could approach a referee 'in a gentlemanly manner'. It was added: 'It is not the intention to shield a bad referee, or to encourage the doctrine that referees are infallible. It must be made quite clear that a referee will not send off the field, or caution, any player, whether he be captain or not, who politely asks a question.'

Typical of the inconsistency that had crept into Bristol City's game, those three points extracted from the Second Division's top two were followed by the loss of all six from their next three matches, sinking them to seventh place. Two of those defeats were suffered at home. Scunthorpe arrived third from the foot of the table, without a win in their eight previous away games. They left winners by an only goal, scored in the second half by Jackie Marriott. The next successful visitors, Derby County, came with an away record scarcely better than Scunthorpe's. They had won just once on their travels, and a fortnight before their defence had been breached five times at Middlesbrough, another club in the bottom half. Such dismal form again counted for nothing. The Rams triumphed 3-1.

Between those setbacks for City, on a cold and foggy afternoon in London, Joe Elwood, a 19-year-old Irish left-winger, did himself a good turn in front of Northern Ireland's team manager by scoring all lowly Leyton Orient's goals in their 4-2 victory over Doherty's men. Sadly, he never did get a full cap.

The match with Derby was the one in which Jimmy Rogers first reappeared in the Bristol City team after his return from Coventry. It was not a scoring comeback, Etheridge netting the consolation goal. Neither did Rogers add to the thirteen he had netted for Coventry in the eight other League games he played for his old club that season, but he made up for lost time by reopening his account in a draw at Scunthorpe on the first day of the next one, and went on to be joint top scorer with Atyeo. He was the third Doherty signing to be brought into the senior side, following Bert Tindill and the other newcomer from Doncaster, Gordon Hopkinson, first choice right-back from the day of his debut in a home defeat by Liverpool in September 1958. Four hours before the deadline for unrestricted transfers on 16 March 1959 there was another – Tommy Casey, an Irish international wing-half who cost £5,000 from Portsmouth after City had haggled. Pompey wanted £6,000.

Casey, a real character full of blarney, was the most popular of Doherty's later signings – with his team-mates, if not the crowd. Five days after signing, he made his debut at left-half, from where Burden moved to left-back (his sixth position for City in two seasons) in place of the rested Thresher. Casey plunged straight into the home highlight of City's League season – the visit of Bristol Rovers. John Atyeo saved a point after Dai Ward had opened the scoring in the first half.

Casey was one of three youngsters from the Irish League club Bangor who joined Leeds United in May 1949. After only one reserve game, he first played for them in the Second Division – in the same team as Tommy Burden – against Preston the following August, at the age of 19. He was transferred back to Bangor a year later, but within a fortnight Leeds had second thoughts and re-signed him. Even so, he had made only three further League appearances when he moved again, to Bournemouth in August 1950. There, after two years in the Third Division South, he was seen in a pre-season trial by Newcastle chairman Wilf Taylor, and Stan Seymour, a former left-winger with the club who then had the unusual title of honorary manager, while they were holidaying at the seaside resort. Casey's £6,000 transfer to Tyneside was promptly completed.

For his first season in the North East Casey was a regular choice, but his subsequent in-and-out existence led him to ask for a move when he was again left out after being in the Cup-winning team against Manchester City in 1955 only as a late replacement for the injured Charlie Crowe. His request was refused, yet a year later Newcastle placed him on the transfer list three days before he helped Northern Ireland to a draw with England in Belfast. 'The board anticipated my decision,' he said. 'I had a feeling that I was in the side for one week and then liable to be left out again even if I played well, so I had been trying to make up my mind about putting in another application for a move after having a few words with Mr Seymour.' He was taken off the list at his own request, saying that his differences with the club had been ironed out, but he had again become unsure of selection, switched to inside-forward for his last few games. He eventually left for Portsmouth, his value raised to £8,000, after his return from the 1958 World Cup finals in Sweden.

A change of club did not solve Casey's problems. Unable to settle at Fratton Park, he dropped out of the first team and had Swansea manager, Trevor Morris back on his trail. Morris had first sought Casey, then at Newcastle, while manager of Cardiff City. He believed his second failure was due to Portsmouth having been drawn to meet Swansea in the FA Cup. A fortnight later, he was again frustrated. As Bristol City originally found when they stepped in soon afterwards, the fee demanded was too big.

Casey, who shared more than 300 matches between his five League clubs, did eventually get to Swansea, as chief trainer, but first he was with Gloucester City as player-manager after leaving Ashton Gate in 1963, and then had a short spell in Canada. Sacked by Swansea in the autumn of 1966, he went into the Welsh League with Ammanford, and into the Irish League as Distillery's player-manager, before joining Everton's coaching staff in 1968. Three years later he was promoted to head coach and trainer at Goodison Park. In 1972 he was briefly manager while Harry Catterick was recuperating from a mild heart attack. Soon afterwards, Casey was appointed first-team coach at Coventry, from where he went into full-time management with Grimsby in 1975.

The confidence with which Casey moved into Blundell Park did not take long to dispel under severe financial constraints, but he left behind the legacy of a fruitful youth policy when, the day after moving into a newly purchased house, he was dismissed in November 1976. Grimsby were waging an unsuccessful battle to escape relegation back to the Fourth Division.

It was also because of the fee demanded that Casey was not preceded at Bristol City by another of Peter Doherty's signings from Doncaster. Towards the end of 1958, the offer for Tommy Cavanagh, a Liverpudlian wing-half/inside-forward, was only half the £4,000 the Yorkshire club were seeking. Cavanagh, at 30 two years older than Casey, was keen to rejoin Doherty, especially as he was not even in Doncaster's reserves after having a transfer request rejected. But he had to wait until the summer of 1959 before getting his wish – three years since Doherty had first signed him for Doncaster from Huddersfield, and only a week after Rovers had persuaded him to re-sign. The deal went through for a fee in the region of £2,500, in the face of interest from Notts County and Rotherham. I remember it particularly well because it was publicised in an emergency daily newspaper called *News of the West* during a dispute that temporarily closed down Bristol's *Evening Post*.

Cavanagh was 21 before he became a full-time professional, signing in 1949 for Preston, with whom he had guested during the war. He did not get into North End's League side, and made only just over 30 first-team appearances for his next club, Stockport, before, in 1952, he followed manager Andy Beattie to Huddersfield. His career really took off at Leeds Road. The Town had just been relegated from the First Division, but he helped them straight back, and then to third in the top flight. Down again, however, Huddersfield went in 1956, and Cavanagh's £1,500 move to Doncaster left him two matches short of a century of appearances for the Terriers. It was also just one of a number of changes Huddersfield made after relegation – among them the promotion of Bill Shankly to succeed Beattie as manager.

A year earlier that post had been offered to Peter Doherty, when Beattie had resigned at the club's annual meeting: 'I do not feel as prepared as I ought to be to face nine more months of mental slogging.' But Doherty's plans of developing young players at Doncaster had then been about to bear fruit, and, in any case, Beattie had soon revoked his decision on being assured by his doctor that he was 'perfectly fit and quite capable of continuing'.

In his three seasons at Doncaster, Cavanagh missed fewer than a dozen League games and was given the captaincy. But in the last two of those seasons Doncaster went down – first from Division Two as the departed Doherty guided Bristol City to safety, then into the wilderness of Division Four in 1958-59. Cavanagh had to contend with much unrest during that most difficult phase, and although he was a natural captain, and admitted that he liked the responsibility, he became so disillusioned that he vowed never again to take on that role after resigning from it near the end of his time at Belle Vue. But with Bristol City he smartly changed his mind. The job was again offered to him by Peter Doherty, and he accepted it in succession to Tommy Burden.

Doherty also went back to Doncaster for three teenagers, full-back Roger Collinson (who comes more fully into this story in the next chapter), Archie Taylor, a half-back or inside-forward, and Mike Quinlan, a centre-half. He also signed two of the outstanding members of the Doncaster Boys team that had just shared the national schools trophy with Brierley Hill – wingers Johnny Cope and Freddie Taylor, but they did not make the first team.

One of the most durable of the other professional signings during Doherty's reign was that of Robert Gordon (Bobby) Williams, known as 'Shadow' because of his slight build, who joined the paid ranks in May 1958 along with Francis Arthur (Frank) Jacobs. Both had played for Bristol Boys, and shown promising form as amateurs after being on the ground staff since leaving school. Williams lived near the Ashton Gate ground. Jacobs, a dark-haired hard tackler, came from the Kingswood district of the city.

Jacobs had a real battle for fitness after undergoing a cartilage operation. He spent many Saturday afternoons in charge of the skip for the Colts, play-ing only when there was a late vacancy, and he was subsequently tried in sev-eral positions, in both attack and defence, before showing a big improvement in form on being moved to wing-half.

Bobby Williams made the first of around 200 League and Cup appearances for City in a home match with Leyton Orient, lost by an only goal, on 18 April 1959. That was the day on which Fulham made certain of promotion as run-ners-up to Sheffield Wednesday by winning at Barnsley after Sheffield United, the only club left with a slender chance of catching them, had been held to a draw at Rotherham in midweek.

'Shadow' Williams, then 19, was originally chosen to make his City debut in the Good Friday home match with Ipswich Town towards the end of March, but dropped out with a slight knee injury. Bobby Etheridge, who had been left out to make room for him after being an ever-present that season, was hurriedly reprieved on arriving to watch the game shortly before the kick-off. He responded not only with the first two goals in a 3-0 win, but also hit a post and had a shot kicked off the line. His second goal came from a penalty awarded in the second half when Hinshelwood was brought down as he was about to shoot.

As if all that was not enough from a man who had not been thought worth his place after a run of disappointing results had put City out of the promo-tion running, Etheridge efficiently took over at centre-half from the injured Alan Williams for the last quarter of an hour. His versatility had stretched to filling every position in City's defence during the season as a result of enforced reshuffles. On successive Saturdays early on, he kept goal for part of games against Sheffield United and Brighton, powerless to prevent defeat on the first occasion but keeping a clean sheet in a 3-0 victory on the second. He next went to right-back when Gordon Hopkinson was injured at Fulham, to left-back as changes were made during the home match with Bristol Rovers, and also occupied both wing-half berths in other rearrangements. 'I think that a defender has a much easier time than a forward,' said Etheridge, who had played at left-half while with Gloucester City. 'I'd like to play in defence every week.'

The Easter home match with Ipswich was the one in which Johnny Watkins burst the net in completing the scoring. And that was also the occasion of one of Tony Cook's penalty saves – his sixth of the season. Five minutes from the end he kept out a spot shot from Ray Crawford, the Suffolk club's all-time leading scorer.

Chapter 14

Jeffrey, Collinson and Crossan problems

Peter Doherty ran into the first of the misfiring transfer deals that contributed to the undermining of his authority as Bristol City's manager when, near the end of February 1958, a month after taking over at Ashton Gate, he sent his former club Doncaster a letter in which he inquired about Alick Jeffrey.

Back in the late 1920s, Bristol had had its own 'Wonder Boy' in Ronnie Dix, still the youngest to score in the Football League with a goal for Rovers against Norwich at the tender age of 15 years and 180 days. In the mid-1950s, Jeffrey became the latest to be given that tag. This well-built son of a Rawmarsh miner, the greatest of Cliff Duffin's discoveries, was described by Doherty as 'without doubt the finest boy prospect I have seen' when he introduced him into Doncaster's attack at the age of 15 for a Second Division home match with Fulham on 15 September 1954. Jeffrey did not score in a 4-0 win, but Doherty said 'he did everything I asked'. Four months later, on 28 January 1955, his 16th birthday, Jeffrey made his FA Cup debut, also at Belle Vue, against Aston Villa.

In opting to turn down invitations to play on the same day for an FA Youth XI against an Arsenal side at Highbury, or for the Sheffield and Hallamshire FA in a youth cup match with Cheshire, Jeffrey became the youngest ever to appear in the fourth round. By the time the tie was decided, he was more than a fortnight older, for it went to a fourth replay in which, amid the snow and slush at West Bromwich on 15 February, he scored two expertly taken goals in the 3-1 defeat of the First Division club that would lift the trophy two years later. Doncaster's players were caught without their shaving kit in hurrying to the Midlands from the previous day's third replay at Hillsborough, where play had been abandoned because of bad light with the score still 0-0 after 90 minutes. But Jeffrey continued reading a magazine while his team-mates went to their hotel's barber's shop. 'It's not my month for shaving,' he said.

Doncaster were required to meet Birmingham City in the fifth round at St Andrew's four days later. They were minus Jeffrey, who was at Milford Haven, doing the hat-trick for England against Wales in a youth international, and they lost their third gruelling Cup-tie of the week. 'We didn't like to ask for Jeffrey's release again,' said a Doncaster official. 'We have had to make so many similar requests this season, and the lad had been promised he could play in that youth game.'

Maintaining his impressive progress, Jeffrey made what he called 'the biggest decision of my life' in signing as a professional with Doncaster the week after his 17th birthday. Amateur soccer had enabled him to indulge an enthusiasm for travelling to other countries, and in leaving it he forfeited the chance of going to Australia with the Olympic team. But he put his faith in Peter Doherty, 'the man to teach me the tricks of the trade,' and all continued well for him until 17 October 1956, when he suffered a double fracture of the right leg nine minutes into his second game for the England Under-23 side, against France under the Ashton Gate floodlights. I was among the onlookers on that clear and starlit night who heard the sickening crack as Jeffrey tumbled out of a tackle with Richard Tylinski, the French centre-half who was to play in the 1958 World Cup. There was no ill intent by either player. After helping to force a scoreless draw with a side for which Colin Booth, of Wolves, substituted, Tylinski visited Jeffrey with the other French players and their officials in hospital the next day, and he brought him a present when he was next in England with the full French team.

Jeffrey was training again, but not yet playing, when Doherty asked in his letter to Doncaster for further details 'if there were any truth in reports that Jeffrey would like to join Bristol City'. He soon got his answer. Jeffrey was most emphatically not for sale. A few weeks later, with Doncaster on the brink of relegation, the player, then 19, put in a written request for a transfer. 'I know I shall be accused of leaving a sinking ship,' he said, 'but I have been unhappy with Rovers for some time. I think my only chance is to get away to another club. I'd like to go to Manchester United, of course. Who wouldn't? I might have gone there as an amateur if Peter Doherty had not been Doncaster's manager at the time I signed.'

But Jeffrey was being over-optimistic. He soon had to admit that the leg, which had been in plaster for eight months 'hadn't mended as quickly as other people's breaks do', and in February 1959, 'fed up and sick to the teeth of waiting,' he at last learned the official verdict: At 20, he was finished as a first-class footballer. Even so, Doherty made another attempt to be reunited with his former protege. He phoned Doncaster's manager, Jack Crayston, and asked if he could sign Jeffrey to try to get him fit for League football again. 'Cliff Duffin and I owe it to the lad to try to get him back into football,' said the City manager. We discovered him and brought him into the game. We want to do something for him. He would have expert attention here.' It was understood that if Jeffrey were re-registered it would be as an amateur.

Once more, however, City were unsuccessful. And later that year any further advances became out of the question. In May, Jeffrey scored three goals for Skegness Town at Louth in his first match, in aid of charity, since his injury. That summer he moved to Skegness with his wife Sheila and their baby son on receiving an offer of help from George Raynor, recently appointed manager of the Midland League club after coaching the Sweden team that lost 5-2 to Brazil in the 1958 World Cup final. Encouraged, Jeffrey was determined to prove the medical experts wrong by making a comeback with Skegness Town, but fate decreed otherwise. Playing with confidence, he scored three more goals in a practice game, but then collided heavily with the goalkeeper and was rushed off to Boston's emergency hospital with a double fracture of his other leg.

After misfortune on such a demoralising scale, the wonder was that Jeffrey reappeared in Doncaster's first team for much of the 1960s, and then for a little while after that in their reserves. Re-signed by Rovers in December 1963, he scored nearly 100 goals in almost 200 League games before finally bowing out in August 1972 at the age of 33. He twice helped Doncaster out of the Fourth Division as champions, and in 1964-65 was leading scorer in the whole League with 36 goals. Bristol City and Peter Doherty were left to reflect what might have been if marksmanship so sharp could have been harnessed to that of John Atyeo.

In view of the courage and commitment Jeffrey showed in making such a successful comeback, it was all the more regrettable that in late May 1984 he became newsworthy in contrastingly unpleasant circumstances. Then 45 and licensee of the Black Bull public house in Doncaster's market place (he was 61 when he died on 22 November 2000), he incurred a six-month prison sentence, suspended for two years, after pleading guilty along with his son, Alick junior, and daughter Tina to wounding Arthur Tretheway, Tina's estranged husband. Young Alick was jailed for six months, Tina fined £75. It was said that Tretheway was beaten until he resembled 'a deflated football'.

After his failure to get the 'Boy Wonder' Jeffrey to Ashton Gate, Peter Doherty encountered further frustration in offering professional terms to Roger Collinson. A farcical situation developed when the 18-year-old full-back he had first acquired as an amateur at Doncaster refused to re-sign for the Yorkshire club, preferring to follow Doherty by becoming a professional with Bristol City. That provoked a protest by Doncaster to the League, whose officials deliberated for two months before refusing to accept the registration. The FA, however, did accept it, which meant that Collinson was barred from playing for City in the League, but could turn out for them in reserve and Cup games.

Doherty professed himself 'amazed and bewildered' by Doncaster's attitude over Collinson: 'He was an amateur with Doncaster Rovers, but I signed him for Bristol City on professional forms. What's wrong with that? It was perfectly normal procedure. No, I didn't approach Doncaster. There was no need to.' City's secretary, Sid Hawkins, agreed that it was 'a perfectly ordinary signing' as far as he was concerned, but his opposite number, Derek Bestall, was equally adamant that Rovers wanted to keep the youngster. 'We think highly of this boy,' he declared, 'and we offered him maximum professional terms for his age. He refused on the grounds that he did not want to play for a Third Division club.'

The deadlock reached the stage of an unusual conference in room 55 of a Sheffield hotel, where Collinson was accompanied by his mother Eva, a friend of both Doherty and Duffin. 'There's no question of Peter Doherty trying to lure my boy away from Rovers,' said Mrs Collinson, whose letter to the City manager, asking him to sign her son at the end of the 1957-58 season, had been the basis for these bizarre negotiations. 'I'm responsible for him signing for Bristol. I'm his unofficial manager and agent, and I wrote to Peter Doherty because I have faith in the man. I couldn't bear to see my boy unhappy, and he was very unhappy with Rovers.' She had entrusted her son to Doherty's care from the outset of his career, and was prepared to move to live in Bristol in his interests.

Across the table from Mrs Collinson and young Roger in that hotel room sat Doncaster's chairman, Jack Garnham, manager Jack Crayston and secretary Bestall. In the background taking notes were, no less, the League's president, Joe Richards, and secretary, Alan Hardaker. At the end of the talks, Hardaker announced there was no statement to make. 'There is no result from the meeting,' he said.

In publicising the League's refusal of the registration, Hardaker stated that it never would be accepted. Yet within two months of that hotel get-together, early in October 1958, by which time Collinson had played half-a-dozen reserve matches in his new colours, Doncaster were persuaded to relent by Bristol City's offer to pay a thousand pounds in compensation. 'We have finally arrived at an amicable agreement,' said Garnham. 'The figure of compensation is acceptable to us, and we have waived our objection to the player playing for Bristol City.' Doncaster were known to be in financial difficulties, so a four-figure sum, though insignificant by today's excessive standards, was certainly not to be sniffed at for an unproven, if promising, teenager.

Almost another year went by, however, before Collinson played his first League game for City, at right-back in a 1-1 draw at Scunthorpe on 22 August 1959. He gave an outstanding display, but his mother was not there to see it, despite having expressed a wish to be there on his debut day. Not realising that he was likely to play in the club's first game of the new season, she had gone off to Skegness on holiday with her younger son. It was therefore left to her husband to attend the game. The news got through to him, and he made the 30-mile trip from his home near Doncaster. There were to be 50 more first-team games with City for Roger Collinson before he left for Stockport County in July 1961. The last 22 of these were back in the Third Division to which City were relegated after Doherty's departure from Ashton Gate. Collinson was later with Hull City, then the Derbyshire club Alfreton Town.

Scarcely had the Collinson problem been resolved than Doherty ran into another one by going back to Ireland to sign, as he thought, 19-year-old Johnny Crossan from Coleraine for a £7,000 fee. This most sought-after young forward in Irish football 'jumped at the chance to play under the supervision of my idol, Peter Doherty, without any talk of money.' He was chosen to play against Birmingham City Reserves in a Football Combination game at Ashton Gate on 18 October 1958, but had to be withdrawn because his registration did not come through in time. Nor did it ever come through. As with Collinson, the Football League refused to accept it. Not only that, they also declared they would not accept it for any of the other clubs in their membership.

Until the previous season Crossan had been an amateur with Derry City, who, in turn, had settled terms for his transfer to Sheffield United, Sunderland and Nottingham Forest, only for the deal to collapse each time. Birmingham and Stoke had also failed with overtures. Crossan had been particularly keen to join Arsenal, whose Irish scout, Joe McCleery, approached him, but the player claimed that 'Derry let that one fall through'. Crossan's father complained that 'hardly a day passed when some English representative did not call for him, and in the end he was getting so fed up that he was even considering giving up football.'

Alleged financial irregularities were at the root of the Crossan controversy. Derry maintained that he had refused to turn professional with them before leaving to join the paid ranks with their neighbours Coleraine a week before agreeing to join Bristol City. Crossan denied Coleraine had offered him any financial inducement, and also that he had been promised a cut of the transfer fee. 'I get no more than the signing-on fee that every player gets,' he was quoted at the time.

Crossan trained with the City players for a few weeks in the hope that the FA would approve his transfer, but then went back to play again for Coleraine. Harry Dolman said that 'after the League banned him the FA asked whether we wanted to go on with our application for his registration, but in view of the League's attitude we said "No".' The City's board later reversed that decision, but any prospect of a more favourable verdict by the FA was snuffed out when in January 1959 a six-man Irish League sub-committee's inquiry into the Crossan affair resulted in the player's suspension for life. With that ban went an automatic suspension by the Irish FA and FIFA. Derry were fined a total of £256, Coleraine £5.

In the *Daily Mail*, Irish international Danny Blanchflower wrote: 'If you want to make any sense of the life ban on Johnny Crossan you have to know something of the sorry, confused mess of Irish and English soccer politics. This distressing business is the outcome of bad and archaic rules. When an Irish player was transferred to an English club his old club used to give him a cut of the transfer fee. That was his inducement to leave. Otherwise, he could hold down a regular job at home [Crossan first earned a living at a gramophone factory near where he lived], play part-time football, and in the end be better off than a full-timer in England. The player's ability was being sold, and he believed he was entitled to profit from it.

'The Irish clubs needed money to remain solvent and maintain their football standard. Of course the English clubs knew that the player had a cut. Although, according to the Football League rules, English clubs were not allowed to pay new players more than the paltry signing-on fee, the English were happy to think that what Irish clubs did was no concern of theirs. But with time resentment arose. Realising the danger of upsetting players in England, the Football League brought pressure to bear on the Irish League, with the result that the rules of both are now more or less consistent.'

In the left-wing political weekly *Tribune*, columnist Llew Gardner said Crossan was 'the latest victim of the dictatorship that the Football League exercises over the lives of hundreds of professional footballers.' He agreed that the League were entitled to investigate any complaints of broken rules, but said there had been no inquiry in this case of a man being 'found guilty and sentenced to the loss of livelihood without ever being allowed to face his accusers or even knowing the nature of the charge against him.' When Gardner suggested to an official at the League's headquarters in Preston that to an outsider their action might appear high-handed, he said he received the answer: 'Yes, I'm afraid it does.' On asking the nature of Crossan's 'crime', the reply was: 'Not for publication.'

Light, however, pierced the gloom in a *Daily Mail* article under Crossan's name in which he said: 'I am not ashamed of what I have done. Others have done it before me. My crime is that I did not get away with it. If the outdated rules of the Football League were brought up-to-date there would be none of this under-the-counter business. All I could get legally for giving up my amateur status, leaving my family and friends in Ireland, turning my whole life upside down and going off as a professional to an English club, was £150 – one year's accrued share of benefit. I tried to get more. From the offers that were flying around my head I was worth it.'

Danny Blanchflower called the ban 'a grave injustice', adding: 'The worst crimes cloak and dagger investigators have unearthed are: 1 – He has admitted receiving as much as £3 per week "expenses" as an amateur; 2 – He sought as much as £3,000 to become a professional footballer. Johnny Crossan never got that £3,000. He did not break the Football League rule, though obviously he intended to do so. He has been punished for a crime he intended to commit. Johnny was not alone in this intention. Many English clubs wanted him. He told [in a *Daily Mail* interview] how their representatives visited his little bedroom to try to coax him to their camps. Some were willing to arrange a transfer deal through Derry City for sums up to £6,000. They must have known the player wouldn't agree unless he got a share. Otherwise, why pay Derry City up to £6,000 for an amateur?'

Interest in Crossan was also shown by two clubs outside the Football League, Bath City and Corby Town (whose player-manager was the former England forward Johnny Morris), but they, too, were thwarted when an appeal against his suspension by the Irish League and Football League failed. The Irish FA, however, then removed a temporary ban to any other Association that might be prepared to register Crossan, and this left him free to join a club on the Continent. Consequently, he soon afterwards left his employment as an £8-a-week groundsman with Coleraine to complete his £7,000 transfer to Sparta of Rotterdam, the reigning Dutch champions. One Belfast report said that Crossan would receive a down payment of £2,500, with a further £2,000 if he signing on again after two years.

The end of that part of the ban also made Crossan available to play for Northern Ireland, and, while still barred from the Football League, he duly followed a 'B' cap against France in Belfast by making the first of two dozen full international appearances in a defeat by England at Wembley in November 1959. The irony of the situation was all too obvious for Peter Doherty in his role as the Irish team manager. 'It could only happen in Ireland,' he said with a chuckle.

From Rotterdam, Crossan went into the Belgian League with Standard Liege, for whom he played in the European Cup before the lifting of the Football League ban enabled him to make his belated entry into English soccer with Sunderland, who paid nearly £27,000 for him in October 1962. In 99 games for the Wearsiders he scored almost 50 goals, 22 of them (plus five in a Cup run that ended after two quarter-final replays against Manchester United) during the 1963-64 season in which they returned to the First Division as runners-up to Leeds. His value rose to £40,000 when he moved to Manchester City in January 1965. The following season he also helped them to promotion, captaining their Second Division champions, besides again reaching the Cup's last eight before defeat in a second replay – by Everton, who went on to recover from two goals down to beat Sheffield Wednesday at Wembley.

After 110 League and Cup games and 28 goals for Manchester City, Crossan went to Middlesbrough for £35,000, then Boro's record fee, in August 1967, but his stay on Teesside was blighted by illness. He suffered so badly from insomnia that he was hospitalised, and also underwent abdominal surgery for the removal of two duodenal ulcers. Released at the end of the 1969-70 season, after increasing his total appearances and goals for his three English clubs to 272 and 85, he went back to Belgium, where he rounded off his career with the Tongren club. As with Alick Jeffrey, Bristol City were left to reflect on what they had missed.

And so, in the next chapter, we come to the big deal Peter Doherty did pull off for the Ashton Gate club, only for it to backfire. As John Atyeo put it: 'On reflection, that had much to do with Peter Doherty's rapid departure later in the 1959-60 season.'

Jimmy Mann bursts through this human sandwich with typical courage

Chapter 15

Ill-fated Signings; City down, Doherty out

Peter Doherty appeared to have landed a real coup when, on 26 May 1959, he signed Barnsley's left-wing pair, Malcolm Graham, a forceful inside-forward with a nose for goals, and Johnny McCann, a Scotland 'B' and Under-23 international, even though the deal took Bert Tindill in part exchange.

Tindill asked for a move the previous December because his wife Peggy, who that month gave birth to their fifth child, wanted to return home to Yorkshire. 'When she agreed to come to Bristol,' said Tindill, 'I gave a promise that if she did not settle down I would take her back north. I will regret leaving Bristol City more than I did my old club, but when Peggy is unhappy then I am unhappy as well, and I fear it will reflect in my play.' Tindill, then 23, had married the 22-year-old Margarita Hannon at the Sacred Heart Church, Hemsworth, five hours before playing at outside-right for Doncaster in their home game against Gateshead in February 1950. The bride had watched the match, after which they had gone to London for their honeymoon. Peggy's sister Julia had been married at the same time to John Williams Dale, and most of the Doncaster players had attended the double reception.

Yorkshire-born Graham and Tindill were both valued at £7,000 in the exchange deal, with the £15,000 McCann cost to be paid in five annual instalments of £3,000. Doherty was also interested in Barnsley's right-winger Arthur Kaye, but he was transferred to Blackpool for £15,000 a few days earlier. 'I'm afraid we've had to sell our three best players because of our shocking financial position,' said Tim Ward, the Barnsley manager, who was one of Doherty's former Derby clubmates. He added: 'I think Johnny McCann will bring the house down in Bristol. He is a real entertainer, and the crowds will flock to see him.' Graham, scorer of four goals in one match with Charlton, had attracted a £12,000 bid by Newcastle, and inquiries from Birmingham and Cardiff, since making his League debut for Barnsley in January 1955 after joining them from an amateur club, Crigglestone, near his Hall Green birthplace in the Wakefield area.

How quickly, however, this infusion of new talent was to run into the trouble that led to Peter Doherty's dismissal with relegation as good as confirmed. During training in preparation for the new season, Graham needed treatment for a knee injury, giving rise to several months' dispute between the two clubs about the player's fitness. Barnsley insisted Graham was fit when they sold him, and they shied away from City's suggestion that they should share any possible liability after two specialists differed in their diagnosis.

Five months had elapsed since the triple deal when a five-man Football League Commission, having sought an independent medical report from Sir

Harry Platt, a knee specialist, decided that Graham's transfer was completed by both sides in good faith. Secretary Alan Hardaker did say, however, that 'subsequent medical evidence has shown aggravation to a previous injury which would have been apparent only by specific and special investigation.' Peter Doherty had been aware of that earlier injury, the recurrence of a knee problem for which Graham had undergone surgery in the autumn of 1955, but said he had been 'given to understand he had fully recovered'. The members of the Commission were Harold Shentall (Chesterfield), Joe Mears (Chelsea), Norman Banks (Bolton), Len Shipman (Leicester) and Dr Andrew Stephen (Sheffield Wednesday).

Two days after the League's ruling, Graham at last played for Bristol City in a competitive game, turning out at inside-left for the reserves at Leyton Orient. This was the line-up: Anderson; Collinson, Briggs; Parr, Williams (A), Jacobs; Coggins, Taylor (A), Rogers, Graham, Bevan. Orient won 1-0, but one of their officials rated Graham the best forward on the field, ahead even of Eddie Baily, the former England forward who was in the home side. The report of City's reserve trainer, 'Lemmo' Southway, was also encouraging, and Graham was again impressive in the following Tuesday's practice match. So, at the end of that week, on 31 October, Graham made his overdue League debut for the Bristol club at Stoke – along with Bristolians Frank Jacobs and Phil Coggins. Only Cook, Thresher, Atyeo and McCann kept their places from the home defeat by Brighton the previous Saturday, in this team: Cook; Collinson (in his second senior game), Thresher; Cavanagh, Williams (A), Jacobs; Coggins, Etheridge, Atyeo, Graham, McCann. This was the match in which City were first captained by Cavanagh.

Coggins had played once before in the first team, in the Gloucestershire Senior Cup final against Bristol Rovers at the end of the previous season. He would have been given his first League chance when Rovers visited Ashton Gate three weeks before the Stoke game – as deputy for Jimmy Rogers, who was serving a suspension – but for a muscle strain. He had few other opportunities, however, before switching to the Eastville club, and was later with Wellington and Trowbridge.

Graham made a success of his debut, scoring twice in a 3-1 victory that was especially welcome after defeats in nine of the thirteen matches played without him. But it was not to last. He was soon back in light training, and before Christmas had to go into hospital for a manipulative operation on his right thigh. There was even talk of City asking Barnsley to take him back and being rebuffed. At the season's end Graham had played only thirteen more League games, scoring six more goals, and City were down in the Third Division again – at the foot of the table, three points behind the other relegated club, Hull City.

In the close season Graham moved to Leyton Orient, and he also had a spell with Queen's Park Rangers before finding his way back to Barnsley. John

Atyeo summed up the City players' view in saying: 'I could never get to the bottom of Graham's injury, and I don't think anyone else could.'

For Johnny McCann, too, things did not turn out well in Bristol. On the form he had displayed for Barnsley, he looked the ideal successor to Johnny Watkins, whose release at the end of 1958-59 had been the big shock of City's retained list. John Atyeo recalled: 'On the day he received his letter, Johnny sat next to me in the dressing room with tears in his eyes. He was a good friend of mine, and I remember telling him that perhaps it could turn out for the best.' It did. Snapped up by Cardiff City for a bargain £3,500, Watkins, to quote Atyeo again, was 'tearing us apart' at Ninian Park inside three months, scoring one of the goals in a 4-2 win for the Welsh club. Watkins was again prominent when Cardiff completed the double by 3-0 at Ashton Gate the following January. Moreover, he ended that 1959-60 season in a side promoted to the First Division, ever present as Cardiff finished runners-up to Aston Villa, whereas Bristol City floundered back to Division Three.

Meanwhile, the scales of football fortune tipped the other way for McCann, and not solely because his transfer to Bristol pitched him into a struggling side. Like Graham, he was dogged by injury. Ten minutes after City's team to visit Lincoln on 28 November 1959 had been announced, he wrenched stomach muscles in training and had to drop out. Then he suffered a broken fibula during what proved to be his only Christmas with the club. Into his place stepped Jantzen Derrick, who had played for Bristol and England as a schoolboy and was still an amateur, aged only sixteen, with just three reserves games behind him, when he made his League debut in the single goal defeat at Sincil Bank.

The month before, Derrick and Adrian Williams, another City recruit with whom he had formed the England Boys left wing, had first played for Gloucestershire in a South-West Counties Senior Amateur Championship game against Wiltshire at Stonehouse. The tall, fair-haired Derrick made four first-team appearances as a groundstaff boy before giving up the chance of an amateur cap and a trip to Rome for the Olympic Games. He turned professional on 21 January 1960, eleven days after his seventeenth birthday – a decision, over which he understandably hesitated, that also compelled his withdrawal from his county's youth team against Hampshire.

That Derrick had done the right thing was made abundantly clear over the ensuing decade. A tricky customer at his best, he had more than 250 games behind him by the time he finally faded from the City scene in the 1970-71 season, leaving first on loan to Mansfield, next on trial to Hereford. He also spent a year in France with the Paris St Germain club, and on his return to England put in a spell with Bath City. At Ashton Gate his versatility was especially valuable. In the 1967-68 season he appeared in all five forward positions in the generally accepted line-up of those days, thus wearing the numbers 7, 8, 9, 10 and 11. He also turned out wearing 12 as substitute.

Derrick and Adrian Williams were among almost all the members of the Bristol Boys side that won the English Schools Trophy in 1958 signed for City by Peter Doherty that summer. Williams had been expected to join Bristol Rovers. He was an avid supporter of that club and his father, a neighbour and friend of Geoff Bradford, was a season-ticket holder at Eastville, but Cliff Duffin was on his trail as soon as he left Baptist Mills School. As it was, the only one of that bumper crop to become a Rover was David Stone, an England Boys trialist. The others who went to City included Peter Prewett, a wing-half taken onto the ground staff with Derrick and Adrian Williams, and Harry Booth (goalkeeper), Michael Thomas (full-back), Terry Burt (right-winger), Brian Clark (inside-forward) and David Summers (centre-forward), who were signed as amateurs.

Adrian Williams became the first Bristol footballer to become an apprentice professional on 1 July 1960, when the new Football League scheme came into force. It provided for a professional club to have a stronger link with a young player than if he were an amateur, allowing a player to decide at seventeen if he wanted to make professional soccer his career. If not, he could revert to being an amateur, provided he did not join another professional club in any capacity within two years of ending his apprenticeship. Williams, like Derrick a schoolboy international, gained an England Youth cap against Wales in March 1960, and went on tour to Austria with an FA youth party that Easter. He turned professional after his seventeenth birthday in August, but of all those youngsters – the nucleus of the City team that reached the FA Youth Cup semi-finals in the 1959-60 season – Derrick and Brian Clark were the only ones to establish themselves at League level. Adrian Williams was given a two-month trial by Exeter City in 1963, and was afterwards with Gloucester City and Minehead.

Johnny McCann's stay at Ashton Gate lasted only until October 1960, when he was transferred to Huddersfield in exchange for Jack Connor, a utility defender who 'didn't want to come to Bristol in the first place', but stayed for more than ten years and made over 400 appearances. At 36, he was the oldest player on the books when he completed his 400th game at QPR on 28 March 1970, as a late replacement for flu-stricken Gordon Parr. Connor told Peter Godsiff: 'I liked Huddersfield. I had been at Leeds Road since joining the club as a 17-year-old nine years before, but the thought of regular first-team football swayed me. I thought I would get more chance at Ashton Gate, but when I played my first game for City I didn't think I'd last four games, let alone 400. I had a terrible game, missing the ball by yards under those old floodlights. I don't know how we managed to beat Coventry that night the way I played, but what a great move it turned out to be for me.'

He could say that again. He was not only the strong-man in City's defence when they returned to the Second Division in 1965, he almost helped them into the First a year later. They were strongly in the running until lapses at

Easter caused them to slip to fifth place, just behind his old club Huddersfield on goal-average.

When McCann left Huddersfield, after making fewer first-team appearances than his 30-odd for Bristol City, he was signed for a second time by Tim Ward, who by then had joined the list of former Derby players who returned to the Rams as manager. The price Ward had paid in taking McCann to Barnsley from Bridgeton Waverley, a Scottish junior club, was just £500. It cost £5,500 more than that to get him to Derby, where he spent a couple of seasons in another ailing Second Division side before following a brief stint at Darlington with another spell in Derbyshire at Chesterfield. After that he went out of League football with Skegness Town.

The McCann-Connor exchange deal rounded off a busy few months for City in the transfer market after the relegation that followed Peter Doherty's exit. In addition to Malcolm Graham's sale to Leyton Orient, Tommy Cavanagh went to Carlisle, Wally Hinshelwood to Millwall, Phil Coggins to Bristol Rovers, Cliff Morris to Nuneaton and Bernard Smith, a reserve inside-forward, on loan to Wellington Town. Newcomers besides Connor during that period included Alex Tait, a centre-forward/winger who cost £5,000 from Newcastle, Harry Nicholson, a goalkeeper from Leyton Orient who had enjoyed his best spell with Nottingham Forest, John Ryan, an inside-forward on a free transfer from Newcastle, and Jack Boxley back from Coventry. Of those, Tait, who had scored three goals against Sunderland in his first home League game for Newcastle, proved the best investment, getting into three figures for appearances and around 40 for goals in the four years before his transfer to Doncaster Rovers for little more than £3,000. He was afterwards player-manager of Burton Albion.

Cavanagh captained Carlisle, and edged past a career total of 300 League appearances before being released to become player-manager of Cheltenham Town, where relationships were soured by his suspension, against which he appealed successfully, for an alleged breach of discipline. Variety continued to be the spice of his life as he was trainer, then manager, at Brentford as they sank into Division Four, trainer-coach at Nottingham Forest, worked with Tommy Docherty, an old pal from their Preston days, at Hull and Manchester United, took over assistant manager at Newcastle, managed Burnley, and coached with Wigan Athletic.

Peter Doherty was shown the Ashton Gate door on 15 March 1960, three days after a five-goal beating away to Brighton had returned City to the drop zone. They had been up against it from the opening weeks of the 1959-60 season, having hit rock bottom as early as a bleak September with five successive defeats – one of them at home to Hull, the other club to go down. Sheffield United and Aston Villa preceded Brighton in scoring five goals against them, and they were hit for six by Huddersfield, Middlesbrough and, in their final match, Swansea Town. The crushing defeat on Teesside avenged one of only eleven victories City gained all season – and on that rare occasion at Ashton Gate Boro were reduced to nine men when centre-half Bryan Phillips was briefly off the field with a cut near an eye after Ray Barnard, their right-back, had been carried off to hospital with a leg injury.

Ten of City's 26 League defeats that season were inflicted at home, and they were also beaten at Ashton Gate in the third round of the FA Cup – by Charlton, one of the seven clubs that did the double over them in the Second Division. These were the final positions at the foot of a table in which Aston Villa were promoted with 59 points, Cardiff with 58:

1959-60	P	W	D	L	F	A	Pts
17 Stoke	42	14	7	21	66	83	35
18 Derby	42	14	7	21	61	77	35
19 Pymouth	42	13	9	20	61	89	35
20 Portsmouth	42	10	12	20	59	77	32
21 Hull	42	10	10	22	48	76	30
22 Bristol City	42	11	5	26	60	97	27

Unrest in the dressing room was behind the deplorable start to the season from which City never recovered. A pay dispute was at the root of it, and the omens were ominous when the rebels were still holding out at the time the players were due to report back from their summer break. Those absent from the 'duty roll call' on 21 July 1959 were skipper Burden, Atyeo and Thresher, survivors from the promoted team of four years before. They each wanted £20 a week to re-sign, whereas Doherty offered them £17 plus a £3 bonus when they were in the first team. 'You can't have favourites in football,' said the manager. 'The old system has got to go. I feel my incentive scheme is fair to all the players.'

The situation, however, was resolved to the players' satisfaction. Atyeo was an ever-present that season; Thresher missed only three games, Burden twelve. But in the first week of November, six days after losing the captaincy to Cavanagh, Burden had another 'discussion' with Doherty. He was on none of the team sheets for the club's games the next day. The manager said he was being rested, but rumours had already started about Burden's retirement. During that week, however, Burden received his full £750 benefit, less tax. He stayed on for another season, too, if with much fewer first-team call-ups, before hanging up his boots to concentrate fully on his time and motion study job at the Street shoe factory. He then received more than £1,000 from the Football League's provident scheme payable to retired players over the age of 35. He was in his 78th year when he died at Street in October 2001.

Peter Doherty's road out of Ashton Gate led, in common with Bert Tindill and Malcolm Graham, back to his first Football League club – if by a round-about route. After eighteen months out of the game (he vowed he would never again manage a struggling club), Doherty resumed the Northern Ireland team manager's post he had relinquished to devote his attention to Bristol City's declining cause. He gathered those reins for the match with Scotland in Belfast on 7 October 1961, but the Irish players had grown old together since those heady heights they had scaled under his direction, and it was not a happy return. The Scots won 6-1, and, although England were held to a draw at Wembley the following month, Doherty resigned in April after another heavy defeat in Cardiff, where Melvyn Charles scored all four Wales goals. Danny Blanchflower said it brought 'perhaps the most successful era in Irish football to an end, for Doherty was the dominating figure'.

After that, Doherty joined Notts County as joint advisor with Andy Beattie, the former Preston and Scotland full-back. He was then chief scout with Aston Villa and assistant manager at Preston, a post he left in 1973, after two years, for economy reasons. Next he was with Sunderland – first on their scouting staff in Lancashire, where he had returned to live, then as assistant to manager Bob Stokoe, the former Newcastle centre-half who piloted the Wearsiders to their shock defeat of Leeds in the 1973 FA Cup final.

In July 1974, a month after his 61st birthday, Doherty relished that new responsibility in an interview with Tony Hardisty for the *Sunday Express*. 'Players talk too much about pressures,' he said. 'I tell you, when I was playing pressure was a joy. Managers have the headaches. I know. I've had some, and there is no harder way to make a living. I resigned from three jobs, and got the sack from two more.' He also likened soccer to smoking – 'so very hard to give up once you've started.' On coaching, he had this thought-provoking comment to make: 'It is just as easy to coach gifts out of a player as to add to them. A good coach should remember that we play this game with our heads as well as the feet, and to fill the mind with rubbish is to destroy the gifts God gives to a player.' Many may consider he was on less secure ground in stating: 'The person who invented the 4-3-3 system should have been shot at dawn. If we fail to destroy this system it will destroy football.'

Finally, the wheel turned full circle for this much-admired Irishman with his appointment as Blackpool's chief scout. He was retired at Fleetwood, largely shunning publicity, when he died on 6 April 1990. He would have been 77 two months later.

As a tailpiece to this chapter, it is worth recalling the impression Peter Doherty made on a young immigrant to whom Doncaster Rovers owed the stabilising of their finances a quarter of a century after the Irishman's move to Bristol City. As a schoolboy new to Britain from South Africa, to which country his father had fled Nazi Germany, Peter Wetzel just happened to go along to watch a Doncaster match. 'They were a good team,' he recalled, 'and I remember Peter Doherty vividly. We lived nearby, and after that first visit to Belle Vue I never missed a home match. Rovers were the first English team I watched. They were *my* team.'

After years at college and travelling the world, Wetzel was back in Britain with a clothing firm built by his late mother. Heir to the S R Gent empire, manufacturers for the biggest fashion outlets, he chose at that time to follow Leeds United, but in November 1983, then 40 and recently ranked thirteenth among Britain's twenty wealthiest men, he joined the Doncaster Rovers board of directors and put money into the club. But for Peter Doherty that, almost certainly, would never have happened.

Chapter 16

Record Victory with Fred Ford in Charge

In the aftermath of Bristol City's relegation in 1960, chairman Harry Dolman offered to pay off the club's debts of £55,000, thus saving them from possible extinction, on condition that two directors, the Rev Wyvyan-Jones and George Jones, resigned. Lionel Smart was invited to join the board along with Stephen Kew, Graham Whittock and Roy Poeton. The stocks and shares the chairman handed over realised £65,000.

Entering professional football had not occurred to Smart until 1951, when Arthur Amor, a City director who ran the general store at Chew Magna – the Somerset village where Harry Dolman had his home, The Rookery – had asked him if he would be interested in joining an executive club that was being formed at Ashton Gate. About six people were then involved, but their number had risen to 21, paying £21 a year, by the time the 51 Club came into existence. It was through that club that Smart first became friendly with Dolman.

Encouraged by the City chairman, Smart also involved himself in transfers. He assisted in the deal that took McCann to Huddersfield in exchange for Jack Connor, who was soon followed from the Yorkshire club to Ashton Gate by the tall and slimly built Gordon Low, a friend and old school-chum of fellow Aberdonian Denis Law, the Scottish international who played for both Manchester clubs, and in Italy for Torino, after beginning his League career at Huddersfield. It took Low some time to gain a regular place with City, but he was only one game short of being a League ever-present through three consecutive seasons in the mid-1960s. He exceeded 200 appearances in seven years at Ashton Gate before leaving for Stockport County in the 1968 close season for a fee £1,500 below the £6,000 paid for him.

The managerial vacancy left by Peter Doherty was filled on 14 June 1960 by Fred Ford. Bristol Rovers were zealously, and justifiably, proud of having finished above their City neighbours in each season since coming together in the Second Division for the first time in 1955, so it was scarcely surprising that the defection of their chief coach to Ashton Gate made Ford something of a traitor in Eastville eyes. Not, of course, that Frederick George Luther Ford was in any way deserving of such a tag. A more cheerful, approachable character would be hard to find, and he could not reasonably be blamed for wanting to better himself by accepting the chance to be his own boss. And, although he had not managed a League club before, having been happy enough at Eastville to turn down an earlier invitation from further afield, his credentials as a coach were impeccable.

Testimony to that came from John Atyeo when he looked back on Ford's reign at the club. 'I always felt there was not a better coach in the country than

Fred,' he said. 'He had the knack of getting the best out of players, whether in training or in a match. The team spirit was always excellent under Fred. He was steady, unspectacular and dependable. Although I never saw him play, I would bet he showed those qualities as a player.' To that tribute, John Gummow, then Bristol Rovers' secretary, added: 'Fred is one of the greatest possible enthusiasts there is for football. You can say he lives for the game.'

Constructive and hard-working best summed up Ford's qualities as a defender before he had to quit playing in 1949 because of a persistent knee injury. Born in Kent at Dartford on 10 February 1916, he was with the Erith and Belvedere club, and at Arsenal as an amateur, before first getting to know Bert Tann on joining Charlton in March 1936. They were mainly team-mates in the reserves while at the Valley, but both had a little experience in the First Division to which the London club soared from the Third South in successive seasons under the guidance of Jimmy Seed.

Shortly before war broke out, Tann's playing career was also curtailed by injury, but Ford had a few more first-team opportunities with Charlton in wartime regional games before and after escaping from Dunkirk with a wound that compelled the amputation of his trigger finger. Early in the transitional season of 1945-46, he also briefly guested for Tottenham at centre-half before his transfer to Millwall, from where he moved to Carlisle United in August 1947.

Around the time Ford had to give up playing two years later, a Scottish firebrand named Bill Shankly ended his own playing career by leaving Preston to rejoin, as manager, the Cumbrian club with which he had entered English football as a tireless and tigerish wing-half in 1932 from the splendidly named Glenbuck Cherrypickers.. Ford stayed with Carlisle – first as assistant trainer, then trainer-coach when Jimmy Wallbanks returned to Millwall – and he and Shankly became close friends for two years before the former Scottish international left to continue a managerial career that took him, via Grimsby, Workington and Huddersfield, to the transformation of Liverpool into one of the greatest club sides in the world. Ford's move from Carlisle to link up again with Bert Tann as Bristol Rovers' chief coach and assistant manager came in 1955.

While in the North-West, Ford was official coach to the Cumberland FA. In the South-West, he held a similar post with the Gloucestershire FA. As a player, he had toured in France, Holland, Belgium, Germany, the United States and Canada. As a coach and trainer, his travels took him with an FA party to South Africa in 1956, and, with England Under-23 teams, to Italy and West Germany in 1959, East Germany, Poland and Israel in 1960. He was also trainer for Under-23 matches in England, and for the England 'B' team. With Bristol City, however, he was required to relinquish such outside posts, and that with the Gloucestershire Association was eventually split into two. The north of the county was given to Tommy Casey, Gloucester City's player-manager. In the south, it went to Bobby Campbell, a former Chelsea and Scotland forward who followed Jackie Pitt as Ford's successor with Bristol Rovers.

Bristol City's faith in Ford, selected from nearly 60 applicants if one estimate is to be believed, was repaid with promotion back to the Second Division – but not until 1965. Indeed, City were so badly let down by their away form in his first season, 1960-61, in charge, with only two wins to set against fifteen defeats, that they ended as low as fourteenth, 24 points behind Bury's champions. From a highest position of eighth at the end of August they slipped to their worst placing of nineteenth in mid-January, and were thankful to be kept out of real trouble by their comparative prosperity at home. All but ten of their 44 points were picked up at Ashton Gate. Their inconsistency was at its peak when they rammed in five goals against visitors from Colchester, then let in five a week later away to Grimsby.

On the bright side, however, a club record was set – albeit at the expense of modest non-League opposition. In the first round of the FA Cup to which City were once more consigned, the draw decreed a trip to Chichester, but the prospect of bigger receipts caused the tie to be switched to Ashton Gate. A crowd of 12,577 saw a slaughter. John Atyeo enjoyed himself with five of the eleven goals City scored without reply, falling just one short of the club's best for one match set by Tommy ('Tot') Walsh against Gillingham in the Third Division South in 1927. Adrian Williams did the hat-trick; the other goals were shared by Alec Tait, Bobby Williams, and one put into his own net by a luckless defender named Bailey. The date was 5 November 1960, and this was the winning team: Cook; Collinson, Thresher; Connor, Williams (Alan), Etheridge; Tait, Williams (Bobby), Atyeo, Williams (Adrian), Derrick.

In the second round, City were again paired away to a non-League club, King's Lynn. This time home advantage was not forfeited, but the issue was still decided at Ashton Gate. After a 2-2 draw, City progressed by 3-0, Atyeo (2) and Jimmy Rogers (3) doing their scoring over the two games. A Bobby Williams goal was sufficient for victory at Plymouth in the next stage, but further progress was emphatically denied at Leicester after the original tie had been abandoned, scoreless, at half-time because of a waterlogged pitch. Leicester, in the top half of the First Division, scored six in the rematch – one of them put into his own net by full-back Richie Norman. It was some small consolation for Bristol City to learn eventually that they had lost to one of that season's finalists. Leicester lost to Tottenham, who completed the first League and Cup double of the 20th century.

The centre-forward in that Leicester team was Hugh McIlmoyle, a man of many clubs who six years later cost Bristol City their then record fee, variously quoted from £25,000 to £27,500, as one of their last signings while Fred Ford was the manager. Matt Gillies, the former Bolton and Leicester defender who was in charge at Filbert Street when McIlmoyle joined Leicester as an apprentice in 1959, considered him the most talented youngster he ever signed.

Hal Stewart, manager of the Morton club with which McIlmoyle was player-coach in the early 1970s, rated him so highly, even though by then turned 30, that he recommended him to Scotland's team manager, Willie Ormond. With Bristol City, however, McIlmoyle was only passing through. He arrived from Wolves on the first day of March in 1967 and rejoined Carlisle in September of the same year, with £22,500 recouped, and played for them in their one season in Division One. McIlmoyle's failure to make an impression with Bristol City was regrettable. In his twenty League games for the Robins he scored four goals.

Another future City player was in the team that knocked the Bristol club out of the inaugural Football League Cup in Fred Ford's first season of 1960-61 as manager. Needing a home replay to get past Aldershot of the Fourth Division, City gave a good account of themselves on being paired at Nottingham Forest, recent winners of the FA Cup, but were beaten by two goals to one scored by Atyeo. Forest's scoring, in front of a crowd of only 3,690, was done by Johnny Quigley, a find from Scottish junior football. Quigley had been their first player to do the hat-trick, against Manchester City, after their return to Division One in 1957.

Quigley moved to Huddersfield for £7,000 in 1965, and in October the following year was transferred to Bristol City in exchange for Brian Clark. By then Quigley was into his 30s, but was a regular choice, missing only one match in 1967-68, before Mansfield paid a small fee for him. He became that club's trainer-coach, helping manager 'Jock' Basford to a revival of fortunes that included a League Cup-tie in which the Stags lost to mighty Liverpool only after extra-time in a replay, but both were dismissed in late 1971 as results fell away following the sale of Stuart Boam to Middlesbrough and Malcolm Partridge to Leicester. Quigley was later coach with Doncaster Rovers, and their caretaker manager between the departure of Maurice Setters and appointment of Stan Anderson.

Brian Donald Clark, captain of Bristol Boys triumphant team of 1958, was an admirable partner for John Atyeo in the years of Fred Ford's reign that included the regaining of Second Division status. On leaving school, he went to Harry Dolman's engineering firm with a view to becoming an apprentice, but left after a week to join Bristol City's groundstaff at a time, on 15 March 1959, when his father Don was scouting for Birmingham City. That was a year to the day before Peter Doherty left Ashton Gate, and one of the Irishman's last acts as manager was to sign this promising Bristol-born forward as a professional on 4 March 1960. Clark had turned seventeen on 13 January, but Doherty delayed signing him then 'because he was not certain of a regular place in the Western League team', adding: 'Had we signed him then, he would have been barred from our amateur youth side and would often have been without a game. Now we feel he can challenge for a place in the professional Western League side.'

Young Clark had a hectic start to life as an amateur with Bristol City. Early in 1959 he was chosen for the youth team against Arsenal at Highbury, but found the date coinciding with his General Certificate of Education examinations at Bristol Technical College at Bedminster Down. So immediately after school, he dashed off to catch the 4.30pm train from Temple Meads to Paddington with goalkeeper Harry Booth, who was similarly placed. They were accompanied by Teddy King, manager of the Bristol Boys team and the Bristol City United side. With the train running sixteen minutes late, both players changed into their kit en route, but others were standing by to take their places if they did not arrive in time. They made it with barely two minutes to spare, hurried across to North London in a taxi that a City director had waiting at Paddington with a ten-shilling (50p) incentive for the driver.

Don Clark watched that game on behalf of Birmingham City, for whom Pat Beasley took over as team manager that month, but he did not want to let his son know he was there. He therefore hid in the shadows at Temple Meads and watched Brian get into a compartment at the front of the train with his two companions. Don then went to the back of the train and sat in an empty compartment, opposite three reserved seats. A few minutes later his secret was out. Yes, those seats were occupied by the trio he had been trying to avoid.

Brian Clark made his League debut for Bristol City in a 3-0 home win against Brentford on the last day of 1960-61 – the match in which Tommy Burden was reinstated as captain for his farewell appearance. John Atyeo did the hat-trick with the aid of a penalty, and on the following Monday evening (May Day) he scored twice more as City made sure of finishing with some silverware by defeating Bristol Rovers 3-1 in the Gloucestershire Cup final at Eastville. Derrick was City's other scorer.

With Alec Tait and Bobby Williams occupying the inside-forward positions on either side of Atyeo, Brian Clark did not get back into the first team until towards the end of the following season, and it was on Easter Tuesday, 24 April 1962, that he opened his senior goals account with a couple in a 3-2 home victory against Coventry. He had then arrived with a vengeance. Over the next four seasons he was absent from only four League matches, an everpresent for the last three, and in two of them he even outscored Atyeo. He left with 81 goals to his name in 195 games – 89 in 215 altogether with the inclusion of Cup-ties.

The move to Huddersfield did not suit Clark, however, and on 2 February 1968 he was snapped up for £8,000 by Cardiff manager Jimmy Scoular, the former 'Iron Man' of Portsmouth and Newcastle. That put him firmly back in the goals groove. He scored twice on his debut in a 4-3 defeat of Derby and went on to be the club's top marksman for three seasons in a row, forming a striking partnership with John Toshack to rival his link-up alongside Atyeo before the Welsh international's departure to League and European glory at Liverpool. Clark also collected Welsh Cup winners' medals, scoring five goals in one match against Barmouth and Dyffryn – one short of the club record set by Derek Tapscott, a Welsh cap who made his name with Arsenal.

In the 1970-71 season, Clark reached the high point of his career when he headed the only goal in the first leg of a third-round European Cup Winners' Cup-tie against Real Madrid (though the Spanish giants won 2-1 on aggregate). He had added 78 goals and 185 games to his League tally when was sold to Bournemouth with Ian Gibson in 1972 for a combined fee of £100,000. After one year on the south coast, then valued at £35,000, he had a short spell with Millwall during which, on 20 January 1974, he scored the winner against Fulham in the first Football League game to be played on a Sunday. On his return to Cardiff for one more season, 1975-76, the Welsh club went back to the Second Division as runners-up to Hereford. Finally, he was with Newport County, taking his career totals to 586 League appearances (plus 25 as a substitute) and 217 goals before winding up as player-manager of several clubs in the Welsh Premier League.

Other players, in addition to Clark, who came up through the ranks into the Bristol City team that Fred Ford steadily rebuilt for another successful promotion push included Terry Bush, Danny Bartley, Tony Ford and Roger Peters. Bush, a bustling type of forward, was originally brought in as a junior from Ingoldisthorpe, a Norfolk village near Hunstanton. Ford, a full-back, and Peters, a winger, were among the club's many local signings – Ford from Thornbury, a few miles up the road on the northern side of Bristol, Peters from Cheltenham. Bartley, a winger who also played at full-back, was a Somerset lad from Paulton who made a quarter of more than 400 Football League appearances for City (the others for Swansea and Hereford) before assisting Trowbridge Town, Forest Green Rovers and several Welsh League clubs. On 10 November 1962, Bush and Peters were with Clark when City first fielded their youngest attack in a home match with Queen's Park Rangers. It had an average age of nineteen: Derrick (19), Clark (19), Bush (19), Bobby Williams (21) and Peters (17).

Chapter 17

Promotion Again – and Atyeo Retires

Bristol City and their supporters were taken on something of a switchback ride under Fred Ford's management before the return to the Second Division as runners-up to Carlisle in 1965.

From the disappointing final position of fourteenth in his first season of 1960-61 in charge, City surged sixth in 1962, slipped back to fourteenth in 1963, and up again to fifth in 1964. And even when promotion was finally attained they got off to no more than an average start. So much so that the directors began to get restless as another downturn appeared increasingly likely, and in January there was talk that Ford might be sacked. It transpired that it had been what was described as 'a touch-and-go affair'.

Of almost 50 players called upon by City through those five seasons, only John Atyeo remained as a regular in the team that went up, compared with the first-choice side Ford inherited – and he was dropped for the only time since becoming established, if briefly, at a stage when, as Atyeo himself put it, 'nothing looked like happening' before the late revival to the rise that reprieved the manager. City's star man played in 196 of the club's 230 Third Division games during that period from 20 August 1960 to 24 April 1965. Jack Connor took part in only four fewer, and would almost certainly have exceeded Atyeo's total but for the fact that the 1960-61 season was into its third month by the time he arrived from Huddersfield.

Seven other players – Alec Briggs (177 League appearances over the five seasons), Terry Bush (52), Brian Clark (138), Jantzen Derrick (141), Gordon Low (111), Mike Thresher (127) and Bobby Williams (178) – played for the club in both that season and the one in which promotion was gained, but were rare selections at either the beginning or end of that half-decade. Clark and Low did not miss any of the club's 46 Third Division matches of 1964-65, along with Tony Ford and the most consistently impressive signing of the Fred Ford era – Mike Gibson, a Derby-born goalkeeper who, three months from his 24th birthday, was brought in from Shrewsbury after the manager and Lionel Smart had seen him play in a match in which he saved a penalty. Gibson just had time to play in City's last two games of 1962-63, and over the next nine seasons he totted up more than 350 before moving on to Gillingham. In three of those seasons he was an ever-present, and in his first six full ones with City he was absent from only ten of their 260 League fixtures.

Gibson's arrival brought an end to Tony Cook's long service with City, and also blocked the path to the first team for Ron Nicholls. Cook's renewed hold on the goalkeeping position, unchallenged for the first two seasons of Fred Ford's reign, had been broken after the transfer of Nicholls from Cardiff City, and off he went to Worcester City in September 1963. Nicholls left for Cheltenham Town during the 1965 close season after being restricted to just four first-team appearances in two seasons as Gibson's deputy. In any case, cricket with Gloucestershire was put first by this dependable batsman.

As briefly mentioned earlier, it was the clash of sporting interests that led to the exit from Eastville of Nicholls and Barrie Meyer, an inside-forward who also played for both Bristol clubs. After failing to meet Rovers' deadline for reporting back for pre-season training in 1958, because of county cricket commitments, Nicholls was offloaded to Cardiff in exchange for full-back John Frowen, and Meyer was swapped for John Timmins, a Plymouth Argyle defender. Obviously, from his own time at Eastville, Fred Ford was well aware of this problem when he added Nicholls and Meyer to his playing strength, so his high opinion of their capabilities was tempered by seeing them as only short-term solutions.

In the case of Meyer, who cost £600 from Newport County after a lean time in Devon, the term was even shorter than the manager might have expected. After only one season with City, 1961-62, in which he made a mere five League appearances, Meyer was put on the free transfer list because he had given priority to Gloucestershire as their wicketkeeper and, to quote Ford, 'we couldn't afford to pay his wages from July to September while he was playing cricket.' In the event, Meyer stayed on for another season after being told he could report back, though still be required to prove his fitness for football, if he did not get fixed up elsewhere before Gloucestershire completed their fixtures. He was, however, to have just three more League games, taking him to a career total of 228, but in the last of them he neatly reached his century for goals with a hat-trick in a 6-3 defeat of Southend in April 1963. After that he was with Glastonbury, then, like Tony Cook, was granted a permit to play as an amateur for Sneyd Park in the Bristol Downs League.

At cricket, Meyer went on to a fifteenth season with Gloucestershire, retiring in 1971 with 826 dismissals to his credit (707 caught, 119 stumped). As a batsman, his highest score was a modest 63, made in a century stand with Arthur Milton when he was promoted to open the innings against the Indian tourists at Cheltenham in 1959, because Martin Young had been injured in a road accident, but Mayer still managed to exceed 5,000 runs in all. Two years after ending his playing career he became a first-class umpire, with such efficiency that he quickly rose to Test standard.

Nicholls, who had started out in soccer as an amateur with Fulham, helped Bristol City do the double over his former Rovers clubmates during the 1962-63 season in which he was the usual goalkeeper before Gibson turned up. In playing almost 40 games for City, he left League football with over 160. For fifteen years he shared his soccer with cricket before deciding with some regret, at the age of 32, to give up goalkeeping at the end of 1965-66, much to the disappointment of Bobby Etheridge, newly installed as Cheltenham's player-manager. With Gloucestershire, for whom he had made his first-class debut in 1951, Nicholls played in the last of his 534 County Championship matches on being called out of retirement in an emergency in 1975. He was still playing cricket at 60, for Cheltenham, only two days before he was taken fatally ill in July 1994. He died in the hospital by the College ground. In his Wisden obituary he was described as 'a quiet, pleasant man, given to occasional wry comments after much thought'.

Of the other Bristol City newcomers while Fred Ford was manager, a place in the promotion season of 1964-65 was most regularly held by Ray Savino, a £4,000 right-winger from Norwich City. He was in a forward line completed by Clark, Atyeo, Bush and Peters until he broke a leg in a 1-1 draw at Carlisle on Good Friday. After his recovery he reached almost 80 first-team appearances before being given a free transfer to King's Lynn in 1968. Tony Ford and Briggs were the full-backs (Thresher the rarely-needed deputy for Briggs), in front of Gibson, with Low and Connor in the half-back line alongside, in the main, Gordon Parr or Charlie ('Chuck') Drury. Drury was a £7,500 signing from West Bromwich after Albion's manager, Jimmy Hagan, had first suggested £12,000. Bobby Williams and Jantzen Derrick played in fewer than 30 League games between them that campaign, after both had been Ford's first choices for the previous four.

Bobby Williams left Ashton Gate in February of that season – reluctantly, in marked contrast to the feelings expressed by his namesake, Alan, when he moved at the end of Fred Ford's first season in charge. Alan Williams first asked for a transfer, in writing, while Peter Doherty was still manager, following special training at Weston-super-Mare before the Cup defeat by Charlton early in 1960, but he was persuaded by the Irishman 'to wait a month or so to see what happens because the club can ill afford to lose you'. Oldham was a surprising destination when the centre-half did depart in May 1961: 'My chief reason for wanting to leave,' he had said, 'is because I want to play in First Division football. That has always been my ambition. I am happy with City, but think I could do better elsewhere.' Yet here he was, for a fee of £1,000, joining a club that had been in the Fourth Division since its formation – and for its first few years in the lower half. In 1960, indeed, they had had to seek re-election.

Alan Williams was back in the Third Division after two seasons in the League basement, ever-present when Oldham went up behind Brentford in 1963. Oldham were again near the bottom when City climbed out two years later, but Williams was one of their most popular players, rising to the captaincy and rated their best central defender of the 1960s. He was absent only ten times in his four seasons at Boundary Park before increasing his overall tally of League games beyond 550 in subsequent moves to Watford, Newport and Swansea. His son Gary, a midfielder, also played for Bristol City and Oldham, and had a short spell as a non-contract player with Bristol Rovers.

Bobby Williams – or 'Shad,' as his nickname was inelegantly shortened – said it was 'a big wrench to leave after seven very enjoyable years' when he was persuaded to join Rotherham. A Bristolian born and bred, he had been with City since leaving Marksbury Road School, where he had played rugby, and, newly married, was settling into a club-owned semi-detached house in the Whitchurch area of Bristol. Rotherham, however, also made a house available, and he found their financial terms 'much too good to turn down'. No wonder. This was made evident when Lionel Smart enlarged on the transfer, which was one that stood out in his memory among those he helped to conduct. 'We were anxious to get the £9,200 fee,' he recalled. 'In private, Shad asked my advice after Fred had told him to demand a signing-on fee of £500. "Tell them you want £2,000," I said. Danny Williams, the Rotherham manager, was staggered by the request, but his chairman agreed to pay up. Shad's wife has often reminded me over the years that they wouldn't have been able to afford to buy a house as early as they did without that £2,000.'

Such a handsome, for those days, signing-on fee had become legal under the structure of soccer finance following the ending in 1961 of the maximum wage system in force since the formation of the Football League in 1888. Matters had been brought to a head by a strike vote by members of the Professional Footballers' Association, having failed to reach agreement with the League over pay and conditions of contract. The calling-off of the strike after meetings between the League management committee and the PFA at the Ministry of Labour offices in London had led to the New Deal from which Bobby Williams benefited.

Williams did not learn of his impending transfer until Fred Ford explained what was happening a fortnight after Rotherham had made their first over-tures. It was not only because they needed the money that City were prepared to part. Williams had lost his scoring touch and first-team place and, with hopes of promotion dwindling, the club's season appeared to be as good as over after defeat by Sheffield United in an FA Cup replay at Bramall Lane. Ironically, that was the match in which Williams gave his best display of the season, watched by Rotherham's impressed representatives. In each of three of his seasons at Ashton Gate he scored 20 or more goals, with a biggest bag of 24 in 1961-62, and he altogether netted 91 in 212 appearances.

To those totals Williams added a dozen goals in under 50 League games for Rotherham. His team-mates included centre-forward John Galley, whose next club was Bristol City. Then, after two years at Turf Moor, 'Shadow' was back in Bristol with Rovers, priced at £6,000, but he played only about two dozen games for them in the Third Division, scoring four goals, before going to Reading on a free transfer.

It was only a few days before Bobby Williams left Bristol City that Fred Ford sprang his biggest bombshell by dropping John Atyeo for the visit to Gillingham on 6 February 1965. After a fine start to the season, Atyeo had scored only three goals in seventeen games. Word got back to me at the *Evening Post*'s offices in Silver Street that the Ashton Gate hierarchy was not pleased by the hefty headlines we used in breaking the news, but this was a Bristol soccer icon we were dealing with, one who only the previous season had reached an unprecedented milestone by scoring his 300th City goal in a 5-1 home victory against Walsall (his 300th in the League alone came in a 4-1 win at Charlton in the October of his final season). The shock waves soon subsided, however. City lost by two goals at Gillingham while Atyeo, on the day before his 33rd birthday, was playing for the reserves against Oxford United's second team at Ashton Gate. He was back for the following week's match at home to Bristol Rovers. That was the turning point. City beat their neighbours 2-1 and afterwards suffered their only further setback on a quagmire of a pitch at promotion rivals Mansfield Town, finding no response to the three goals they conceded.

One goal that year John Atyeo said he would never forget was scored by Terry Bush away to Grimsby. This was how he remembered it: 'Everything went wrong that weekend before the game. The driver of our coach lost his way, we were late getting to our hotel, and the rooms were freezing cold. The ground was virtually empty, the weather was icy, and for 25 minutes we were given a real hammering. Then Terry chased a loose ball down the right, hooked it into the middle from the dead-ball line, and it hit the inside of the far post and spun a foot over the goal-line. It was the most incredible goal I've ever seen, and it was greeted with utter silence.'

City had only an outside chance of going up when they began their Easter programme in fifth place, taking a point from the Good Friday match at Carlisle in which Savino's season ended. Their next fixture was not until the Easter Monday evening, at Shrewsbury. The players heard that afternoon's results while they were travelling to Gay Meadow by coach. They all went in City's favour, and they realised for the first time that promotion was a real possibility. That prospect became even brighter when they won 5-1, Atyeo scoring four, and next day a 3-0 victory in the return game hoisted City into second place for the first time.

There was then only one game to go. 'All we had to do was beat Oldham and we were up,' said Atyeo in looking back many years later. 'I was on holiday from Redland Training College in Bristol [where he was studying to be a schoolteacher]. I just moped around for the rest of the week, hardly eating a thing. I really got so carried away with it all that I wasn't in a fit state to play on the Saturday. It meant a lot to me, and I had serious thoughts about finishing at that time. Oldham were a poor side, but the goals wouldn't come. Then, just before half-time, Brian Clark scored a goal that had a dubious look about it. I hadn't done much in the game, but near the end I had a dip and the ball ended in the top right-hand corner for our second goal. I couldn't remember the last ten minutes. I was crying for much of the time through sheer joy.'

How desperately close it was though. If City had not taken both points they would have been pipped for the second promotion place by Mansfield, who ended with a 3-2 win at Barnsley. Goal-average was therefore the deciding factor, with Mansfield let down by their away record:

1964-65	P	W	D	L	F	A	Pts
1 Carlisle	46	25	10	11	76	53	60
2 Bristol City	46	24	11	11	92	55	59
3 Mansfield	46	24	11	11	95	61	59
4 Hull	46	23	12	11	91	57	58
5 Brentford	46	24	9	13	83	55	57
6 Bristol Rov	46	20	15	11	82	58	55
7 Gillingham	46	23	9	14	70	50	55

Of City's 92 goals, Clark scored 24, Atyeo 23 and Bush 16.

City's fringe players that season included two others not already mentioned: Peter Hooper and Gerald Sharpe. Hooper, another to play for both Bristol clubs, was reunited with Fred Ford from Cardiff City at a cost of £11,000 in July 1963. A left-winger with a cannonball shot, he made an immediate impact by scoring on his debut in a 3-0 victory against Bristol Rovers, for whom he had completed a century of goals in more than 300 games before his move to Ninian Park. In 38 League games in that 1963-64 season he contributed a dozen goals, the fourth into double figures behind Atyeo (21), Bobby Williams (20) and Clark (18), but lost his place to Peters in the side that won promotion. He went into the Southern League with Worcester City in 1966, and also played for Glastonbury and Barnstaple before becoming licensee of a Devon public house, and then a probation officer.

Gerry Sharpe, an adaptable forward, was signed from Gloucester City, turning full-time professional on his 18th birthday, 16 March 1964. Over the next seven seasons he exceeded 50 goals and 150 games before suffering a double fracture of his right leg in a match with Middlesbrough. He afterwards gave further service on the backroom staff, and ten years on, in May 1982, he was caretaker manager before Terry Cooper, the former Leeds and England full-back who had ended his playing career with City, was given the unenviable job of trying to revitalise the club that had just been saved from extinction. More about that traumatic time later.

Promotion in 1965 changed John Atyeo's mind about packing up playing. He wanted to finish in the Second Division, intending to have just one more season, but he would have been faced with a difficult decision if City had immediately risen to the First – as they had a chance of doing until Easter. For some time they were in the top six, but on the Good Friday of 1966 they suffered a crucial home defeat by Southampton, Jack Connor putting the only goal of the game into his own net

City won at Plymouth the next day, but on the Monday they were denied both points in the return at Southampton after leading 2 1 until Terry Paine broke away to equalise in injury-time. 'I could have headed the ball away,' Connor said later, 'but Alec Briggs shouted for offside. I ducked out of the way, but the whistle didn't go.' So it was that the season ended with Saints elevated to the First Division for the first time, runners-up to Manchester City with 54 points. City finished fifth with 51. If the three points yielded in the two games with Southampton had gone the other way those positions would have been reversed.

Atyeo admitted he would probably have wanted to carry on if he could have stepped down at the League's highest level, but some weeks before the promotion issue was decided he had quietly told Fred Ford that he intended to finish playing, and also informed Harry Dolman by letter. He played through that final season of 1965-66 as a part-timer again, with his future outside the game already assured. He had qualified as a teacher of maths and in physical education on completing his two years at Redland, and had been assured by Peter Kay, his headmaster at the Kingdown School at Warminster, that he could go on playing for as long as he wished. The time had come however, when he felt he could not go on playing so many matches a season. 'I had so much on at school,' he said. 'Leading a double life like I did for most of my career had become a physical and mental strain.' Even so, he concluded his fifteen years with City by saying that 'the happy, contented side Fred has built up in the past five years has been a pleasure to play in. He's done it all on a shoe-string budget.'

On 10 May 1966, at home to Ipswich, Atyeo played his last League game – just one short of 600 with the inclusion of his two with Portsmouth. When ties in the FA Cup and League Cup were taken into account, it was his 645th appearance for the Bristol club. He needed two goals to reach 350 in those matches for City – and he got them in a 4-1 win. Moreover, he stepped down with a clean record, never sent off and not even booked. His only regrets were not winning League or Cup honours, though he said that neither would have been as important to him as his England caps because they were achieved by individual ability, not team effort.

'I've got a lot to thank football for,' he told George Baker in an *Evening Post* interview many years later. 'I've maintained a good standard of living. I've got a bit of money behind me. I've got a good status in life. I've been widely travelled, visiting a dozen countries and many towns and cities in this country. But above all I've met some wonderful people and made many good friends from football. I wouldn't have changed my life one bit.'

In the season after his retirement from football Atyeo made his farewell appearance at Ashton Gate in his testimonial against Leeds. A £4,000 cheque was given him by the Lord Mayor of Bristol, Alderman Cyril Hebblethwaite. Some years later, one of the many phone calls I took at my desk in the sports department of *The Daily Telegraph*, whose offices were then at Canary Wharf on the Isle of Dogs, came from John Atyeo. I forget now what he was ringing about, but during our little chat I thought how fit and well he sounded and remarked on it. How great was the shock, therefore, when not long afterwards, on 9 June 1993, came news of his death at the early age of 61.

His name will live on, given tangible form in 1994 when, as previously with Billy Wedlock and Harry Dolman, a stand was named after him at Ashton Gate. The Britannia Atyeo Stand, which replaced the old terracing for away fans at the Park End, cost £1.8 million The price was £235,000 when the Dolman Stand, sponsored by the *Evening Post* and incorporating indoor bowling rinks, was opened in 1970.

Chapter 18

Sacked for not Spending enough Money

Time ran out for Fred Ford as manager of Bristol City sixteen months after John Atyeo left. Far from building on the progress made over the previous three seasons, the club slithered back to the lower regions of the Second Division, undermined by a falling-off in their scoring power through the loss of not only Atyeo but also Brian Clark.

Atyeo had confidently expected Clark to succeed him as the club's main source of goals, but the player who had been his admirable foil in their double spearhead played in only ten more matches, scoring just once, before his move to Huddersfield in October 1966. Attempts were made to shore up the striking force by bringing in Chris Crowe, an England forward, the following January, and Hugh McIlmoyle shortly before the March transfer deadline, but at the end of that 1966-67 season the sorry state of City's attack was made all too plain: none of their players got into double figures for goals in the League. Peters was top scorer with nine; Sharpe netted eight. The team's total of 56 was City's lowest since their 44 of 1948-49.

Neither Harry Dolman nor Fred Ford had tried to dissuade John Atyeo from retiring, both having agreed that it was a good time to go. Only a few games into that first season without him, however, there were what Atyeo called 'vague suggestions' that he should return, but he never took them seriously. Soon afterwards rumours began to be bandied about that Atyeo might come back in another capacity – as a director. These originated from newspaper and television interviews in which he said, shortly before giving up playing, that perhaps his future would be as a member of the City board. This was more than just wishful thinking, for Harry Dolman had told him that he would like him to become a director 'in due course', and that moment arrived towards the end of the 1960s when the chairman put the invitation in writing.

It came, however, in a form not quite what Atyeo had expected. This was how he recalled it: 'I would have been considered for a seat on the board if I had been prepared to put in "a substantial amount of money" into the club. I don't think the amount was mentioned, but I knew it was £3,000 because I'd read about it in the newspapers. The position had obviously changed drastically since I had left the club. Then the only financial requirement had been to guarantee £1,000 at the bank.'

Atyeo, who had never fancied staying in the game as a manager because it was 'too much of a rat race', explained why he turned down the chance to return to it as a director by saying: 'I have always felt that if I were to become a director my asset would be my experience in football. I never really had money to offer in any quantity, but after fifteen years in the professional game my contacts and friends could have been a great help to the club. I thought this was of just as much value as a few thousand pounds. When it became really a question of money I had to back out. Still, Harry Dolman kept his word and did invite me to join, as he had said he would. He said that it wasn't the right time when I finished playing because I knew so many of the players and had played with them in the same side. I was a little disappointed, I must confess. The club seemed desperate for money, and it was made pretty clear by Mr Dolman that large sums were required.'

All the more strange, therefore, that when, on 19 September 1967, Fred Ford became the 643rd manager to leave a Football League club since the Second World War, the reason given was that 'he refused to spend money on new players.' And even then that was something of a delayed reaction, for he had come most under fire from City supporters five years earlier for not signing new players before the transfer deadline. He could then have borrowed a five-figure sum from Harry Dolman, free of interest, but had replied: 'We have been paying our own way this season [1961-62], and I was reluctant to rely on Mr Dolman's generosity any more.'

The irony of that situation was increased when £15,000 was spent on Crowe, and £10,000 more than that on McIlmoyle, during the last months of Ford's reign. McIlmoyle has cropped up in a previous chapter. Crowe, then 27, came from Nottingham Forest after twice asking them for a transfer. 'I prefer playing at inside-forward,' he said, 'but I suppose about 85 per cent of my 120-odd first-team games for Forest were on the right wing. I was content to play there if it meant a first-team place, but I was out again when Barry Lyons was bought from Rotherham. Then John Barnwell was injured and I thought I would come back at inside-forward but Jeff Whitefoot, who normally plays at wing-half, was moved up. I didn't think there was much future for me in that. As far as I know, Bristol City were the only club to come for me.'

The negotiations were quickly completed. Fred Ford phoned the Forest manager, Johnny Carey, to inquire about both Crowe and Alan Hinton, Forest's other transfer-listed former international languishing in their reserves. Hinton's price was prohibitive, Crowe's more realistic – even though City had never before paid so much for a player. Crowe agreed to meet Ford and Lionel Smart at a Leicester hotel that evening, and the final snags were sorted out next day after he had travelled to Bristol with his wife and their two children. He had visited the city only once before, for a League Cup-tie with Rovers while with Blackburn. Hinton moved the short distance to Derby – and to teams that topped the Second and First divisions.

Crowe was born at Newcastle-upon-Tyne, but moved with his family to Edinburgh at an early age, learned his football in the streets of a suburb in the Scottish capital, and played for Scotland Boys. As a teenager with a rich Scottish accent, he talked of Scotland as his home country. Discovered in an Edinburgh junior team, he was still only fifteen when Leeds brought him back to England in the autumn of 1954, and at Elland Road he had the benefit of having his career as an inside-right shaped by manager Raich Carter, one of England's best occupiers of that position in the twentieth century. By the time Crowe turned professional nearly two years later he was the winner of eight England Youth caps, and the most sought-after young player in the country. After moving to Blackburn for £25,000, then to Wolves for £28,000, he added to four Under-23 appearances by gaining his one full England cap in a drawn game with France in October 1962.

Forest succeeded where, among others, Tottenham, Birmingham, Newcastle and Preston had failed in signing Crowe, though it cost them £30,000. 'I was happy with Wolves,' he said, 'but suddenly they bought Jimmy Melia from Liverpool. The next thing I knew was that Wolves had agreed terms with Forest for my transfer, so I signed.' On leaving Nottingham, his stay at Ashton Gate lasted until May in 1969, when City recouped £2,000 from his transfer to the Australian club Auburn – or, to be exact, they did do when Walsall handed over the £690 balance of that fee still owed in signing him on his return to England the following September. Crowe then completed his Football League career with a total of almost 400 appearances – 66 with Bristol City, for whom he scored a dozen of nearly 90 career goals. Afterwards he ran a public house in Leeds, a newsagent's business in Bristol, and had a final footballing fling with Bath City.

Two other forwards who made their names elsewhere would have joined Bristol City if Fred Ford had had his way – ironically, again, because it was Harry Dolman's refusal to sanction the fees required that caused the proposed deals to fall through. Ford was convinced that City would become strong contenders for promotion to the First Division with the signing of Ernie Hunt and Mike Summerbee from Swindon – and he knew through his friend Bert Head, the Wiltshire club's manager, that they could be bought. Head, however, said that a joint offer of £60,000 was the lowest Swindon would accept, and Ford had to pull out when City's chairman suggested that £40,000 was the most his club could afford. Hunt went to Wolves for £35,000, Summerbee to Manchester City for £30,000.

Hunt did get to Ashton Gate at the tail-end of his career, and Summerbee might have done so even before joining Swindon. In December 1957, shortly after his fifteenth birthday, Summerbee was invited to join the City ground-staff, but, in his words, the trial he was given 'didn't work out'. Everything certainly worked out all right for him after that. He was in the Swindon team that won promotion for the first time in the club's history in 1963. And while with Manchester City, during the Joe Mercer-Malcolm Allison era, he played eight times for England besides gaining winner's medals in the Second and First divisions, the FA Cup, League Cup and European Cup-Winners' Cup. Mercer had kept a close eye on him since being a team-mate of his father, George, when they were wartime guests with Aldershot

The path to Bristol for Hunt, winner of three England Under-23 caps, led from Wolves by way of Everton, Coventry and a loan spell at Doncaster. He originally came from Coventry on a six-match loan in December 1973, then was signed for about £7,000 towards the end of January, two months before his 31st birthday. At Molineux, where McIlmoyle was among his team-mates, Hunt had the off-putting experience of seeing Andy Beattie resign as Wolves' manager four hours after completing the deal, and then of watching his new club let in nine goals next day as Southampton romped to their record League victory. The only way to go after that was up – and up Wolves went to the First Division the next season, with 20-goal Hunt their leading scorer. By then McIlmoyle had left for Bristol City, and Hunt followed him out, to Everton, six months later, his price tag boosted to around £70,000. That amount was recouped by the Goodison Park club when Hunt soon ended an unhappy time on Merseyside with his move to Coventry, where his career took off again with more than 50 goals in over 170 games for the Sky Blues.

One of those goals, seen by millions on television's Match of the Day, will be remembered by many – the innovative and controversial 'donkey kick' with which Hunt scored against Everton in connivance with Scottish international Willie Carr. Would-be imitators of Carr's free kick, a backwards two-footed flick of the ball into the air for Hunt to volley home, were foiled when that kind of spectacular trick was outlawed.

Hunt, whose real first name was Roger, ended his career with Bristol City, retiring in May 1975 with a total of 165 goals in 467 League appearances. He became a publican at Ledbury, near Hereford, and was later a window cleaner.

Despite the infusion into their team of Crowe and McIlmoyle, who resumed his wanderings around the clubs only four days after Fred Ford's dismissal, Bristol City were again struggling when the directors decided that the time had come for another change of manager. All of them, that is, except Lionel Smart, who was away on holiday in Majorca and subsequently refused to make the sacking unanimous.

'When I returned,' he said, 'I discovered that the other directors had gathered informally and agreed to get rid of Fred. A board meeting had been called for the following Tuesday. When the proposal to dismiss the manager was put forward, I said I would resign. Harry Dolman asked me what I was going to tell the press. I said: "The truth – that you all decided to sack Fred without my being able to speak up in his defence." Harry decided to let me have my say. I outlined his record, how he had taken the club into the Second Division, and that the troubles arose directly from John Atyeo's retirement and the inability at that time to replace him. But it made no difference. Fred went. I stayed because it was a democratic vote and I'd been allowed to have my say.'

Within a month, Ford was appointed as Swindon Town's chief coach. By then Bert Head was manager of Crystal Palace, having first left Swindon to rejoin Bury (for whom he had been a stolid centre-half), and the reins at the

Wiltshire club were being held by Danny Williams. It was Williams whom Ford succeeded as Swindon's manager when the former Rotherham player and manager left for Sheffield Wednesday in July 1969, but in the meantime Fred spent just over a season back at Eastville as successor to Bert Tann, who 'moved upstairs' as Bristol Rovers' secretary and first general manager.

It could be said that Ford's defection to Bristol City, so upsetting for Rovers at the time, was forgiven when his name topped the list the Football Association supplied in response to the Eastville club's request for recommendations. 'No-one is happier than I am that Fred has got the job,' said Tann. 'We were looking for a capable, confident, ambitious man, and Fred fulfils all these requirements.' But Ford left his coaching post at Swindon to take over at a most difficult time, on the first day of April in 1968. Rovers were only three points clear of the Third Division's relegation zone, and, although that margin was doubled by the season's end, they were back to being just three from safety the following campaign. That summer Ford resigned, much to Rovers' repeated disappointment (perhaps too mild a word), to fill the Swindon vacancy Williams had suddenly left.

On that occasion Ford went back to a club buoyant after headline-catching success. Only four months before Swindon had pulled off one of the great giant-killing acts by beating Arsenal in the League Cup final at Wembley. They had also regained, as runners-up to Watford, the Second Division status they had lost in 1965. Ford got off to a decent start in 1969-70 by piloting them to fifth place in the table and to an FA Cup quarter-final with Leeds. He therefore had good reason to be his usual cheerful self when I last met him when Swindon visited (and drew with) Sheffield Wednesday early in 1971, but in the following May a shadow was cast over his future at the County Ground with the arrival of David Mackay, a player who could truly be described as a legend in his own lifetime.

Mackay, captain of Derby's promotion team of 1969, a Scottish international powerhouse with Hearts' Scottish League champions and Tottenham's double winners, was ostensibly transferred to Swindon as a player only, declaring himself ready to carry on 'for a couple of seasons at least'. But within six months, during the November of 1971 in which he celebrated his 37th birthday, it was announced that he would take over team selection and discipline 'with a view to management when he decides ro give up playing'. Ford, his position irretrievably undermined, left 'by mutual agreement'. Mackay officially embarked upon a managerial career that took him to Nottingham Forest a year later – then to a tempestuous start as successor to Brian Clough at Derby before he guided the Rams to their second First Division title in four years.

Ford soon found another post as coach and assistant manager of Torquay United, but left there early in 1973 as economy cuts were made. He was then youth coach and chief scout with Oxford United until his death at 65 on 16 October 1981.

After putting Les Bardsley in temporary charge, Bristol City's choice of manager to follow Ford fell, in October 1967, on a Londoner who, by his own admission, had been little more than an average player, but had built up an impressive reputation inside the game as a coach, while assistant to Jimmy Hill at Coventry. Alan Dicks arrived unknown to Ashton Gate followers, among whom that backroom reputation had not spread, yet he was the longest-serving contemporary manager in the Football League by the time he left City in September 1980. His high point was promotion to the First Division in 1976, but there were also lows – above all, the relegation in 1980 that resulted in his dismissal.

Lionel Smart missed the meeting at which Dicks was appointed. 'We never got on,' he admitted, 'even though he proved to be the most successful manager in the club's history over thirteen years. We were soon at loggerheads. I was in charge of the pitch, but Alan insisted on training on it in all weathers, which did the surface no good at all.'

Dicks, younger brother of Ronnie, a Middlesbrough and England 'B' defender, and father of Julian, a full-back with Birmingham, West Ham and Liverpool, was born at Kennington on 29 August 1934. He played at wing-half for Dulwich Hamlet and Rainham Town before joining Millwall as an amateur in June 1950. A bright future was predicted for him by Sam Weaver, the former Newcastle, Chelsea and England half-back who was then trainer at the Den, but he was mainly a reserve on moving to Chelsea, where Roy Bentley was among his clubmates. He made only one first-team appearance when the Stamford Bridge club were League champions for the first time in 1954-55, and played most of his 33 League games for them (there were also five FA Cup-ties) in the 1956-57 season, after being switched to centre-half. In November 1958, after six years chiefly spent as a mainstay of the Combination team's defence, he was transferred to Southend United with Les Stubbs, a forceful forward who had been a regular member of Chelsea's title-winning side, for a combined fee of £12,000.

Dicks had looked to the future by obtaining a coaching badge at the early age of 23, and that served him in good stead when he went to Coventry in February 1962. Over the next five years he was an integral part of the behind-the-scenes team as the Midlanders soared from Third Division to First under the dynamic managership of Jimmy Hill, who preceded Dicks at Highfield Road by three months after having his playing career with Fulham ended by a knee injury. That remarkable rise had barely been completed when, in May 1967, Hill caused a sensation by suddenly resigning to embark upon a new career with London Weekend Television. He agreed to stay on for five months during which Malcolm Allison and Brian Clough were touted as possible successors (Allison talked himself out of it by jumping the gun; Clough decided to stay at Derby) before the post went to Noel Cantwell, former captain of West Ham, Manchester United and the Republic of Ireland.

Dicks, available to Bristol City through the break-up of his prosperous partnership with Hill, was faced with the demanding task of trying to revive a team wallowing in the depths of the Second Division. The first newcomer to the playing staff after his appointment was Ken Wimshurst, a 29-year-old half-back or forward who cost £10,000 from Southampton and played in more than a hundred games before stepping down to become the club's reserve-team coach – then promoted to that role with the senior side when John Sillett left to manage Hereford. Sillett guided Hereford to the Third Division championship before forming with George Curtis a managerial partnership that in 1987 took Coventry City to victory over Tottenham in one of the best FA Cup finals.

Shortly before Sillett's departure from Ashton Gate, City lost their youth coach, Dave Merrington, who had been signed as a half-back from Burnley. He returned to Turf Moor as coach. Other experienced players who were also with City for a short time included half-back Ken Waterhouse and defenders George Showell, Tony Knapp and Roger Kenyon. Waterhouse moved to Darlington in 1964, the year after costing £1,000 from Rotherham; Showell, recruited from Wolves, also stayed only a year before joining Wrexham in 1966; Knapp, formerly of Leicester, Southampton and Coventry, was signed in March 1969 on his return from playing for Los Angeles Wolves, but released two months later; Kenyon, brought in towards the end of Alan Dicks' reign after helping Vancouver Whitecaps to the North American League title, had played more than 300 times for Everton, but made only four appearances in the red of the Robins before having his contract cancelled early in 1980.

Bristol City's next important signing after Wimshurst, before Christmas 1967, was John Galley, a 23-year-old centre-forward for whom Rotherham were paid £25,000. In his first City game, a 3-0 win at Huddersfield, Galley did what he had done on his debut for Rotherham in their 5-3 victory at Coventry three years before – he scored a hat-trick. He was a dab hand at getting straight off the mark for a new club around Christmas. With Wolves in 1962, he scored just the once in a 5-0 frolic at Fulham. In 1972, also at Craven Cottage, he opened his account for Nottingham Forest three days after his £30,000 transfer from Bristol City. On that last occasion, however, Fulham were the winners, by 3-1.

Galley's goals were a key factor in City's escape from relegation in 1967-68 – 17 of them in 21 games. But there were many anxious moments before safety was assured, down in 19th place with 36 points. Only Preston, one point worse off, were below them, immediately above the trapdoor through which Rotherham and Plymouth plunged.

City's next highest scorer in the League that season, with eight goals, was Chris Garland, one of their biggest local finds of the Fred Ford era. He was among six members of the current Bristol Boys team signed in December 1963, directly after a new FA ruling that permitted professional clubs to sign boys from the age of thirteen. They were able to go to City for training and coaching, but were not allowed to play in any of their teams until they finished with school Then they were offered either apprentice professional or amateur forms, and the fair-haired Garland, who lived in a flat overlooking the Ashton Gate ground, was signed as an amateur as soon as he left Southville School in 1964.

On becoming an apprentice, he played regularly in the reserve and youth teams in the 1965-66 season, and in the week before he was summoned to Fred Ford's office to sign as a full-time professional on Friday, 29 April 1966 (five days after his 17th birthday), he was in line for a place in the first team's friendly with the Finnish club Haka until an ankle injury put him out of the reckoning. Having completed his final chore as an apprentice by cleaning out the dressing rooms, he left next day for another friendly match, with the reserves in Guernsey.

The five other Bristol Boys players who were snapped up by City with Garland were John Munday, Tony Bray, who had just scored four goals against Somerset Boys at Paulton, Keith Moore, whose brother Colin had been a City apprentice before crossing over to Rovers, Roger Oldfield, whose cousin Terry was also at Eastville, and David Lewis, a Connaught Road School team-mate of Munday's who had the misfortune to break a leg in a match a week before being signed. Munday, Garland's right-wing partner with Bristol Boys, was described by Willie Evans, the former Tottenham and Wales winger, as 'the best schoolboy prospect I've seen for years', but Garland was the only one of the six to make good with Bristol City. He had to be nursed along carefully, however, his strength having been sapped by growing about six inches in the last few months before accepting full-time terms, and that was the reason why he was given just one League game during Fred Ford's last full season as the club's manager.

Alan Dicks reaped the benefit as Garland bore out Ford's prediction that he was a natural footballer who had 'a great chance of becoming a very good player if he dedicates himself to the task'. Garland was still only 22, and had scored nearly 40 goals in some 150 League and Cup games, when he was sold to Chelsea for £100,000 in September 1971 because City, £140,000 in the red, desperately needed the money. Only the previous summer they had resisted an offer of just over £80,000 from Leicester, the club Garland did join in March 1975, for another six-figure fee, after also exceeding a century of appearances for Chelsea in which he netted over 30 times.

Garland was back at Ashton Gate in December 1976, midway through City's first season in the First Division for 65 years, but the paupers of the days when he had left them went well down to road to becoming paupers again – this time in circumstances much more dire. He became the costliest player City had either bought or sold in answering Leicester's demand for £110,000. Such a big outlay, for those days, was far from reaping the desired reward. Garland considered himself 'twice the player I was when I left Ashton Gate', but his return was bedevilled by injury and his contract was cancelled in 1981 as City tumbled into the Third Division with a second successive relegation. He was reinstated, but dispensed with again, in February 1982, when he was one of the players, known as the Bristol City Eight, whose agreement to give up their contracts warded off the threat of bankruptcy. It could not stave off the club's descent from First Division to Fourth in consecutive years – a free-fall then unprecedented, but promptly also the fate of Wolves.

Even after all that, City had still not seen the last of Garland. They were at the foot of Division Four when he was signed for a fourth time in December 1982, on an expenses-only basis. The nine games he played, two of them as a substitute, before finally fading out at the end of a season the team ended in mid-table, took him past 200 for the club in the League alone. He scored the last of more than 60 goals for City in a draw at Darlington, watched by a crowd of fewer than 1,500. Overall, his career totals for games and goals in League and Cups were raised to the regions of 400 and 100. From the trauma of his last years at Ashton Gate, he went to finishing playing with Gloucester City and Minehead, and to a life outside football that dealt him a very raw deal indeed.

In their book *A Life of Two Halves – the Chris Garland Story*, James Ryan and Mark Leesdad have told of how he tried to run a fruit and vegetable business that failed, a wine company that went bankrupt, and was then made redundant from a job in insurance. Gambling made him bankrupt again, but the biggest blow of all came when, at just turned 40, he was diagnosed with Parkinson's disease, the degenerative brain condition for which he later underwent surgery. Medical opinion attributed it to his heading of leather footballs, which in his time were considerably heavier, especially when wet, than those that are pinged about these days. 'At Chelsea,' he recalled, 'we always ended a training session by doing 100 sit-ups and headers.'

Left homeless after the break-up of his first marriage, he was reduced to sleeping under the pier at Weston-super-Mare before finding happiness again with his second wife, a Welsh woman he calls 'my saviour', and with whom he set up a new home at Newport in Gwent.

Gerry Sharpe (No 11) exceeded 50 goals and 150 games for Bristol City.

Centre-half Dickie Rooks spent three seasons as Ashton Gate, 1969-72

Chapter 19

Dreams dashed of all-Bristol Wembley final

Alan Dicks endured some tough times both before and after steering Bristol City back to the First Division as runners-up to Sunderland in 1976. With final placings of 19th (twice), 16th and 14th in his first four seasons, the main highlights of that period were reaching the semi-finals of the League Cup in 1970-71 and the quarter-finals of the FA Cup in 1973-74.

Cup cheer had been in short supply for City in the League Cup since its inception ten years before, with only four wins in eighteen ties (including replays) and one thumping five-goal defeat at home by Everton's aristocrats. Nor had it been all that plentiful in the FA Cup since City and Rovers had both reached the fifth round together for the first time in 1951, and then met at that stage in 1958 – the year of the Eastville club's memorable 4-3 win. Only twice after that had City gone so far in the FA Cup, losing to Tottenham in 1967 and Leeds in 1968.

It was Spurs who prevented City reaching Wembley in the League Cup. There had been dreams of an all-Bristol final until Rovers' quarter-final replay defeat by Third Division Aston Villa, the day after City had qualified for the last four by beating Fulham at the second attempt with a first-half penalty by Gerry Sharpe. City had also needed a replay to account for Rotherham in the second round and for Leicester's coming Second Division champions, after extra-time, in the fourth. In between, a Sharpe goal edged them through against Blackpool, who that season dropped out of the First Division.

The first leg of City's semi-final was drawn 1-1 in front of an Ashton Gate crowd of 30,000, more than treble that for the 4-0 eclipse of Rotherham which had set them on their way. The scorer of the goal that countered Alan Gilzean's for Tottenham was Alan Skirton, a 6ft, 13st winger who had been released by Bristol City as 'not good enough' before coming to prominence with Bath City, his home club then managed by Bob Hewison, in an attack that also included former internationals Stan Mortensen and Charlie ('Cannonball') Fleming. Skirton had been a private in the Royal Army Pay Corps at Devizes when he chose Arsenal from among several Football League clubs on his trail in costing the Gunners £5,000 on 20 January 1959, three days before his 20th birthday. Prominent among those disappointed were Newcastle United, whose management could hardly have rated him more highly in hailing him as 'a second Jackie Milburn'. They were first in the hunt, but he turned them down on the advice of his father, who thought it best for him to keep playing part-time and not go so far from home, where he had a job in the treasurer's department at Bath's Guildhall to which he could return on completing his National Service.

Shortly afterwards, Peter Doherty, as Bristol City's manager, went to see for himself if the club had made a mistake over Skirton by attending a Southern League Cup match at Twerton Park. He could not fail to have been impressed. Bath City defeated Exeter City Reserves 5-0, and Skirton scored in the second minute. Unfortunately for Doherty, however, the onlookers also included George Swindin, the Arsenal manager, and his assistant Ron Greenwood, a future England manager. They, too, liked what they saw, and the lure of London and its famous Gunners pre-empted any offer Doherty might have considered making. Bristol, though much nearer to Skirton's home, would have to wait.

Skirton was given a rousing send-off at the Bath City Supporters' Club annual ball in the Pump Room three days after the deal had been done, also departing with a travelling case presented to him by chairman Ken Ollis. But fate was soon to take an unpleasant hand. After almost making an early Arsenal first-team debut at Manchester City – on stand-by because of a fitness doubt about David Herd for the centre-forward position Skirton so disliked that he had once refused a chance to play there for the Army. – he fell ill with pleurisy and pneumonia, and the following September he was discharged from the Army on medical grounds. Consequently, almost another year went by before he first played in the Gunners' First Division side, in a defeat at Burnley on the opening day of the 1960-61 season.

With the inclusion of cup-ties, Skirton made over 150 further appearances, scoring 54 goals, before his transfer in September 1966 to Blackpool, who could have saved themselves most of the £30,000 fee if they had followed up the tip-off from Mortensen while their former ace marksman was with Bath City. The first of Skirton's 80-plus games for the Seasiders was at Highbury of all places – and he scored the goal that held Arsenal to a draw.

An encouraging influence in both the dressing room and out on the pitch, Skirton became one of Blackpool's most popular players. He was their joint top scorer when they missed an immediate return to the First Division on goal average in 1967-68, and his departure to Bristol City the following November was viewed with regret by fans among whom he was something of a folk hero. The man who made the decision to part with him, for £15,000, was none other than Mortensen, by then the club's manager. He felt he had enough promising young talent coming through to make it affordable, but was himself the victim of an unpopular move when dismissed the following April, a year before Blackpool were promoted.

Skirton was substituted through injury during the second leg of the League Cup semi-final in which, on 23 December 1970, Bristol City had no answer to Tottenham goals scored by Martin Chivers and Jimmy Pearce. Aston Villa, surprise semi-final conquerors of Manchester United, were Spurs' opponents at Wembley, but their hopes of emulating QPR and Swindon as Third Division winners of the trophy were dashed by two late Chivers goals.

Skirton's place at White Hart Lane was taken by Trevor Tainton, a versatile former Bristol Boys captain and England schoolboy international who had been signed as an amateur as far back as 1963, then progressed from being made an apprentice professional a year later at the age of sixteen. He was to be a mainstay of the side throughout the 1970s, becoming second only to John Atyeo for senior appearances, totalling over 580. And he could have chalked up even more but for being one of the Bristol City Eight who, after much agonising, decided in City's favour when weighing up saving the club from extinction against risking their families' financial security.

Two other members of the team against Tottenham were with Tainton at the heart of City's 1975-76 promotion winners. One was Brian Drysdale, a full-back bargain at £10,000 from Hartlepool, the other Gerry Gow, an adaptable Scot who was signed around the same time, during the summer of 1969, as an apprentice professional along with another Glaswegian, Billy Menmuir, a half-back who was released after only one League appearance. Drysdale, briefly with Lincoln before exceeding 170 games for Hartlepool, played in all of City's 126 League games and 18 cup-ties in his first three seasons with the club, and had totalled nearly 300 appearances when he left in 1977 – first on loan to Reading, then on a free transfer to Oxford United.

Gow was even longer-lasting, with around 450 outings before moving to Manchester City in October 1980 for a fee said to range from £175,000 to £227,700 with the inclusion of the League levy and VAT. That price was down to £75,000 when Gow, then in his 30th year, joined Rotherham fifteen months later.

Always a wholehearted, fiery type of player, never one to shirk a tackle, Gow was sent off in the third minute of his second game for Rotherham for a challenge in which Steve Emery, a Derby full-back, suffered a compound fracture of the right leg. John Newman, Derby's manager, considered it 'one of the worst fouls I have ever seen, and I've been around some rough and tough games in my time', but his opposite number, Emlyn Hughes, the former skipper of Liverpool and England dubbed 'Crazy Horse,' said that Emery, whom he had visited in hospital, 'bore no grudge against Gerry whatever; he says the ball was there to be won, and it was just one of those things.'

While with Bristol City, Gow got into double figures for penalties amid some 50 goals, but he failed with a crucial one against Luton when Rotherham were in the running for promotion from the Second Division in April 1982. He volunteered for the job after the club's previous two spot-kicks had been missed, but confessed to changing his mind on the run-up in trying to place the ball instead of hitting it with power. Rotherham dropped a precious point, provoking the wry joking comment from Hughes that 'the next time we get a penalty I'm going to ask one of the spectators to come down out of the stands and take it.' As it happened, Rotherham were awarded another penalty two games later, and player-manager Hughes himself took it – successfully. Again, however, the result was a draw. And promotion eluded the Millmoor club in a season when Bristol City completed their crash dive into Division Four.

From Rotherham, Gow went for a short stay at Burnley – then to Yeovil Town as manager in succession to Ian MacFarlane, who took the opposite route to Turf Moor as the Lancashire club's first-team coach after only fourteen weeks in Somerset. Gow was later manager at Weymouth before leaving football to work in the engineering trade.

During his years with Bristol City Gow occupied half-a-dozen different positions – mainly as an inside or wing forward, but latterly on the right of the half-back line. As a midfielder, he was an excellent successor to Bobby Kellard, who did the rounds with Southend, Crystal Palace, Ipswich and Portsmouth before becoming one of Alan Dicks' early signings, soon after the arrival of Wimshurst and Galley. In a stay of two years, Kellard displayed delightful creative skills, then brought a profit of some £20,000 on the £30,000 fee paid for him in leaving for Leicester. From there, he rounded off a career circle with returns to Palace and Pompey.

For City's semi-final against Spurs, Gow was inside-left, with Gerry Sharpe as his partner in the first leg and Peter Spiring in the second because Sharpe was switched to head the attack in the absence of the injured Galley. The Glastonbury-born Spiring, who joined City as a junior, played in over 60 first-team games before Liverpool paid £60,000 for him in March 1973, and when he moved again, in November the next year, Luton forked out a few thousands more, even though he had never been in the Anfield club's First Division side. With Luton he had just fifteen League opportunities, three of them as a substitute, but then found his niche in repaying Hereford'a £8,000 outlay with more than 250 appearances. Luton, a First Division club less than nine months before that deal, had to sell because of serious financial difficulties.

Drysdale and Gow were just two of the astute signings Alan Dicks made during the 1969 close season. He had been warned that there would not be too much money available for dabbles in the transfer market, so he landed another bargain in snapping up Dickie Rooks from Middlesbrough for £15,000. Rooks began with his home club, Sunderland, as centre-half understudy to Irish international Charlie Hurley. Raich Carter, then the Boro manager, satisfied his thirst for regular first-team football by seeing him as an ideal replacement for another capped player after Welshman Mel Nurse's transfer to Swindon Town.

Rooks could scarcely have had a more harrowing debut for the Tees-siders. Huddersfield hammered in six goals, three of them by the man he was marking, Allan Gilliver. On the last day of that 1965-66 season, Rooks strayed from his defensive duties to do the hat-trick himself. It was not enough, however, to avert the defeat at Cardiff that sent Boro down from Division Two, but he helped them straight back and clocked up exactly 150 League and Cup appearances. His omission two games from the end of the 1968-69 season cost him an ever-present record and provoked the transfer request that led him to Ashton Gate. Many Boro fans were sad to see him go.

With Bristol City, Rooks, as captain, took over the position held for so long and efficiently by Jack Connor, who was by then into his mid-30s. Connor went to Everton as reserve-team trainer, but left there in the summer of 1973 when backroom changes were made with the appointment of Billy Bingham as manager. Later, Connor was with Formby in the Cheshire League, and worked as a representative for a cargo control firm.

Rooks reached another century of League and Cup games in City's colours before being given a free transfer at the end of 1971-72. He went back to the North-East as the Willington club's player-coach, then had an unhappy experience of management at Scunthorpe, where he was unable to avoid an application for re-election and was sacked soon afterwards as the team continued to struggle in the depths of Division Four.

Towards the end of 1972 Alan Dicks was allowed to break City's transfer record by paying West Bromwich £63,000 for Bobby Gould as the attacking spearhead replacement for John Galley, who moved to Nottingham Forest the day before for roughly half that amount. Galley had given good value in averaging a goal every two League games – 87 in 174. Gould made up for a lack of finesse with a bustling and fearless style of play, but he was a man of many clubs, and it did not take him long to find another. After only eleven months, he was listed at his own request and went to West Ham for £70,000. Four years later, following a second spell with Wolves, he was back in Bristol as Rovers' player-coach, his price reduced to £10,000. He then had half-a-dozen other coaching posts, one of them in Norway, before his roamings took in a couple of stints as manager back at Eastville. Coventry, West Brom and Wimbledon were other clubs to which he returned, culminating in the shock victory the London club's 'Crazy Gang' gained against Liverpool in the 1987 FA Cup final.

Alan Dicks augmented his excursions into the transfer market for experienced players by developing a youth policy. He had persuaded the board to invest £10,000 each year for that purpose. He also reorganised City's scouting system, taking an important step in that direction by putting it in charge of Tony Collins, who was left to roam at will from his Lancashire home, at the centre of some of England's most fertile footballing country. Collins, who had been a tricky left-winger with Watford, Norwich, Torquay and Rochdale, was brought in closer touch within five months of his appointment when, in April 1968, he was also made assistant manager. He left in June 1972 to become chief scout and coach with Leeds, but returned three years later and stayed with City in his former posts until he went back to Elland Road in October 1980, the month after Dicks' long reign at Ashton Gate came to an end. Leeds parted with him again after only another year as one of their economy measures, but he found other scouting posts with Manchester United, QPR and Newcastle.

The shrewd Collins eye, at its sharpest in spotting for the Old Trafford club a raw talent as rich as that of Paul McGrath, a coming Republic of Ireland international, was behind many of Bristol City's signings while Alan Dicks was manager. From Scotland, after Gow, came such other outstanding finds as Donnie Gillies and Gerry Sweeney, for both of whom Morton were paid a reasonable fee, and Tom Ritchie, who accompanied his younger brother Steve on the strength of one good trial game. Homesick Steve, a full-back, played only one League game before joining Morton, but was afterwards among Spiring's clubmates at Hereford and did not miss a match when that club won promotion as Third Division champions under John Sillett's management in 1975-76. Tom stayed at Ashton Gate – for two spells over which he joined the select band of those who have made more than 500 appearances for Bristol City. Sweeney was just ten short of the fifth century when he became one of the 'Eight.'

Tom Ritchie was converted from midfielder to striker so effectively that Arsenal were prepared to pay £100,000 for him before Sunderland succeeded with a bid of £180,000 early in 1981. He had rejected the then Roker club's first approach, leading them to take Ian Bowyer from Nottingham Forest instead, because he decided it was not in his best financial interests to leave Ashton Gate – such were the ridiculously long and lucrative contracts that City gave their players while in the First Division. An increased offer by Sunderland forced City's hand as they were striving to avoid a second successive relegation, but Ritchie was on their books for only eighteen months, during which time he was on loan in a Carlisle team that rose from Division Three as runners-up to Burnley, before he rejoined City with two years of his lucrative contract still to run.

Sunderland, once the prosperous 'Bank of England team', were so desperate to reduce their wage bill (shades of the situation in which Bristol City were to find themselves) that Ritchie was their third costly purchase, following the Argentine Claudio Marangoni and Bowyer, to be given a free transfer. 'We have come to an agreement with Tom over the contract,' said manager Alan Durban. When Ritchie finally left City in 1985, he was second only to John Atyeo for goals for the club with 132, having pushed Arnold Rodgers (111) and Jimmy Rogers (108) down to third and fourth.

Arsenal failed to obtain not only Ritchie but also Geoff Merrick, a Bristol-born former England Boys captain who was another prime legacy of the Fred Ford regime, when they made inquiries in January 1976 after being similarly thwarted in an approach to Preston for winger Tony Morley, later winner of six England caps with Aston Villa. 'They are prepared to take either player, or both,' said Robert Hobbs, who was then City's chairman. 'They have been after them all season, and recently have been pressing us hard. We are doing our best to keep both players because we have a side good enough to take us into the First Division, but, unfortunately, we also have an overdraft of £200,000, and are losing £1,000 a week.' City's gates were then averaging only 12,000, whereas they needed a break-even figure of 16,000 for the Second Division.

Alan Dicks would therefore have been forced to sell if City had not won promotion that season. He had already been under great pressure while the team had continued to struggle during those early years of his tenure, invoking frequent criticism from fans. He also had to carry on under the threat of a take-over bid by a group of builders from East Bristol who were involved in the expansion of the town of Yate a few miles to the north of Bristol. Harry Dolman decided the directors had to cough up more cash to counter the offer proposed by Duggie Leonard, former player Arnie White, George Burnside and Wally Allen, and this led to the resignation of Lionel Smart.

'I was prepared to raise my stake to £3,000,' he said, 'provided the others side the same. When the time came for the money to be put in, not all the board complied. I was furious. Then I had a call from Harry's wife, Marina, to see him urgently at his home at Chew Magna. "I don't want you to leave because I had you lined up as a future chairman," he told me, but I resigned on principle. When there were changes on the board later I was asked to rejoin, but my application was blocked.'

Smart soon went into the Southern League as chairman and owner of Bath City, but left almost as quickly. He took control at Twerton Park for less than £1,000 after being told by Denis Follows, then the FA secretary, that the directors were preparing to put the club into liquidation, and was joined on the new board by Brian Frost, an existing member of it, and David Counsell, an estate agent who was a former League referee. However, Smart's decision to reappoint ex-Bristol City forward Arnold Rodgers as general manager did not prove popular. Bath's player-manager, Johnny Petts, formerly a wing-half with Bristol Rovers, departed in protest, and Smart also decided to leave when his fellow directors agreed that Rodgers had to go too. Counsell took over as chairman and, with the help of the brothers Gilbert and Tony Walshaw, gradually returned the club to the financial stability lost since the death of Arthur Mortimer, who for many years had been Bath City's equivalent of Ashton Gate's Harry Dolman.

Smart was later on the boards of Bournemouth and Swindon Town. He resigned after five years with Bournemouth when he disagreed with his fellow directors in considering the fee of £55,000 too low for the transfer of striker Kevin Reeves to Norwich City, the club to which John Bond had moved from Bournemouth as manager. Reeves was reported to have cost £1,250,000 when he left Norwich for Manchester City, and he played for England.

As Bristol City's results in the League continued disappointing in the early 1970s, Alan Dicks was convinced that Leeds kept him in his job by losing a fifth-round FA Cup replay at Elland Road in 1974. He could more directly have given his thanks to Donnie Gillies, scorer of the tie's only goal in the 73rd minute. It was indeed a major scalp, for Leeds were First Division champions that year and went into their clashes with City (the original tie at Ashton Gate was drawn 1-1) on the back of an unbeaten League run of 29 matches since the season's start. Only Ipswich, in the League Cup, and Vitoria Setubal, in the UEFA Cup, defeated Leeds during that period, but four days after being so sensationally knocked off the road to Wembley the Yorkshire giants also lost in the League at Stoke – after taking an early two-goal lead. Centre-half Denis Smith, later a Bristol City manager, headed the Potters' winning third goal.

In the Cup's last eight, Bristol City came up against Liverpool, the other dominant team of the day, and they again did themselves proud despite failing to reach another semi-final. An Ashton Gate crowd of 37,671 saw them beaten by an only goal, scored in the second half by Welsh international John Toshack. On the same March afternoon, Burnley won by the same score at home to Wrexham, who the previous month had ended an undefeated Third Division sequence of 28 games by promotion-bound Bristol Rovers, and crowd trouble at Newcastle nullified a 4-3 victory over Nottingham Forest. Newcastle won the replay at neutral Goodison Park, but after accounting for Burnley in their semi-final they were comprehensively beaten at Wembley by Liverpool, runners-up to Leeds in their defence of the League title.

A minor knock-out competition in which Bristol City promised to offset some of the Second Division disappointments of Alan Dicks' early years was the short-lived Watney Cup, open to the previous season's two highest scoring teams in each section of the Football League who did not gain promotion or qualify for a major European tournament. It was introduced with the intention of encouraging attacking play, but quickly went out of favour after experimenting unsuccessfully with the offside law. The 18-yard line of the penalty area was extended to both touchlines, and a player could be offside only in that end of the field. A similar trial in Scotland was also soon abandoned.

In finishing fifth, but fifteen points from a promotion place, in 1972-73, City were the Second Division's representatives on the eve of the ensuing season along with Hull, six points behind them down in thirteenth place. Stoke and West Ham qualified from Division One, Bristol Rovers and Plymouth from Division Three, Mansfield and Peterborough from Division Four. Again, as in the League Cup of 1970-71, there was the prospect of an all-Bristol final, for City and Rovers both got through to the last four. With only one win required to do so in such a small entry, Rovers gained theirs at home to the Hammers – by 6-5 on penalties after a 1-1 draw. City edged through 2-1 at Peterborough. Again, however, hopes that Bristol would have a trophy to flourish were dashed. Stoke went from a narrow win at Plymouth to a 4-1 defeat of City in the Potteries, and one goal by Hull, easy first-round winners at Mansfield, was sufficient to beat Rovers at Eastville. In the final, the fourth and last, Stoke made the most of home advantage.

For Bristol City, despite Alan Dicks' perceptive rebuilding, the long overdue climb into the First Division was then still three seasons away.

Chapter 20

First Division Birthday Present
for Skipper Merrick

Harry Dolman OBE was deposed as Bristol City's chairman in 1974, but continued with the club as president, a post he held until his death at his Chew Magna home on 9 November 1977. After numerous frustrations during his 35 years as a director since 1939, he saw a lifetime's ambition fulfilled with the return to the First Division in 1976, though he was in failing health from the March of that year in which he underwent a major operation. He had to return to hospital for a few days in March 1977, but attended a public dinner to celebrate his 80th birthday shortly before being confined to his home the following August.

By then City were embarking upon a second season of unremitting struggle among the big guns of the Football League's top flight, but at least the man known as 'Bristol's Mr Football' was spared seeing the club for which he had for so long been such an inspiring figure plunge to the verge of bankruptcy over the next few years. It had been torment enough traversing the prolonged and twisting path to a promotion last achieved as far back as 1906. After the first four seasons of Alan Dicks' management, haunted by fears of a fall rather than the hoped-for rise, the next three before the summit was finally scaled brought two fifth-place false dawns divided by another depressing dip to sixteenth, perilously close to a Third Division return.

In 1972-73, City's healthy final position belied the fact that they were never serious contenders, hovering around mid-table until uplifted by the loss of only one of their last nine games, six of which they won. With 46 points, they finished 15 adrift of QPR, who went up as runners-up to Burnley. In 1974-75, they were never outside the top six from the halfway point, but crucially faltered on the run-in with two successive defeats in which they failed to score. Their 50 points left them eight behind Aston Villa, the club promoted with champions Manchester United. The first of those decisive setbacks was inflicted at Leyton Orient, where skipper Geoff Merrick, another destined to be among 'The Bristol City Eight', led his men off the field when the floodlights fused. Referee Lester Shapter ordered them back after repairs – and City yielded precious points to a first-half goal scored by Derek Possee. Other defeats by the same score, at York and at home to Norwich, and the dropping of a home point to Bristol Rovers, contributed to another missed opportunity, but it was the failure at Brisbane Road that scuppered the last hopes.

Patience had indeed a virtue as City took time to gell into a consistently successful combination. All but three of the seventeen players used for League

games in the 1973-74 season of slump were among the seventeen who contributed towards promotion in 1975-76. The big difference was that the side
was so unsettled on that former occasion, either through injury or loss of
form, that only left-back Brian Drysdale was not called upon to change position among the outfield players, whereas the team that went up contained four
ever-presents besides goalkeeper Ray Cashley (right-half Gerry Gow, left-half
Geoff Merrick, Trevor Tainton and Tom Ritchie) who did so for all but one
match. Tainton made 41 of his appearances on the right wing, the other at
inside-right for a home match with Chelsea during the final month in which
Ritchie, who scored both City's goals in the 2-2 draw, was switched from being
his partner to lead the attack.

The promoted side also had stability at centre-half, where Gary Collier
missed only two games, and at full-back, where Drysdale, absent for just three,
was usually partnered by Gerry Sweeney in succession to Trevor Jacobs, a
Bristolian former junior. Paul Cheesley and Jimmy Mann mainly shared the
inside-left and centre-forward berths. Clive Whitehead returned for the run-in
at outside-left after facing competition from Mike Brolly, a Scot signed on a
free transfer from Chelsea, and Keith Fear, a versatile ex-Bristol Boys forward.
That left Donnie Gillies the other player most often called upon in showing
his adaptability in both defence and attack over some two dozen games.

Collier, who joined City from school, was one of a dozen Bristol-born
players then on the books. He took over as successor to Dickie Rooks from
another Bristolian, Arnold Rodgers' son David, a former Cotham Grammar
School boy and Bristol Boys captain. Rodgers was first signed as amateur in
1967, while Fred Ford was manager, four months after scoring for both sides
on his debut at the age of fifteen for England, who won 3-2, in a schools international against Northern Ireland at Windsor Park, Belfast. Twice there were
echoes of scoring both for and against his team, after he had regained his place
from Collier while City were in the First Division during 1978-79. In four successive games, he scored the lone goal that earned the points at home to Aston
Villa, had one of the two goals in a defeat at Wolves debited against him, put
the ball into his own net for the winner at Tottenham, and scored at the right
end in a 3-1 victory over Southampton at Ashton Gate.

Rodgers was introduced early in his fourth season with the club after being
converted from wing-half to centre-half. He did not gain a regular place until
three seasons later – and then, halfway through the next one, 1973-74, he
faded into the background as Collier's claims became too strong to be ignored.
Over the next three seasons, Collier was absent only three times. Rodgers was
recalled for the first of those matches; on the two other occasions the deputy
was Steve Harding, also a Bristolian, who soon afterwards was given a free
transfer to Bristol Rovers after being loaned to Southend and Grimsby.

The way for Rodgers to re-establish himself was opened, however, when
Collier rejected City's new terms and started a storm over the new freedom of

contract. His resulting move to Coventry for £325,000 in July 1979, after Derby had been cleared of trying to poach him, was the first under the ruling that allowed players whose contracts had expired to negotiate their own transfer. Coventry had been tracking him since a teenager, and five years earlier they had offered £200,000. Two months before he joined them they increased their bid to £250,000, then to £300,000 before the final figure was reached. He had approached them and, as he put it, 'asked them for a job.'

Alan Dicks complained that the freedom of contract was being abused. 'Coventry have not broken any rules,' he said, 'but I am unhappy about a situation where the club which loses a player does not have the right to further talks. We know Collier was not 100 per cent happy. He turned down our new terms a few months ago, and I told him we would talk again at the end of the season. What has made it even more disappointing is that the first I heard of the move came from the other club. Frankly, I think Collier has restricted his horizons. Several other clubs might have been interested, but he has now made his choice. I told Coventry I was not interested in selling, and that I hoped to persuade Collier to stay. On May 4 he handed me a letter saying he wanted to go. The following day he played his 250th match for us away to Manchester City, and three days later I had a call from Gordon Milne, the Coventry manager, saying Collier wanted to go to them and asking how much we wanted.'

After all that, Collier was seen only twice in Coventry's first team – and then not in his best centre-half position, and only by those fans who travelled to away matches. He was at left-half at Stoke on the first day of the 1979-80 season, and at right-half at Liverpool four games later. Coventry conceded seven goals in those matches, losing both. At least they got their money back, with a little extra, when he crossed the Atlantic to join Portland Timbers in February 1980. The fee of £365,000 set an Anglo-USA record. This followed an aborted re-signing of the player by Bristol City, who controversially pulled out of a proposed £440,000 deal. It would have increased their overdraft to £750,000.

The reinstated David Rodgers went on to increase his League and Cup appearances for the Ashton Gate club to around 200 before joining the ranks of the 'Bristol City Eight'. He accompanied Trevor Tainton on a free transfer to Torquay in February 1982, but neither stayed there long. No fee was again involved when Rodgers moved to Lincoln the next month. Tainton's contract in Devon was cancelled at the end of that season – as was Rodgers' at Sincil Bank.

Ray Cashley, another of the home-grown players City produced in such abundance, started out as a full-back, but he was encouraged to take up goalkeeping while John Sillett was the club's coach. With Len Bond, formerly of Somerset Boys, as his deputy, he made the switch so successfully that he was just the man when the time came for Mike Gibson to be replaced. Gibson was a hard act to follow, rated by Jack Connor as 'the outstanding City player of my time with the club', but for the two seasons that culminated in the rise to the First Division Cashley was firmly in possession, suitably completing a century of successive League appearances on the April evening when promotion was assured.

His hold was not to last much longer, however. Only nine games into the club's first season in the top echelon for 65 years, Cashley was ousted by John Shaw, a Scot signed on Tony Collins' say-so along with midfielder Jimmy Mann after both had been given a free transfer by Leeds. Not until well into the second half of 1979-80 was Cashley back in favour, but he then missed only one match in 36, taking him to an overall total of 262, before going on loan to Hereford at the beginning of 1981. He subsequently went out of the Football League with Clevedon Town, back into it with Bristol Rovers, out again with Trowbridge Town, back once more with Chester, and finally out again with the Somerset clubs East Worle and Weston-super-Mare.

Shaw played only twice in the Leeds first team, and on both occasions he was substituted. He was among the reserves manager Don Revie mistakenly felt he could afford for the home leg of a UEFA Cup-tie with Lierse SK in 1971 after Leeds had won 2-0 in Belgium. Leeds crashed out on aggregate, conceding four goals without reply, and Shaw was replaced by Welsh international Gary Sprake. Two years later, after Leeds had been held to a 0-0 home draw by Hibernian in the same competition, Shaw was brought back for the second leg in Edinburgh, and this time remained unbeaten until he had to go off injured. Glan Letheran, a Welsh youth international, took his place, Sprake having moved to Birmingham. There were still no goals after extra-time, and although Leeds won 5-4 on penalties they were knocked out in the next round by the Portuguese club Vitoria Setubal.

With Bristol City, Shaw had to wait in the background for the two seasons while Cashley was undisputed first choice, but then established himself with a sequence of 110 League and Cup games before missing a couple through injury. That number rose beyond 150 before Cashley's reinstatement, after which Shaw also made a comeback, ever-present for two consecutive seasons and an absentee only five times in the next, 1984-85. He then left for Exeter, having exceeded 300 appearances for the Ashton Gate club, 295 in the League, and he completed another century while in Devon. After that he was with Gloucester City, the strain of goalkeeping by then evident through a severe loss of hair as the result of a nervous complaint.

Jimmy Mann, who played for Yorkshire Boys before joining Leeds as an apprentice, also proved a sound investment for City after being given little first-team scope at Elland Road. To the five senior appearances he made for Leeds, he added over 200 before, as another of the 'Eight', he moved early in 1982 to Barnsley. The Tykes were then managed by Norman Hunter, the former England player and clubmate at Leeds and Ashton Gate. From Barnsley, Mann soon went to Scunthorpe, then Doncaster on a free transfer.

Clive Whitehead, who came from the Northfield district of Birmingham, joined Bristol City in 1973 after a trial with Wolves, and over the next eight years played in more than 200 matches before bringing in a much-needed fee of £100,000 from his transfer to West Bromwich. He was afterwards on loan to Wolves, then took his career total of appearances beyond 500 in free transfers to Portsmouth and Exeter. After that, he followed a spell as Yeovil Town's player-manager by rejoining Bristol City as an academy coach and scout, later becoming a football agent and referees' assessor.

Paul Cheesley was a rarity – a Bristol-born player who cost Bristol City a fee. He began with Norwich, breaking into their senior side in November 1971 as a substitute in a fifth-round League Cup-tie at home to Chelsea. He scored just one goal, earning a home draw with Liverpool, in his two dozen games for Norwich, but repaid Bristol City for their £30,000 outlay by forming an efficient strike partnership with Tom Ritchie in their promotion season of 1975-76. It produced 34 goals – 18 to Ritchie, 16 (one of them in the League Cup) to Cheesley.

Of the six penalties converted for City that season, the one credited to Cheesley helped him to a hat-trick in a 4-1 win at York, who were on their way down in company with Oxford and Portsmouth. The other successful spot-kicks were shared by Sweeney and Gow. Sweeney took the first two, starting on the opening day in mid-August with the one that earned a home victory against Bolton in front of a disappointing crowd of 10,000. That number was trebled on the April evening when victory over Portsmouth (Whitehead the marksman) clinched the long-awaited return to the First Division.

City gave one of their best displays of the season, following victory over Bolton, with a 3-0 midweek win (Brolly, Mann 2) against visiting Sunderland. Both victims were to be among City's rivals for the hotly contested leadership. Bolton briefly held it in late February, but faltered to finish a point outside the promoted three – Sunderland, Bristol City and West Bromwich. City were never out of those positions from early October, although they had sunk to sixth at the end of August in losing at Hull and Southampton, and held to a home draw by Bristol Rovers. Cheesley opened his account in that derby match and the hirsute striker scored ten more goals in the next seven League games – plus another in a League Cup replay home defeat by West Ham.

Cheesley's purple patch was crowned by the hat-trick in the victory at York that lifted City to the top for the first time, only for them to fail to score in their next four games. West Bromwich, who were to be late promotion contenders, yet never out of the bottom half until November, inflicted City's first home League defeat. Their new player-manager, the former Leeds and Eire midfielder Johnny Giles, sprang a surprise by omitting Geoff Hurst, England's World Cup hat-trick hero of 1966, but his reshaped attack paid off with goals from the unrelated Browns, Alistair and Tony. Hurst, signed from Stoke, left for Seattle Sounders without again appearing in Albion's first team.

Points gained during City's scoreless matches at Luton and at home to Orient, before defeat at Nottingham Forest, ensured they dropped no lower than third. They then got back into the winning groove by repeating their 4-1 beating of York, at Bootham Crescent, a hat-trick this time registered by Ritchie, and followed up with a win at Fulham in which the Scot scored twice more. The loss of a home point to Carlisle, who spent most of the season fighting off relegation, was offset by a 3-0 revenge victory against Hull, but next came a crucial clash at Bolton, second to Sunderland. City lost to a second-half goal.

That, however, was City's last League reverse until Forest, reinvigorated by a trip to Majorca, completed the double in late February with a 2-0 win at Ashton Gate. The intervening unbeaten run of seven League games, interrupted by an early FA Cup exit at Coventry, began with a Boxing Day draw with Plymouth, but the all-important goal-difference (newly introduced in place of goal-average) was improved as the defence was only twice breached in the six matches leading up to Forest's visit. One of those goals came in a home draw with Southampton, who might well have pressed home a stronger promotion challenge but for the distraction of an FA Cup run that carried them to a shock defeat of Manchester United at Wembley

City's second failure at Forest's hands cost them the second place they had regained with victory over Blackburn, but three days later they rose back to the top by beating lowly Oldham, also at Ashton Gate, with another of Cheesley's goals. That set off another undefeated sequence of seven matches in which they took three precious points off their main promotion rivals, winning at West Bromwich and drawing at Sunderland. Gerry Sweeney, fresh from snatching a late equaliser at Charlton, scored the only goal of a game as Albion were foiled by a resolute City defence. At Roker Park where the midweek crowd of 38,395 included a planeload of fans from Bristol, he gave City a lead that was not wiped out until six minutes from time. Sunderland's equaliser was scored by Mel Holden, in his first season with the club after costing £120,000 from Preston. Since the turn of the year Sunderland had also bolstered their promotion push by paying a similar amount for Roy Greenwood from Hull, and beating the transfer deadline to sign Ray Train from Carlisle for £80,000. Although money does not always buy success, it did pay off for Sunderland as they surged to the title by dropping only three of the sixteen points they had remaining at stake after Bristol City's visit.

City left Wearside four points above second-placed Sunderland, who had two games in hand as the result of a run to the sixth round of the FA Cup, which Third Division Crystal Palace had surprisingly ended. From the North-East, City crossed over to Cumbria to meet Carlisle on the last Saturday of March, when they maintained their lead with the third of Gow's successful penalties (he had failed a few weeks earlier in hitting the bar in a home win over Luton), while Sunderland beat their next visitors, Southampton.

On the following Tuesday, Sunderland halved their deficit by again winning at home, against York, in the first of their games in hand, and, although they then drew at Notts County the gap narrowed to just one point as City were undone by two defensive errors at Blackpool, after Ritchie had put them ahead in the third minute. And on the Saturday after that, three matches from the finish, Sunderland dislodged City on goal-difference by winning 3-0 at home to Blackburn while Merrick and his not quite so merry men were being held to a home draw by Chelsea, despite twice taking the lead through Ritchie.

City did not leave Bristol for any of their last four games, but on Good Friday at Eastville, struggling Rovers were eager to improve upon their draw at Ashton Gate back in August. The honours were again shared, but, with Sunderland not playing the 0-0 draw was sufficient for City to regain the lead – if only for 24 hours. City themselves did not play on the Saturday, when Sunderland went back to the top to stay with a 4-1 humbling of Hull. On the Monday, with City again without a game, Sunderland pulled three points clear in surviving a Bolton second-half revival to gain a home win with the aid of a penalty.

The next day City got out the champagne on making sure of promotion by beating relegated Portsmouth. Sunderland slipped up at Blackpool, but the three-point gap was restored four days later on the final Saturday, 24 April, when City lost 1-2 to Notts County. Hapless Pompey had to wind up at Sunderland and suffered a 26th defeat that left them also three points adrift – at the foot of the table.

City's line-up for their final match was: Cashley; Gillies (Mann), Drysdale; Gow, Collier, Merrick; Tainton, Ritchie, Cheesley, Sweeney, Whitehead. This showed three changes from the team on the opening day, when Sweeney was in his more usual position of right-back, and Mann was linked with Brolly on the left of the attack. Although unable to sustain their ready scoring of the first three months, City were sustained by a defence that kept a clean sheet in 19 of their 42 matches. Even so, it was their 'goals for' total, nine superior, that enabled them to deprive WBA of second place on goal-difference. Albion conceded two fewer than City's 35 in the 'against' column.

Albion went into their last match, at Oldham, knowing that they needed both points to make sure of warding off Bolton's challenge for the third promotion spot. They took encouragement from having won more away matches than any other club in the division, but Oldham had been beaten only once on their own turf – by Bristol City back in October, when Mann, Gillies, Cheesley and Whitehead had shared the Robins' goals in a 4-2 win. It was therefore no surprise that Albion were made to work hard for their victory, gained in what one of their players called 'a Cup final atmosphere' with a goal by Tony Brown in the 54th minute. That enabled them to join City on 53 points, and put them out of Bolton's reach, even though Wanderers won 4-0 at Charlton and had one more match to play. The following Wednesday,

Bolton defeated Bristol Rovers 3-1 at Burnden Park to finish fourth with 52 points – and a better goal-difference would have sent them up instead of WBA if Albion had only drawn at Oldham. These were the leading positions:

1975-76	P	W	D	L	F	A	Pts
1 Sunderland	42	24	8	10	67	36	56
2 Bristol City	42	19	15	8	59	35	53
3 West Brom	42	20	13	9	50	33	53
4 Bolton	42	20	12	10	64	38	52
5 Notts Co	42	19	11	12	60	41	49
6 Southampton	42	21	7	14	66	50	49

Promotion to Division One was an ideal birthday present for skipper Geoff Merrick, who turned 25 on 29 April. It was also the perfect reward for a dozen years' loyal service since first joining the club as an associate schoolboy. And at the annual dinner of the Professional Footballers' Association he received another accolade. His fellow professionals voted him the best Second Division defender in his left-half position during that 1975-76 season.

To get to that pinnacle, however, he had had to overcome early adversity. While still a teenager he had suffered a serious knee injury in stretching into a tackle. He had barely recovered from that setback when he dislocated both elbows – one in a match at Sheffield United, the other in training. He therefore needed determination as well as ability to become so firmly established in the side for so many seasons, moving into the top ten of the club's appearances list with a final total of 433. A born leader, one older players readily accepted, he was the youngest captain in the Football League, at the age of 20, when he first led out the City team at Blackpool on 22 January 1972.

Chapter 21

A Deceptive Start – Then Relegation Again

The start Bristol City made to their first season in the First Division for 65 years could hardly have been more deceptive. After four games they were second in the table, one point behind Aston Villa, after two wins and two draws. From then onwards, however, it was all downhill – first to a finish only a point clear of relegation, then to three more seasons of almost unremitting struggle, culminating in a financial crisis that plunged the club to the brink of oblivion and the dizzy drop straight through to Division Four.

On 21 August 1976, for their first match at the League's highest level since 15 April 1911 when they bowed out with a 5-1 home win over Nottingham Forest, who went down with them, City faced a daunting visit from an Arsenal side containing such charismatic figures as World Cup winner Alan Ball and Malcolm Macdonald. Indeed, there was a special incentive for Macdonald. It was his debut for the Gunners, following his summer transfer from Newcastle at the figuratively alliterative transfer fee of £333,333.

Supermac ended the season in his customary role as his club's top scorer, totalling 29 goals in League and Cup, but not one of them went into Bristol City's net. At Highbury and in the return he was firmly in the grip of Gary Collier. In fact, no Arsenal player scored in either match. City won in London with a second-half header by Paul Cheesley. In Bristol in January, Arsenal were beaten by two goals from Peter Cormack, one of the players of international experience Alan Dicks signed in the hope of making the team better prepared to cope with more demanding opposition.

By then, however, the luckless Cheesley was out of the reckoning. In the very next match after the win at Highbury, in midweek at Stoke, he seriously damaged his right knee at full stretch in challenging Peter Shilton for a cross. Don Gillies went on as substitute and scored the second-half goal that countered the one netted by future City manager Denis Smith. Cheesley made just one further first team appearance, in a home defeat by Birmingham in October before being forced to give up his attempted comeback. His contract cancelled after 64 games (three as a substitute) and 20 goals, he eventually played for a few non-League clubs, notably Yeovil Town, and found a new occupation outside football as a publican in the Knowle district of Bristol.

After prising a point from the Potteries, City also drew at Newcastle and gained what would be their biggest win all season, 4-1 at home to Sunderland with goals from Mann, Tainton, Ritchie and Gillies. But between those games they made an immediate exit from the League Cup to Coventry, and they tumbled into the drop zone after failing to win again until the tenth attempt – at Tottenham. Keith Fear broke the deadlock in the only First Division match played because of postponements permitted before midweek internationals. Alan Hardaker, the League secretary, warned that calling-off games for that reason caused concern and financial hardship. This provoked Engand manager Don Revie to say 'it is murder to sit by the phone on a Saturday night, waiting for notification of injuries and withdrawals.'

The two capped players in Bristol City's team at Tottenham were past being in contention. Cormack, who made his debut that afternoon, was nine times a Scottish selection while with Hibernian and Nottingham Forest – but, surprisingly, he did not add to that number with Liverpool sides that won the League title, UEFA Cup and FA Cup before his £50,000 move to Bristol. He was preceded in the City side, two games earlier, by Norman Hunter, a veteran of nearly 550 games for Leeds who made the last of his 28 England appearances in 1974 as the PFA's first Player of the Year. Hunter was said to relish his 'Bites Yer Legs' reputation, though the thunder of his tackling often disguised the quality of his play. Nevertheless, he was booked on his City debut in a defeat at Derby, and was twice ordered off during a century of appearances with which he repaid their £40,000 investment.

Hunter and Cormack were followed into the City team by the returning Chris Garland. Compared with the line-up for that opening game against Arsenal, only Collier, Tainton and Whitehead retained their positions when Garland first reappeared for the visit of Middlesbrough on the Saturday before Christmas, though Merrick and Sweeney also played on both occasions. Merrick, who scored in the defeat by Boro, was switched to replace Drysdale at left-back after Hunter's arrival; Sweeney had a run at right-half in addition to being used in both full-back berths and on the right wing. Sweeney and Collier were ever-presents that season, Whitehead was absent just once.

City's main weakness was evident from their paltry tally of 38 goals, Ritchie and Garland top-scoring with seven apiece. They had the best defensive record among their fellow strugglers, conceding 48, but sank to last place in early March when they lost at title contenders Ipswich, also the scene of their immediate FA Cup exit. After hopes had been revived by four games unbeaten, they were dumped back at the foot of the table by their heaviest League defeat, conceding three goals without reply at Birmingham, and they stayed bottom until only two matches were left. The first of these was at home to Liverpool, in the running for a treble having become the first champions to retain the League title since Wolves in 1959.

Liverpool had to 'make do' with a double, carrying off the European Cup against Borussia Monchengladbach in Rome after losing to Manchester United in the FA Cup final at the end of the week in which they were also beaten by Bristol City. No doubt, with championship safely stashed, the Merseysiders were somewhat preoccupied by their two looming finals, but City gave one of their best displays of the season in winning with two Garland goals to one by David Johnson. On the same Monday afternoon of 16 May, Stoke City lost to an Andy Gray penalty at Villa Park in their final match and went down in company with already doomed Tottenham. With three clubs being relegated instead of two since 1973-74, that left one more for the drop to be decided – and the issue rested between Bristol City, Coventry and Sunderland, each on 34 points with one fixture to fulfil.

Coventry was the venue for this traumatic tale of the two Cities, with Sunderland also facing a formidable task in having to visit Everton the same day, Thursday, 19 May. And, by another twist of fate, the kick-off at Coventry was five minutes late, leading to a League inquiry that brought the home club a reprimand. With the score 2-2 at Highfield Road and those five minutes still to be played, word came through that Sunderland had lost 0-2. This was duly announced publicly, so the Coventry and Bristol players were content to settle for the draw that kept both clubs up and sent Sunderland straight back to the Second Division. 'Not one of our directors feels guilty of any malpractice,' said Jimmy Hill, then Coventry's managing director, after the League's censure, 'yet we have been found guilty without any trial.' A 'fight through the courts' was threatened, but second thoughts prevailed in the light of being thankful to have survived. This was how the bottom clubs finished:

1976-77	P	W	D	L	F	A	Pts
17 West Ham	42	11	14	17	46	65	36
18 Bristol City	42	11	13	18	38	48	35
19 Coventry	42	10	15	17	48	59	35
20 Sunderland	42	11	12	19	46	54	34
21 Stoke	42	10	14	18	28	51	34
22 Tottenham	42	12	9	21	48	72	33

Midway through that season, a young Plymouth-born forward named Colin Lee who never played in Bristol City's first team and had been loaned out to Hereford, was released to Torquay. A few months later, in the autumn of 1977, he was sold to Tottenham for a Torquay record fee of £60,000, and on his League debut for Spurs scored four goals in a 9-0 defeat of Bristol Rovers at White Hart Lane. Lee helped Tottenham to prompt promotion and totalled just over 30 goals in nearly a hundred first-team games, latterly converted into a full-back, before moving to Chelsea for £200,000. At Stamford Bridge, as both striker and defender, he was in another promotion-winning side, the Second Division champions of 1984. After more than 200 appearances and 40 goals for Chelsea, he moved to Brentford as player-coach for £17,500, then managed Watford and the youth team at Reading. Certainly, as far as Bristol City were concerned, one that got away.

One youngster who did not, who earned a fee of £100,000, plus defender Terry Boyle, when he moved to Crystal Palace in October 1981, was Kevin Mabbutt, Bristol-born son of Ray Mabbutt, a long-serving Bristol Rovers half-back during Rovers' successful Bert Tann era. Kevin's younger brother Gary started out with Rovers and also commanded a six-figure fee when transferred to Tottenham, where he continued to be an inspiration to diabetics in more than 500 League and Cup games and sixteen full international as he coped uncomplainingly with that condition. Both brothers already had over 100 senior appearances to their credit when they left Bristol, their departures dictated by Gary's wish to play in the First Division (Rovers had dropped back into the Third) and City's desperate need of the money. Offers for Kevin were invited, because, as much as City wanted to keep him, he was clearly their most saleable asset as an England Under-21 striker, still only 22.

The deal that took Kevin from Ashton Gate was completed at a time when City were reported to be losing £3,000 a week and had shown a deficit of £461,969 on the 1980-81 season after a second successive relegation. They then had a bank overdraft of £242,864, and their total liabilities had soared to £757,072, including £120,000 owed in Income Tax and VAT. They were far from alone in their plight, but that was small comfort in the knowledge that they had brought it upon themselves by spending beyond their means in attempting to preserve their hard-won premier status. Next in after Hunter, Cormack and Garland among those costly captures came Joe Royle, an England centre-forward who had played the first of nearly 300 games for Everton at the age of 16. He was originally signed on loan from Manchester City on 23 November 1977, the day on which City defeated St Mirren 2-1 with goals from Mabbutt and Cormack in the first leg of the Anglo-Scottish Cup final. Three days later, Royle scored all City's goals in a 4-1 home win against Middlesbrough, and in the middle of the following month his transfer was completed at a fee of £90,000.

A 1-1 draw with St Mirren (Mabbutt again) in the second leg at Ashton Gate was sufficient to give City a trophy that succeeded the Texaco Cup, but that welcome silverware was not put into the boardroom cabinet without rancour. With goal-difference having been introduced instead of goal-average to decide positions, City qualified from their group of four because theirs was superior to Birmingham City's at the top of a table in which Bristol Rovers came last behind Plymouth Argyle. City began the knock-out stages by recovering from a two-goal deficit in the away leg to overcome Partick Thistle, but then had Hunter and Cormack sent off in the first leg of their semi-final, drawn 1-1 at Hibernian. Next day, the Scottish club's management declared they were not going to play the return leg against what they called 'the Bristol Butchers'. They said they were willing to forfeit the tie rather than risk the safety of their players, but climbed down after being warned by Alan Hardaker that they would be fined £2,000 if they failed to turn up. Bristol City won through 5-3, fielding the team that also played in the second leg of the final: Shaw; Gillies, Sweeney; Gow, Collier, Merrick; Tainton, Ritchie, Mabbutt, Mann, Whitehead.

Being accused of rough play was, unfortunately, nothing new for the bat-tling Bristol City of those tormented times. The previous January, Tommy Docherty, manager of Manchester United, had complained about their 'strong-arm tactics' after his team had wiped out a first-half lead gained by Keith Fear to win 2-1. And in the return game at Ashton Gate, from which the Manchester club's fans were banned because of the unruly element among them, Stewart Houston, the United's left-back, was carried off with a broken leg and his team-mate Sammy McIlroy was ordered off with Gerry Gow. Docherty blamed Norman Hunter for the ill-temper of the match, which was drawn after City, through Garland, had again taken the lead.

Bristol City's unwanted reputation for over-robust play, to put it politely, worsened when two more players were sent off, both at home, within a week in March 1978. Alan Dicks promised strong action after the dismissal of Trevor Tainton, along with Chelsea's central defender Micky Droy, had been followed by a red card for Gerry Sweeney against Birmingham. But the most sobering influence was imposed when City were among a dozen clubs fined by the FA for accumulating more than 175 disciplinary points during that 1977-78 season.

It might be said, however, that the effect did not last long. Two more City players, Norman Hunter and Tom Ritchie, were ordered off in an FA Cup defeat the following season by Crystal Palace. It was the fourth time Hunter had been banished in his career, but he and Ritchie were generally considered harshly treated, even though City were showing frustration in being outplayed by the coming Second Division champions, who had also knocked them out of the League Cup. Hunter accepted a booking for a foul on Steve Kember shortly after half-time, but claimed he should not have been shown a red card for his tackle on Jim Cannon a minute later. 'It was an accident,' he said. 'I just clipped him.' Ritchie was pointed to the dressing room a minute from time for kicking at Billy Gilbert.

The double defeat by Palace was a repeat of that inflicted on City in the 1977-78 season by Wrexham, another club heading for promotion from their division (the Third) as champions. A second-half goal put paid to City in the third round of the League Cup, and they again made a fruitless trip into Wales, this time beaten by three goals, after a pulsating 4-4 draw at the same stage of the FA Cup. Wrexham went out in the fifth round to Liverpool, who were beaten by Nottingham Forest in a replayed final at Old Trafford.

Liverpool failed on all three domestic fronts, but were still a formidable force and won the European Cup for a second successive year. It was there-fore much to Bristol City's credit that they twice drew with them that season, despite again being involved in a struggle against relegation. They were fortu-nate to visit Anfield while the reigning champions were going through a rare lean spell, having followed a home draw against Everton with three consecu-tive defeats, but Liverpool's recovery to draw at Ashton Gate with a goal from

Cormack against his old club was made when Liverpool were in the middle of a concluding run of a dozen games without defeat.

In or around the drop zone until the beginning of February 1978, City climbed to mid-table after their second away win, at Leeds, just three weeks after the first, at West Ham. They stood fifteenth following a draw at home to Coventry in their last match, but finished two places lower in the final reckoning because Wolves and Chelsea gained points from their two matches still to play. City ended on 35 points for the second successive season, but this time with a safety margin of three. West Ham went down ten points above their companions, Newcastle and Leicester.

Compared with their first two seasons back in Division One, Bristol City improved in the third, 1978-79. As high as fifth in the early weeks, and eighth during the closing ones, they never fell below 14th and finished 13th. With a points total up to 40, they had six clubs below them before the relegation cut-off point and were 15 clear of QPR, the first of a relegated trio completed by Birmingham and Chelsea. Highlights included hat-tricks by Mabbutt, in a 3-1 win at Manchester United, and Royle, in a 5-0 home win against Coventry. Another Royle goal earned victory at Ashton Gate over Liverpool, who went on to reclaim the League title, and Leeds, who finished fifth, were twice held to a draw.

In the 1978 close season, Norman Hunter was rejoined at Ashton Gate by his former Leeds and England colleague Terry Cooper, a winger turned attacking full-back who was 34 when signing from Middlesbrough for £20,000. Cooper made fewer than a dozen League appearances in his one season with City before leaving to join Bristol Rovers as player-coach, but he more than doubled that number as a substitute after returning to Ashton Gate as player-manager for the 1983-84 campaign in Division Four. He was the oldest to play for City when he last appeared in a 2-0 win at York on 6 October 1984, aged 40 years and 86 days. His longevity was truly remarkable considering the complications that set in after he had broken a leg while playing for Leeds at Stoke in 1972, putting him out of the game for twenty months and virtually ending his international career. He was substituted in his only other game for England after a three-year absence.

Cooper was sacked as Bristol Rovers' coach after a disagreement with manager Bobby Campbell over tactics, but stayed on as a player and eventually became manager himself following a second blocking of his appointment by the board. Eighteen months later Cooper was the fourth member of England's 1970 World Cup team, after Geoff Hurst, Alan Ball and Martin Peters, to be dismissed from management, and he briefly assisted his former Leeds captain Billy Bremner at Doncaster before going back to Bristol City. In his second spell with the club, which included his becoming Britain's first player-director since Vivian Woodward in the early years of the twentieth century, he led them up from Division Three and to two successive Freight Rover Trophy finals at

Wembley (one won, the other lost on penalties), but it ended in another dismissal in 1988 when he was replaced by Joe Jordan, another former Leeds colleague.

Towards the end of the season in which they first signed Cooper, in March 1979, Bristol City turned to Europe for their next two newcomers. Dutchman Gert Meijer, a tall left-winger, came from the Amsterdam club Ajax for £95,000, and Pertti Jantunen, a Finnish international inside-forward from the Swedish club IFK Eskilstuna for £55,000. Meijer went straight into the side when City were in danger of the drop after a slump in which they picked up just one point out of fourteen. Their next two matches were at home in the space of four days against clubs that would go down. Meijer made a scoring debut against Birmingham, then helped to beat a QPR team from which star player Stan Bowles was omitted. Meijer scored one more goal, at home to Chelsea, in being retained for the remaining seven games in which safety was ensured with three more victories – one of them against third-placed West Bromwich – and the home draw with Leeds. Jantunen was restricted to one appearance as a substitute in one of the three defeats during that run-in – inflicted by Kenny Dalglish at Liverpool.

Another City import in December 1980 was goalkeeper Jan Moller, a member of Sweden's squad for the 1978 World Cup and Sweden's Footballer of the Year in 1979 – the year in which he was in the Malmo team beaten by Nottingham Forest in the European Cup final. Moller played over 50 times for City before being sold to Toronto Blizzard for £85,000 in March 1982 when the Ashton Gate club's financial situation was at its most desperate, but Meijer and Jantunen made only 30 appearances between them, both leaving as cash problems were compounded by the unavailing struggle to avoid the loss of First Division status. The month before going to Canada, Moller was on the verge of a £150,000 move to Birmingham, but that deal fell through when the Midlanders parted with manager Jim Smith.

City recouped £50,000 when Meijer went back to the Netherlands in February 1980, joining Sparta Rotterdam; Jantunen had his contract cancelled a year later, and he rejoined the Reipas club with which he had started out in his home city of Lahti. He and Meijer both scored twice for City. One of Jantunen's goals was a spectacular effort in a drawn home game with Leeds on the first day of the 1979-80 season, the other the opener in a 4-0 win against Peterborough during a League Cup run that ended in a fourth-round replay defeat by Nottingham Forest.

Jantunen's last full game for City (he finally appeared in the first team as a substitute in a League Cup-tie with Birmingham) was the second leg of the Anglo-Scottish Cup final of 1980 in which St Mirren avenged their defeat of two years earlier with a 3-1 home victory that made them the first Scottish winners of the trophy, 5-1 on aggregate. St Mirren had also beaten City in the quarter-finals in the intervening season. City failed to progress beyond the group stages in 1980-81. Thereafter the Scots no longer wished to take part. They considered the competition devalued and could not obtain a guarantee of stronger English opposition. Their argument was somewhat weakened, however, when Chesterfield, of the Football League's Third Division, eliminated mighty Rangers on their way to beating Notts County over two legs of that 1981 final. It was the Derbyshire club's first 'major' trophy in 114 years.

For Bristol City to reach the final of this tournament for the second time in two years was small consolation for the relegation from the First Division that so swiftly followed. But there was much, very much, worse still to come.

Chapter 22

'Ashton Gate Eight' help to avoid oblivion

With a mixture of optimism and desperation, Bristol City embarked upon the 1979-80 season a month after sinking even deeper into the financial mire by raising their record fee to £235,000 on Glaswegian Tony Fitzpatrick. The 23-year-old midfielder had impressed against them for St Mirren in the Anglo-Scottish Cup.

A few weeks before that deal City's wage bill was reduced by the departures of Terry Cooper and Norman Hunter, and six days later came the stormy £325,000 transfer of Gary Collier to Coventry. Nevertheless, the cash flow remained critical, so much so that a £1 million clearance sale was launched on 4 February 1980 as the club floundered in the First Division relegation zone from which there was to be no escape. Manager Dicks was prepared to consider offers for Kevin Mabbutt, Clive Whitehead, Geoff Merrick, Joe Royle, Chris Garland and skipper Gerry Gow (though none of them left at that time), and the contracts of Peter Cormack, Roger Kenyon and Geert Meijer were cancelled.

Hunter went as player-coach to Barnsley, where Allan Clarke, another of his former Leeds and England colleagues, was manager; Cormack was freed to rejoin Hibernian. Both later entered management – Hunter with Barnsley and Rotherham, Cormack at Partick Thistle. Hunter was twice more ordered off after having his debut for Barnsley delayed by a second Achilles tendon operation. On succeeding Clarke, who returned to Leeds as manager, he guided the Oakwell club back to the Second Division, and did not play again for more than two years before making a surprise comeback in a defeat of Grimsby on the first day of 1983. It lasted for only twenty minutes. 'Although I was frightened to death before I went on, I really enjoyed those twenty minutes,' he said. 'Then a calf muscle seized up on me. I'm nearly forty now, and it's time to pack it in. At least my wife will be pleased.'

After Hunter's exit from Ashton Gate, Geoff Merrick reverted to the left of midfield, and Clive Whitehead was switched from the left wing to take his place at left-back alongside Gerry Sweeney. Those three – with Fitzpatrick, who, like Sweeney, missed only one match – remained the most regular members of the side as the unsuccessful battle to avoid the drop was waged, with Ritchie, Tainton, Royle and Gow not far behind. Ritchie was the main source of goals, six penalties helping him to 13 of City's miserly 37 in the League. Royle managed only three in the 34 games that neatly took him to 100 full League appearances for the club before his £60,000 transfer to Norwich during the summer of 1980. A knee injury forced him into retirement two years later, with career totals of almost 550 League and Cup matches and 180 goals

– 20 of them for Bristol City. After that, he managed Oldham (whom he took from next to the bottom of Division Four to the Premiership), Everton, Manchester City and Ipswich Town, and also coached the England Under-21 team.

On his way to take the Oldham job after spending the night at his parents' home in Liverpool, Royle's maroon-coloured Daimler-Jaguar broke down with heating problems as he was leaving the motorway, and he had to leave it on a traffic island with the hazard warning lights flashing. He thumbed a lift in the cab of a coal lorry for the last mile to Boundary Park, leaving him open to the quip of being the first manager to turn up with the sack for his inaugural press conference.

It was during Royle's three-match absence from the Bristol City team just after Christmas in the 1979-80 season that the Ashton Gate club finally fell into one of the three relegation places. At the beginning of September they had been as high as sixth after a home win over Wolves, and they had ended that month eighth with a draw at Goodson Park. After that, however, they gained only three victories in twenty League games before winning the return match with Everton, another of the strugglers, then won just three of their last thirteen fixtures. One of those successes in the closing weeks, 2-1 at home with the aid of a Ritchie penalty, ended Bolton's hopes of avoiding a return to the Second Division. A fortnight later, City's own fate was virtually sealed when they lost at home to Norwich, then confirmed as they conceded five goals in their penultimate match at Southampton. That left them with a concluding trip to Tottenham, where they bade farewell to the top flight with a draw, but failed to score for the 21st time that season.

Those blanks included defeat at Nottingham Forest in a fourth-round League Cup replay, and a first-leg defeat in the Anglo-Scottish Cup final in which Tony Fitzpatrick played against his former club (which he was to rejoin for £170,000 after one more season). In the FA Cup, City cast off their goal-shyness to score six against a Derby side demoralised by the disciplining of two players, full-back David Langan and midfielder Bruce Rioch, who were sent back home before the kick-off, but the benefit of another home draw in the next round could not avert defeat by Ipswich. Derby, who were to be City's other relegation companions, accused Langan of deliberately arriving late. He did not travel with the rest of the team, they said, because he was eager for a move and did not want to be cup-tied. Rioch, a former captain of Scotland, was banished for speaking up too forcefully for the Eire defender.

Chris Garland and Welshman Howard Pritchard both scored twice in the demolition of Derby, City's other goals coming from Whitehead and Mann. The Rams replied twice, repeating the tally of their previous visit two months before which had earned one of the only two away wins all season (the other one at Bolton). City's crucial return game at the Baseball Ground resulted in a pulsating 3-3 draw. Two goals from Ritchie, one a penalty, and one from Mann countered a hat-trick by Alan Biley, a costly newcomer from Cambridge United. City critically lost their other relegation battle at Stoke, and this was how the bottom teams finished:

1979-80	P	W	D	L	F	A	Pts
18 Stoke	42	13	10	19	44	58	36
19 Everton	42	9	17	16	43	51	35
20 Bristol City	42	9	13	20	37	66	31
21 Derby	42	11	8	23	47	67	30
22 Bolton	42	5	15	22	38	73	25

Despite the drop, City gave Alan Dicks a new five-year contract, reputedly worth £125,000, in May 1980, yet the following season was only five games old when, on 8 September, he was dismissed – after declining the chance to 'move upstairs'. The longest reign among current managers was one month short of thirteen years. During it, frustration had often bitten deeply and criticism had frequently been harsh, but he had firmly turned down attractive offers from other clubs to stay in Bristol, a city he described as 'a lovely place to live'. He had looked forward to being able to take up the year's option at the end of his new contract, saying that it would take him up to 50, 'the age at which I plan to retire.'

Ironically, the month before he failed to survive in his job, Dicks was in a Secretaries, Managers and Coaches Association study group that drew up a charter entitled 'Soccer – The Fight For Survival'. A blueprint for the future, it was discussed in October by representatives, mainly chairmen, of the 92 Football League clubs at a two-day seminar at Solihull, and then voted upon at an extraordinary meeting the following February. Resolutions passed included three points for a win instead of two, introduced for the 1981-82 season, and – most significantly as it was to prove for Bristol City – no players to be bought by a club until previous transfer debts had been settled. A proposal that half a transfer fee be paid immediately, and the rest within twelve months, was rejected.

City drew the first three of those five Second Division matches before Dicks' dismissal, one of them goalless at home to their Rovers neighbours, and lost the next two. The unenviable task of trying to extricate them from their morass of debt and decline fell to Bristolian Bob Houghton, a former player with Fulham and Brighton who had been managing the Greek club Ethnikos after taking Malmo to four Swedish League titles and a European Cup final in which they lost to Nottingham Forest. He was appointed after Norman Hunter had had the chance to fill the vacancy before becoming Barnsley's manager.

Houghton fulfilled an ambition in managing an English club, but he was powerless to revive City's fortunes. Down they went to the Third Division,

winning just seven of their remaining 37 League matches – and with them, at
the lowest point in Bristol soccer history, went Rovers under the management
of Terry Cooper. With only a dozen victories between them, they occupied the
last two places, Rovers bringing up the rear seven points adrift. City's goals-for
total was reduced further to 29, supplanting the 32 of 1923-24 as their lowest-
ever for a League season. These were the final bottom positions:

1980-81	P	W	D	L	F	A	Pts
19 Cardiff	42	12	12	18	44	60	36
20 Preston	42	11	14	17	41	62	36
21 Bristol City	42	7	16	19	29	51	30
22 Bristol Rov	42	5	13	24	34	65	23

City's solitary away win was not achieved until three games from the finish,
by 3-2 at Cardiff. Rovers gained theirs by 3-1 at Cambridge early in March.

The decline in City's playing fortunes came on top of the financial crisis
that put Alan Dicks in the position of being able to bankrupt City even without the intervention of their other angry creditors. In March 1981, he was presented with a cheque for £10,000, the final instalment of his £58,000 pay-off
from the club. It was post-dated 31 January, but he was told that City's bank
account had been closed the previous week, and their finances placed in the
hands of independent auditors. 'My immediate feeling was to push the club
into liquidation,' he said, 'but I am not a spiteful person, and it will be a sad
day for me if the club folds.' He left the matter in the hands of his solicitor.

Nearly ten years were to go by before Dicks reappeared in English soccer.
After leaving City, he worked for a promotions company involved in golf and
snooker, and was also a director of a travel agency. He afterwards had a season as coach with the Greek club Houghton had left, and, following a spell
working for the BBC, took other coaching posts in Cyprus, Qatar, Sweden and
the United States before his appointment as assistant to Fulham manager Ray
Lewington in 1990. That reunited him with Jimmy Hill, by then the club's
chairman. Dicks and Lewington soon had their roles reversed, but Dicks was
sacked near the end of 1991 after a run of poor results had put the Cottagers
in danger of the relegation to the Fourth Division that they only just managed
to avoid.

At Ashton Gate, Bob Houghton was handicapped by having to sell two of
his best players, Gerry Gow and Tom Ritchie. Those departures – together
with the free transfers given to Pertti Jantunen and reserve Ian Doyle, plus the
loaning of Ray Cashley to Hereford – saved £80,000 in wages. Redundancies
among office staff and maintenance departments sliced another £68,000 off
the annual salary bill, and other economies increased the saving to £250,000 in
all. Even so, with several players still on Division One contracts, and at least
one on a basic £450 a week, City struggled to pay summer wages. There was

a glimmer of hope late in 1981 when two local businessmen, Deryn Coller and Ken Sage, promised to raise more than half a million pounds for the club – but it came with the proviso that two directors, Stephen Kew and Peter West, had to resign. Only the year before, Kew, a solicitor, had been succeeded as chairman (the second, after Robert Hobbs, since Harry Dolman) by Archie Gooch, a company director and president of the National Federation of Supporters' Clubs.

Next, three days into 1982, came the resignation of Bob Houghton, who later coached in China. 'There's nothing more I can do,' he said, after a fourth home defeat had left City heading for a third consecutive relegation. His assistant, Croydon-born Roy Hodgson, who had also been his deputy with Malmo, took over to the dismal backdrop of a financial investigation of the club. Barely had Hodgson settled into the manager's chair than City were banned by the League from buying players after falling behind with their payments to Newcastle for striker Mick Harford. This soon led to the farcical situation whereby Harford went back to Newcastle on a free transfer, but on the same day was transferred to Birmingham for £100,000, the amount the Ashton Gate club still owed on their £160,000 deal with the Tynesiders. More than £1½m changed hands in Harford's subsequent moves as his number of clubs rose into double figures until injury forced him to give up playing at the age of 39 while with Wimbledon.

Before January 1982 was out, Archie Gooch warned that the club would have to close down 'within two weeks' under the burden of their huge debts, said to be around £700,000, if agreement were not reached with the eight leading players to whom they planned to give immediate transfers to cut the £350,000 annual wage bill. The players looked to the Professional Footballers' Association for help, and Lionel Smart came back into the picture because City were one of the clubs he represented on the Football Association.

'I had a phone call from Peter Godsiff, Sports Editor of the *Evening Post*,' he recalled. 'He was very close to all sides in what was a bitter dispute, and he suggested matters had become so serious that I ought to step in as the FA representative to seek a solution. I met the famous Ashton Gate Eight at the 51 Club – Geoff Merrick, David Rodgers, Jimmy Mann, Gerry Sweeney, Trevor Tainton, Chris Garland, Peter Aitken and Julian Marshall.'

Aitken, a Welsh Under-23 international midfielder, had the unique distinction of captaining both Bristol clubs. He played more than 200 times for Rovers, who recruited him from their Cardiff-based nursery club, before he was listed because of a contract dispute, and made his next half-century or so appearances for City. He left Ashton Gate with Sweeney for York City and afterwards followed a short spell at Bournemouth as assistant to his former Eastville clubmate Lindsay Parsons with Cheltenham. Marshall, a Swansea-born defender who had joined City from Hereford, went on trial to Blackburn Rovers.

Smart continued: 'It was vital, if the settlement worked out by accountants was to be implemented, that the Eight tore up their contracts in exchange for a fraction of their value. Geoff, and, in particular, David, were hostile, and the others showed their anger as well. I offered a way out by arranging a friendly match between Southampton and Ipswich Town at Ashton Gate as a testimonial, the proceeds being used to boost their compensation. Reluctantly they agreed. Geoff said: "I'll never be happy about what has happened, but it is the best we can do. Otherwise, the club will be wound up and we'll be left with nothing."'

Merrick threw in his lot with Yeovil Town, also complaining that he had lost £1,000 on his testimonial game at Ashton Gate two years before – around the time when shareholders met to protest about the way the club's affairs were being run. Coller and Sage stated that City had 'lacked direction and control for the past five years' after their examination of the books. The 'Eight' were incensed that their decision should be the ultimate one. 'Why should we be the sacrificial lambs?' demanded Merrick. 'Blackmail is the only word for what the club are doing to us. If I were a City director I would not be part and parcel of it.'

For their first match after the cancellation of the contracts of the 'Eight,' 0-0 at home to Fulham on the first Saturday of February 1982, City fielded four young debutants, three of whom, Rob Newman, Wayne Bray and Mark Smith (a substitute), made up the six Bristolians in the squad with Paul Stevens, Gary Williams and Ricky Chandler. The other newcomer was Londoner Jon Economou. With so much inexperience in the side, the descent to Division Four was accelerated by a sequence of twelve games without a win, in nine of which City failed to score. They finished next to the foot of the table and went down with Wimbledon, Swindon and Chester. These were the details:

1981-82	P	W	D	L	F	A	Pts
20 Walsall	46	13	14	19	51	55	53
21 Wimbledon	46	14	11	21	61	75	53
22 Swindon	46	13	13	20	55	74	52
23 Bristol City	46	11	13	22	40	65	46
24 Chester	46	7	11	28	36	78	32

The FA Cup provided some slight lifting of the gloom for City with a run from the first round that ended in defeat by only one goal at home to First Division Aston Villa in the fourth.

Welsh international Terry Boyle, City's centre-half and captain against Villa, found himself on the transfer list three months after his arrival from Crystal Palace as part of the deal that took Kevin Mabbutt to Selhurst Park. Boyle, who was living in a Bristol hotel while negotiating the sale of his house in London, went to Wales with his wife for the weekend after the Cup exit. 'I spent the time moping about that defeat,' he said. 'It could have been a draw, we did well enough. Then, when I reported back at Ashton Gate for training, an apprentice told me about the troubles and added: "By the way, you're on the list." It was quite a shock, but I don't regret coming here. It's a great club, and there are some good people around.' As it turned out, Boyle saw out the rest of that season with City, then was with Newport, Cardiff and Swansea before playing for several clubs, including Merthyr Tydfil and Barry Town, in the Welsh League. He later worked for the Football Association of Wales Trust and was assistant manager at Welshpool Town.

Within weeks of severely pruning the playing staff, City got the wrong side of the PFA by signing Les Carter, a midfielder, from Crystal Palace and Aiden McCaffery, a former Newcastle and Derby centre-half, from Bristol Rovers. Gordon Taylor, the PFA secretary, felt moved to warn club chairmen in general: 'We shall have to force clubs into liquidation if they copy what Bristol City are doing. The club have signed two new players, and are moving for a third, despite axing eight who were on contracts.' The outcome was an order to return all three. Ray Gooding, a Coventry City midfielder, was the third man.

Not until the end of April were City finally saved from extinction. The Football League waived a £250,000 guarantee that the next season's fixtures would be fulfilled, with the proviso that the club's £95,000 share-out from the League Cup pool would be withheld for a year. Although City's share issue realised only £90,000 towards the £300,000 target, the caretaker board raised the balance from the several businessmen they contacted. Bristol City FC (1982) Ltd was formed, replacing the one that had been in existence since 1894. Gooch was succeeded as chairman by Des Williams, who, as already recalled, has had a stand at Ashton Gate named after him – the old grandstand opposite the Dolman Stand. Williams, the director of a building company, was something of a compromise choice. Coller, a former Metropolitan policeman, and Sage were among the new directors, with Leslie Kew, a distant relative of Stephen, and Ivor Williams the only survivors from the old board. Kew became vice-chairman, and after the death of Des Williams at 66 in 1991 he took over as chairman until ousted in another coup five years later.

The boardroom changes of 1982 also brought a change of manager. On 20 May, two days after City, two goals down at half-time, had ended the season with a draw at Doncaster, Terry Cooper returned to fill the vacancy left by the luckless Roy Hodgson. Back abroad went Hodgson – first rejoining Malmo, whom he guided to a trio of league titles and cup wins, then also managing the Neuchatel Xamas club in Switzerland and the Swiss national team before Inter Milan appointed him 'technical consultant', a title devised to get round the ban in Italy on foreign coaches. From Italy he returned to England as manager of Blackburn, and he was on the FA's short list to replace Kevin Keegan as England's coach before the appointment of Sven Goran Eriksson.

He later coached in the United Arab Emirates, Finland, and again with Inter-Milan, before reviving Fulham's fortunes in the Premiership.

From having been in the top six of the First Division three years earlier, City were dumped at the very foot of the Fourth in December 1982, with home gates below 5,000. Not until February did they escape the bottom four, but an improvement in form was consolidated the following season when they secured the last promotion place, if with attendances at Ashton Gate mostly below five figures. Their biggest home crowd was 16,107 for a third-round FA Cup replay they lost to Notts County after knocking out their neighbours at Eastville. This was how they finished at the top of Division Four:

1983-84	P	W	D	L	F	A	Pts
1 York	46	31	8	7	96	39	101
2 Doncaster	46	24	13	9	82	54	85
3 Reading	46	22	16	8	84	56	82
4 Bristol City	46	24	10	12	70	44	82
5 Aldershot	46	22	9	15	76	69	75

It was the start of a roller-coaster ride, with three more promotions offset by two relegations, that carried City through fifteen changes of manager since Alan Dicks to the brink of the FA Premiership in 2008. Their narrow defeat by Hull in the Championship play-off final that year added a fourth Wembley appearance to those they had made (one successful) since 1986 in the knock-out competition that began as the Associate Members Cup for clubs in the two lowest divisions of the Football League

Printed in Great Britain
by Amazon

26807409R00112